DISCARD

D1611802

AMERICAN
HAUNTINGS

AMERICAN HAUNTINGS

The True Stories behind Hollywood's Scariest Movies—from *The Exorcist* to *The Conjuring*

ROBERT E. BARTHOLOMEW
AND JOE NICKELL

PRAEGER™

An Imprint of ABC-CLIO, LLC
Santa Barbara, California • Denver, Colorado

Library of Congress Cataloging-in-Publication Data

Bartholomew, Robert E.
    American hauntings : the true stories behind Hollywood's scariest movies—from The exorcist to The conjuring / Robert E. Bartholomew and Joe Nickell.
        pages cm
    Includes bibliographical references and index.
    ISBN 978-1-4408-3968-9 (print : alk. paper) — ISBN 978-1-4408-3969-6 (e-book)
    1. Ghosts—United States. 2. Parapsychology—United States. 3. Occultism—United States. 4. Horror films—United States—History and criticism. 5. Motion pictures—Influence. I. Nickell, Joe. II. Title.
    BF1472.U6B3738 2015
    133.10973—dc23   2015003962

ISBN: 978-1-4408-3968-9
EISBN: 978-1-4408-3969-6

19 18 17 16 15   1 2 3 4 5

This book is also available on the World Wide Web as an eBook.
Visit www.abc-clio.com for details.

Praeger
An Imprint of ABC-CLIO, LLC

ABC-CLIO, LLC
130 Cremona Drive, P.O. Box 1911
Santa Barbara, California 93116-1911

This book is printed on acid-free paper ∞

Manufactured in the United States of America

Contents

Acknowledgments

We are grateful to many people for their assistance, including the Center for Inquiry, its director of libraries, Timothy Binga, and the staff of its science magazine, *Skeptical Inquirer*. We also wish to thank Michael Shermer, Christina Tatu, Chris Mele, Jesse Glass, Jack Cook, and Fred Rolater. Special thanks to Jamilah and Paul Bartholomew.

Introduction

Those who do not study history are forced to get it from Hollywood.
—Alan Barra[1]

We will examine seven of the most compelling and thoroughly documented hauntings on record, baffling cases that have been affirmed by witnesses and hailed as genuine by researchers in the field of parapsychology. Each story has been promoted by Hollywood producers as having been "based on a true story." We will scrutinize the evidence behind such films as *The Exorcist*, *The Amityville Horror*, *The Conjuring*, and *The Haunting in Connecticut*. The belief in ghosts is an integral part of American society, as reflected in opinion polls and the recent upsurge in paranormal investigation groups, which now number in the thousands.[2] There is little doubt that Hollywood plays an influential role in promoting supernatural beliefs, but how factual are these productions and the stories they are based on?

Each case shares classic poltergeist elements. For centuries, people have reported encountering these invisible entities or forces. The word refers to a "noisy ghost" or "spirit" and is derived from the German *poltern* (to make noise) and *Geist* (ghost).[3] While the earliest cases predate Christianity, it was not until 1848 that the word first entered the English lexicon with the publication of Catherine Crowe's book, *The Night-Side of Nature*. The term was popularized during the 1920s in the works of British psychic investigator Harry Price (1881–1948).[4] Poltergeist hauntings are a Hollywood staple, and over the past century they have featured prominently in a number of accounts that have been immortalized by producers, who have titillated audience interest by claiming they depict real-life events. We will carefully sift through the evidence and assess whether these stories are Hollywood hype or there is substance behind the claims.

It is important to distinguish between accounts that are "based on a true story" and documentaries. A documentary is a reenactment based entirely on factual information, although there may be differing perspectives as to exactly what occurred and a multitude of interpretations of the same event by different participants. A film or TV show that is "based on a true story" is known as a docudrama. While historical events form the basis of the narrative, a certain amount of literary license is taken to increase the story's appeal. Hence, some events may be embellished or fabricated altogether. In short, documentaries are based on facts; docudramas are dramatized reenactments of supposedly real events and place a heavy emphasis on maintaining viewer interest by telling a good story. Despite the distinction, some viewers erroneously assume that "based on a true story" is synonymous with "factual." During our investigations, we will ask two key questions: How faithful are media portrayals to the accounts given by the witnesses, and what evidence is there that these paranormal events took place at all?

Parapsychology is rife with controversy and conflicting claims. At one end of the spectrum are the true believers; at the other end are the dogmatic skeptics. The subject of poltergeists is typical. Read through any sampling of books and articles on the topic, and it is hard to know what to believe. Some investigators note that these strange occurrences often appear in the presence of angry or frustrated children or adolescents who are thought to have the temporary ability to control their environment by moving objects and projecting visions using only their minds. Others believe that instead of creating these effects, the accused is the victim of harassment by a restless spirit that represents proof of life after death. Skeptics observe that the principal figure is often suspected of feigning events, and they suggest that *all* poltergeist claims result from fraud and deception.

As we delve into these cases and evaluate the evidence, we will seek to answer questions that have long puzzled observers. Why do most cases revolve around one person? How likely is it that the central figure created the effects? An examination of the literature presents us with a conundrum: on the one hand, there are scores of reports from every part of the world, dating back centuries. British researchers Alan Gauld and Tony Cornell collected information on 500 poltergeist cases. Many contain eerily similar features, from reports of airborne pebbles and stones, to heavy objects being tossed about or destroyed. Despite the impressive accumulation of testimony, their evidence is overwhelmingly composed of eyewitness descriptions, which are notoriously unreliable.

During earlier times, poltergeists were commonly associated with spirits of the dead, witchcraft, and demons. The term even appears in the writings of German theologian Martin Luther (1483–1546), who, like most of his contemporaries, attributed the presence of these "noisy ghosts" to Satan.[5] Encounters have been recorded as early as the year 858, when a farm family at Bingen, in what is now southwestern Germany, reported flying stones and mysterious sounds.[6] Their appearance typically begins with strange knocks and noises and slowly escalates to flying objects, broken furniture, levitating people, strange visions, and disembodied voices. While their conduct is usually confined to harmless antics and mischievous acts such as knocking over sugar bowls and pulling blankets from sleeping children, they occasionally turn sinister, setting fires and ripping doors off hinges. In rare instances, their appearance is accompanied by the demonic possession of occupants and frightful images in windows and mirrors. Sometimes an eerie, threatening voice will order people to leave their home. Other times, they seem to be playing a game of cat and mouse with bewildered family members. In modern times, electrical disturbances are common, such as flickering or exploding lightbulbs. Occasionally, victims report bruising, bleeding, and welts after allegedly being pinched, scratched, bitten, or struck by an unseen force, in addition to psychological trauma and exhaustion from the harassment. Eerie noises often accompany appearances, such as groaning, laughing, weeping, and talking.

Gauld and Cornell found the most common poltergeist activity to be the appearance of small objects such as pebbles or stones that fly through the air (64 percent). Occasionally they will pelt the exterior of a building. Large furniture was reported to have moved or been tossed about in 36 percent of cases, while nearly half of all episodes were associated with rapping sounds (48 percent). Poltergeists are most active at night, and their presence usually lasts from a few hours to several weeks or months. Occasionally they persist for years (24 percent).[7] When the activity stops, it usually does so abruptly and coincides with the central figure leaving the household. The strange happenings may follow this person to their next residence. Sometimes those affected will look into a mirror or window and report seeing an evil or hideous face. Some outbreaks are accompanied by the mysterious appearance of water, which may seep through walls. Investigators may have difficulty in uncovering the source. These cases make up 5 percent of the survey.[8] Since the

1970s, the appearance of a strange, gooey substance has been reported oozing from walls, ceilings, and keyholes.

 Paranormal researchers often suggest that poltergeists target adolescents because they feed off energy generated from the rapid physical and psychological changes associated with puberty. They have long noted that most people who attract poltergeists are experiencing extreme anger, trauma, or distress, which is believed to generate "psychic energy" in sensitive people who can temporarily exhibit psychokinesis: the ability to move or alter the shape of objects, such as bending a spoon using mental power alone. The word is derived from the Greek *psyche* (mind or soul) and *kinesis* (movement).[9] The trouble is that the ability to manipulate objects and create visions using pent-up mental energy has yet to be proven and is looked upon with suspicion by most scientists. Another explanation is that poltergeists are spirits of the dead who are drawn to distressed persons who are generating high amounts of psychic energy.

 Most scientists would explain the presence of preexisting tension and anger in poltergeist households as resulting from the focus person engaging in deception by throwing and breaking objects and making mysterious noises. People hoax for many reasons: fame, fortune, revenge, jealousy. Some do it for the thrill and challenge of outwitting an opponent; others may feel important by being part of a mystery. The hoax explanation does not require hypothesizing about unproven psychic energy and supernatural forces that defy the known laws of physics. This would explain a curious observation through the centuries: subjects around which cases revolve are typically in distress, prior to—and not necessarily from—the poltergeist. After surveying the literature and investigating numerous cases firsthand, veteran parapsychologist Guy Playfair concludes that poltergeists "feed on fear, anxiety and tension." There is usually so much conflict and distress swirling around the household that he recommends calling in a psychiatrist to figure out what is causing it within the family dynamic![10] However, the deception hypothesis can explain this pattern and why, to date, no scientist has been able to replicate poltergeist activities in a controlled setting where the target is under constant, rigorous scrutiny.

 In Chapter 1, we investigate the supposed real-life events behind the 2006 film *An American Haunting*. Often touted as the most famous 19th-century haunting in U.S. history, the story of Tennessee farmer John Bell and his reported death by a female poltergeist has baffled researchers ever since it first came to light in 1886. The case is remarkable in that it is said to have persisted over several years and attracted people from hundreds of miles away to observe the strange goings-on, including a soon-to-be president of the United States, Andrew Jackson. Many paranormal researchers consider the case to be genuine. It is one of the most challenging and complex reports on record, and we will present new information that offers fresh clues to solving the mystery.

The Exorcist is one of the most recognizable and successful horror films in cinematic history and was nominated for ten Academy Awards. The extraordinary claims behind the movie are the focus of Chapter 2. The film's release in 1973 left audiences gasping as they watched the adaptation of William Peter Blatty's bestselling book by the same name. The events were inspired by the real-life diary of Father Frank Bishop, who documented the exorcism of a boy known as "Robbie" in St. Louis, Missouri, in 1949. The "true story" subtitle has helped to stoke the anxieties of those watching the film version of events, to the point where several viewers have experienced psychotic episodes requiring hospitalization.[11] How accurate are reports that the boy was demonically possessed; that words would mysteriously appear on his body in the form of deep, bloody scratches; and that he had the ability to send crockery and books whizzing through the air?

Popper the Poltergeist is the subject of Chapter 3. In 1958, journalists from across the United States descended on 1648 Redwood Path in Seaford, Long Island, hoping to glimpse the mysterious happenings that seemed to follow little Jimmy Herrmann. The inspiration for Steven Spielberg's *Poltergeist*, the case marks the first scientific investigation of such an outbreak, as researchers from the Duke University Parapsychology Lab stayed with the family. More mischievous than malevolent, more naughty than nefarious, Popper was named for its penchant for popping bottle tops. The affair was chronicled by the *New York Times* and featured in *Life* magazine. Popper attained such notoriety that the Nassau County Police Department even assigned one of its detectives to investigate the mysterious goings-on full-time. Popper is one of the most meticulously investigated cases on record, and when we examine the wealth of evidence more closely, a clear pattern emerges. Is this the first instance where scientists have proven the existence of a poltergeist, or is there another explanation?

The events that gave rise to the supernatural thriller *The Conjuring* are examined in Chapter 4. The 2013 film tells the story of paranormal investigators Ed and Lorraine Warren, who attempt to exorcise an array of spirits from the Rhode Island farmhouse of Roger and Carolyn Perron. After the family moved into its new home in 1971, strange happenings were recorded by Mrs. Perron and her five daughters. Over the next decade, they reported hundreds of mysterious occurrences, from levitating beds to terrifying visions and ghostly presences. On several occasions a broom was reported to sweep by itself; a "haunted" fridge would routinely expel food onto the kitchen floor; a mysterious cloud-like force was said to routinely attack family members. Hollywood producers claim that the saga of the Perron family is a true story—but is it?

The Amityville Horror, which frightened a generation of filmgoers during the 1970s, is examined in Chapter 5. Based on the bestselling book by Jay Anson, it tells the story of George and Kathy Lutz, who reported a series of chilling and bizarre encounters after moving into their "dream home" at 112 Ocean Avenue in Amityville, Long Island, a home they bought at a bargain-basement price after it was the scene of a gruesome mass murder thirteen months earlier. Soon family members reported personality changes and visions of demonic figures. An unseen force was said to have attacked the Lutzes, causing lacerations, welts, and bruises. On one occasion, Kathy reportedly floated two feet into the air. We are told that cloven footprints were found in the snow outside the house; a 250-pound door was ripped from its hinges; tempered locks were inexplicably bent; a green slime oozed from keyholes and walls. When a Catholic priest was asked to bless the house, a chilling voice ordered him to get out. What evidence is there that these events took place? Were the Lutzes, as some suggest, master manipulators who fabricated the affair to get rich, or were they victims of a malevolent force that was determined to expel them from the house?

Don Decker, the young Pennsylvania man who reportedly levitated and made it rain, is the subject of Chapter 6. At first glance, these claims seem beyond belief, yet his abilities were observed by two couples, a restaurant owner, four police officers, a prison warden, and two guards. It is arguably the most credible case of paranormal activity ever recorded. Featured on the TV show *Paranormal Witness*, the segment was presented as a series of interviews with eyewitnesses who all swear that the events took place. Producers of another respected TV program, *Unsolved Mysteries*, also interviewed many of those who observed the events first-hand. When we probe deeper by examining the circumstances of these remarkable claims and compare the various testimonies of those present, a remarkable pattern emerges. Does this case prove the existence of the paranormal, or is there a more mundane explanation?

In Chapter 7, we explore the truth behind the 2009 film *The Haunting in Connecticut*, which was based on the claims of the Snedeker family after moving into a former funeral home in the town of Southington in 1986. In addition to seeing ghosts and levitating objects, Mr. and Mrs. Snedeker claimed to have been sexually violated by a mysterious paralyzing force while lying in bed. Their niece reported being groped in the night by an unseen hand. Most of the strange events centered on the Snedekers' thirteen-year-old son Philip, who was angry and frustrated while undergoing an experimental treatment for blood cancer. How close does the film reflect the family's claims, and what evidence is there that the events took place?

While it is not possible to examine every alleged haunted house that has gained the attention of Hollywood, to our knowledge this is the first study to systematically examine the evidence for the most compelling "based on a true story" productions—creations that have undoubtedly had an impact on popular culture.[12] In Chapter 8, we summarize the findings of our case studies and highlight patterns within the literature. How accurate is Hollywood in portraying "based on a true story" hauntings when compared to the original claims? What evidence is there that those claims are genuine? These are important questions, if we are to better understand the impact of Hollywood on our perceptions of the world around us. It is a question that has been around as long as Hollywood producers themselves. To what extent do their productions reflect reality, and to what extent are they creations of the human imagination?

Robert Bartholomew, Auckland, New Zealand
Joe Nickell, Buffalo, New York

CHAPTER 1

An American Haunting: Terror and Torment in Tennessee

I ought to know by this time that when a fact appears to be opposed to a long train of deductions it invariably proves to be capable of bearing some other interpretation.

—Sherlock Holmes[1]

In spring 2006, *An American Haunting* opened in theaters across the United States, and it has since grossed nearly $30 million in global ticket sales.[2] Set in the present, with flashbacks to the early 1800s, the backdrop to the film is rural Tennessee, where a recently divorced mother comforts her daughter, who is haunted by a series of nightmares. The mother soon finds a binder of old letters from the house's previous occupants, which tell the story of the Bell Witch, whose vengeful spirit once haunted the family of pioneer farmer John Bell, played by Donald Sutherland, and his daughter Betsy, portrayed by Rachel Hurd-Wood. The father and daughter were tormented nearly two centuries earlier, after John got into a property dispute with an eccentric local named Katy Batts, who was rumored to have been a witch. After she vowed revenge, strange things began to happen, as the Bell family was harassed by a spirit that was believed to have been of her creation. The attacks unleashed the repressed memories of John's wife, Lucy, played by Sissy Spacek, and of Betsy's abuse at the hands of her father. Betsy then kills her father with poison. Fast-forward to the present, when the young woman, about Betsy's age, is tormented by bad dreams and a series of events that are reminiscent of the Bell haunting. At the end of the film, the ghost of Betsy Bell appears and warns the mother of similar abuse.

The movie is loosely based on the legend of the Bell Witch, which is well known to folklorists and paranormal researchers. The word "witch" was used because such happenings were typically associated with witchcraft. The film's release was promoted as "the most documented haunting in American history"[3] and an event that was "validated by the State of Tennessee as the only case in U.S. history where a spirit has caused the death of a human being."[4] Believers argue that the haunting, the subject of many books, is based on real events. Tennessee historian Fred Rolater observes that the story has developed "an almost radical following of believers" who staunchly defend its reality,[5] while skeptics contend that it is either a hoax or a tall tale that may or may not have been based on an earlier alleged haunting. Neither side has been able to muster the evidence needed to conclusively document its claims.

Long a staple of Southern folklore, stories of the Witch have frightened children and adults alike as they listened attentively to different versions of the tale at slumber parties, sitting around campfires, and huddled in college dormitories late at night. During the early nineteenth century, a series of strange happenings reportedly befell the John Bell family on and near their farm in Middle Tennessee. An invisible force would punch, pinch, and slap bemused family members and occasionally pelt them with stones and other objects. Mysterious knocks, tapping, and scratching noises frightened the family, and animals were spooked for no apparent reason. A disembodied voice was soon heard, which kept the household in a state of turmoil. It would sing, shriek, curse, and send furniture and other objects crashing to the floor. The offending spirit was said to be a witch named Katy Batts who felt cheated by Bell after he purchased land from her—or so the story goes.[6] She reportedly swore that she would haunt John Bell and "his kith and kin to their graves."[7] As in the film, John Bell and his young daughter Elizabeth, popularly known as Betsy, bore the brunt of her wrath. The attacks culminated in the death of John Bell Sr. in 1820, when the spirit reportedly took credit for murdering him with a vial of poison. The anomalous events then subsided, although mysterious occurrences attributed to the Witch continue to be reported sporadically in the area where the farmstead once stood, including the nearby Bell Witch Cave.[8] The first published book on the haunting did not appear until 1894, after Bell's son Richard reportedly wrote a summary of the events and gave them to a local newspaperman, Martin Ingram (1832–1909).[9] By this time, there were no living witnesses.

The Bell Witch saga is frequently touted as one of the most credible and inexplicable cases of poltergeist activity ever. In 1894, a journalist for *The Hartford Herald* noted, "In its day it was the sensation of two states."[10] Over forty years later, in 1937, residents living in the vicinity of the original hauntings were reported to have been fearful amid rumors of the spirit's predicted return,[11] and they were relieved when it failed to materialize.[12] A feature story on the haunting appeared in a 1955 edition of *Family Weekly Magazine,* with the observation, "Nobody has ever satisfactorily explained the Bell Witch mystery."[13] In 1973, Alan Spraggett wrote about the Witch in his syndicated newspaper column, "The Unexplained," prefacing the story as follows: "And every word of it is true."[14] In his 2009 book, *The Bell Witch: The Full Account,* Southern U.S. mystery writer Pat Fitzhugh boldly states, "The astonishing events that took place . . . have baffled scholars and researchers for nearly two centuries."[15] Paranormal investigator Stephen Wagner also holds the episode to be significant, calling it "America's best-known poltergeist case." He notes that the outbreak "has remained unexplained for nearly 200 years."[16] Even geography professor Charles Stansfield Jr. of Rowan University in New Jersey describes it as one of America's "best documented hauntings,"[17] while journalist Michael Schmicker writes that it is "one of the most intriguing and believable spirit/poltergeist cases in American history."[18] Surely a case that is held in such high regard by so many researchers and writers deserves to be examined more closely. It is a remarkable story of a haunting that persisted over many years, during which time residents from hundreds of miles away flocked to the Bell farmstead to witness the strange happenings.

The American public has long been captivated by the story. In 1948, Charles Bryan's composition *The Bell Witch Cantata* helped spread the Witch's fame when it premiered at Carnegie Hall in New York City.[19] *Playboy* even featured a story on the legend in November 1968.[20] Eight years later, hundreds of residents living in the vicinity of where the Bell farm once stood came for the opening of Audrey Campbell's play about the Witch, *Our Family Trouble,*[21] while 2002 saw the premier of another play: David Alford's *Spirit: The Authentic Story of the Bell Witch of Tennessee.* This dramatic production has become an annual favorite in the region and is billed as a historically accurate re-creation.[22] In recent years the story has become a popular Hollywood drawing card due to its association with real people and events, giving rise to a series of low-budget films promoted as based on true events. This includes *The Bell Witch Haunting,* released in 2004,[23] and *Bell Witch: The Movie,* which premiered the following year.[24] In 2008, the nearby Bell Witch Cave was placed on the National Register of Historic Places and was a significant boost for the local economy, averaging 117,000 visitors annually.[25] The cave has been the scene of an annual Halloween party that has attracted several thousand visitors.[26] The tiny city of Adams, Tennessee (pop. 633 in 2010), hosts an annual Bell Witch Festival,[27] and there is even a Bell Witch Fan Club.[28]

Historical Enigma

Historians seek out primary sources: artifacts or documents that are from the period under study. They are the gold standard of research: newspaper articles, letters, diary entries, police records, church documents, and court papers written at the time. Given the volume of people who were reported to have visited the Bells, this should prove to be fertile ground for researchers. The primary narrative of the Bell Witch story is *Our Family Trouble*, written, we are told, by John Bell's son, Richard Williams Bell, in 1846.[29] Born in 1811, he was a child of about six at the time the strange events reportedly began. He tells how his father, John Bell Sr., having settled his family on a farm in Robertson County, Tennessee, was plagued by what today would be called a poltergeist. The strange happenings supposedly began in about 1817. In 1894, Martin Ingram published *Authenticated History of the Bell Witch and Other Stories of the World's Greatest Unexplained Phenomenon*, containing an edited version of Richard Bell's diary. In it he added letters and interviews from area residents who recalled stories about the Witch from their ancestors. In the introduction to the book, Ingram writes that the story will be familiar "to thousands who have heard graphic accounts from the lips of the old people who witnessed the excitement and have, perhaps, also read short newspaper sketches."[30] He says that Richard Bell gave him *Our Family Trouble* to set the record straight, as there were rumors at the time that the story was a hoax.[31] There is something odd about these claims. For such a popular story that was said to have appeared in many papers during the first half of the nineteenth century, there is not one known reference to the Bell Witch prior to 1886: no diary entries, letters, newspaper or magazine accounts, or official documents of any kind.[32] Let us look closer at the Bell Witch story, using the only known primary source: the diary of Richard Bell.

A Mystery Begins: The Witch Appears

The episode began in classic poltergeist fashion with mysterious noises that grew more frequent and intense. There were eerie knocks at the door, but no one was there. Another noise sounded like a rat gnawing at a bedpost, yet the wood was unblemished, and no rodent was seen. Sometimes the noises sounded like heavy stones striking the floor. The racket typically stopped between 1:00 and 3:00 a.m., before which point, we are told, it was impossible to fall asleep. Even then, the children were often targeted by having their hair yanked and bedcovers pulled off. Richard Bell describes the scene in his diary: "Soon after we had all retired, the disturbance commenced as usual; gnawing, scratching, knocking on the wall, overturning chairs, pulling the cover off of beds, etc., every act being exhibited . . . and so soon as a light would appear, the noise would cease, and the trouble begin in another room."[33] The spirit harassed Betsy the most. Just twelve years old when the trouble began, Betsy was sent to stay with different neighbors, in the hope that the harassment would end, but it followed her wherever she went.[34] Curiously, there are no known accounts from these homes.

Soon the spirit began to communicate by rapping. Bell writes, "When asked a question in a way, that it could be answered by numbers, for instance, 'How many persons present? How many horses in the barn? How many miles to a certain place?' The answers would come in raps, like a man knocking on the wall, the bureau or the bedpost with his fist, or by so many scratches on the wall like the noise of a nail or claws, and the answers were invariably correct."[35] During this time, lights resembling those from candles or lamps were often seen "flitting across the yard and through the field." On many occasions, Mr. Bell, his boys, and the hired hands would be returning late from work, only to be pelted with "chunks of wood and stones" as they neared the farm.[36] There was no apparent source for the lights. Bell observed that some of the antics intensified—the spirit "took to slapping people on the face, especially those who resisted the action of pulling the cover from the bed, and those who came as detectives to expose the trick. The blows were heard distinctly, like the open palm of a heavy hand, while the sting was keenly felt, and it did not neglect to pull my hair."[37]

Soon the spirit began to speak—first in whispers and then in a feeble voice; later in a strong, clear tone. When someone asked aloud, "Who are you and what do you want?" there was a response: "I am a spirit; I was once very happy but have been disturbed." As the voice gained strength, those who suspected Betsy of trickery accused her of ventriloquism.[38] When pressed about its unhappiness, it said, "I am the spirit of a person who was buried in the woods near by, and the grave has been disturbed, my bones disinterred and scattered, and one of my teeth was lost under this house, and I am here looking for that tooth."[39] Mr. Bell was said to have conducted a careful search for the tooth—to the point of pulling up floorboards where it was believed to have fallen and sifting the dirt underneath—but nothing was found. Bell's son wrote that the Witch then laughed at his father for his gullibility.

Buried Treasure

Bell recounts that after a skull and other bones were found to have been taken from a nearby grave, the Witch claimed that she was the spirit of an early immigrant who had hidden treasure for safekeeping but died before divulging the location. The voice proclaimed, "I have returned in the spirit for the purpose of making known the hiding place, and I want Betsy Bell to have the money." The treasure was said to be under a "great stone" near a spring at "the southwest corner" of the farm. Soon a group of men raised the stone. Finding no treasure, they continued digging until they had opened a hole about "six feet square and nearly as many feet deep." They found nothing and were later mocked by the witch for being easily fooled.[40] Bell's story grows increasingly bizarre and incredible, and it continues through other fantastic adventures, including attacks on John Bell, which culminate in his death at the hands of the witch. One odd incident stands out. Bell's son wrote, "We had not gone far before one of his shoes was jerked off. I replaced it on his foot, drawing the strings tight, tying a double hard knot. After going a few steps farther, the other shoe flew off in the same manner." The ordeal intensified, and the Witch struck him in the face.[41]

There is something odd about these accounts written by Ingram and Bell, which read like breezy dime novels. While the cornerstone of Ingram's book is the handwritten diary of John Bell's son Richard, it is suspicious that he never produced the diary. Showing it publicly and allowing it to be examined—including the ink, paper, and handwriting—would have lent credibility to its authenticity and very existence. The remarkable aspect of the Bell Witch story is that so many modern-day writers and researchers consider the account to be credible. These investigators either have failed to read the original account or are incredibly gullible, because it is a far-fetched claim that sounds more like hearsay and folklore, with little supporting evidence. In fact, the more one scrutinizes the evidence, the more suspicions are aroused, to the point of calling into question whether the story has *any* basis in fact.

A Masonic Tall Tale

Ingram's story about the Bell Witch and the diary supposedly given to him by Richard Bell may be a Masonic spoof. The book takes on an entirely different meaning if it is seen as representing—with a wink from those in on the meaning—key tenets of Freemasonry. Arthur Waite's authoritative *Encyclopedia of Freemasonry* defines it as "a system of morality veiled in allegory and illustrated by symbols."[42] An *allegory* is an extended metaphor in which its components carry one or more meanings in addition to the seemingly literal one—symbols that stand for something else. Waite stresses that in Masonic stories and rituals, "the significance is in the allegory which may lie behind it."[43] Masonry focuses on the Mystery of Death, whereby "the Mason is taught how to die,"[44] utilizing symbols such as the skull and grave. Masonry's Secret Vault symbolism pertains to the grave, buried treasure, and lost secrets that can never be known.[45] Much Masonic symbolism is based on the stonemason's trade, such as the Rough Ashlar—a stone in its original form—symbolizing man's natural state of ignorance.[46] Masonic rituals focus on the death of Hiram, master mason and architect of Solomon's Temple, whose allegorical grave measured $6 \times 6 \times 6$ cubic feet—the cube in Masonry being a symbol of truth. Significantly, in Bell's account of the treasure search, the cube is not quite completed. In Masonry, Hiram's name is Hiram Abif, whose legend—including his murder—represents "the dogma of the immortality of the soul."[47]

The location of the Bell Witch treasure at the southwest corner of the farm corresponds to the southwest corner of the Masonic lodge. This is one of the four corners to which the "hoodwinked" (blindfolded) initiate is conducted in the second (or Fellow Craft) degree in search of light, being opposite to the starting and ending point.[48] Near the end of *Our Family Trouble,* there is a most peculiar incident in which the elder John Bell has first one and then the other of his shoes yanked from his feet, presumably by the Witch.[49] Surely this invokes the Masonic Rite of Discalceation—from the Latin *discalceare,* to pluck off one's shoes. One does this when approaching a sacred place.[50] In the Bell narrative, the pledges the men make and their agreement to maintain secrecy evoke the Masonic society's penchant for keeping secrecy. So does the section "The Mysterious Hand Shaking," suggesting the Masons' secret hand-shake.[51] Other Masonic references abound.[52]

More Strange Encounters: The Andrew Jackson Affair

Before we finish examining the link between the Bell Witch and the Masons, it is worth looking at another account from Ingram's book: that of General Andrew Jackson, war hero and future president, having visited the Bell farm at the time of the haunting, as recounted by a neighbor of the Bells.[53] According to the story, as General Jackson's party approached the farmstead, men on horseback were following behind a wagon when the wheels froze, even though the roadway was smooth and level. The driver "whooped and shouted" at the team of horses, but the wagon would not budge. Each wheel was removed and examined, found to be in good working order, and reattached. Again the wagon would not budge. General Jackson then "threw up his hands" and blamed the witch, at which point a metallic voice from the bushes called out, "'All right General, let the wagon move on, I will see you again to-night.' . . . The horses then started unexpectedly of their own accord, and the wagon rolled along as light and smoothly as ever."[54] Jackson brought with him a "witch layer" or hunter, intent on casting the spirit from the house. He and his party spent the night in a candlelit room with the witch layer, who sat confidently in a chair, cradling a gun loaded with a silver bullet and boasting of his previous exploits and what he would do if the Witch appeared. Suddenly there were footsteps and a metallic voice: "All right, General, I am on hand ready for business." The voice then addressed the witch layer: "Now, Mr. Smarty, here I am, shoot." The witch layer was unable to fire his pistol. An unseen force struck him, knocking him to the floor. He quickly rose to his feet but immediately began crying out that something was grabbing his nose, before he ran off in fright—or so the story goes.[55]

Jackson's diary for the period makes no mention of such a visit.[56] The story is almost certainly fictional, yet writers continue to promote it without qualification. In "The Strange, True Story of the Bell Witch," journalist Don Wick writes that the Witch "is unique because of the large number of people who had direct experiences with it. Many of these people, General Andrew Jackson among them, were of unimpeachable reputation and unquestionable reliability." Wick recounts the story of Jackson as if it were historical fact.[57] Other writers also treat the account with little skepticism.[58] In 1828, Andrew Jackson fought a bitter campaign for president against John Quincy Adams, in what has been termed the dirtiest presidential election in U.S.history.[59] If the story had been true, it certainly would have been used against him in a campaign that saw Jackson accused of being anti-Christian, a gambler, a drunkard, a womanizer, and even a mass murderer.[60] But why include a visit by the seventh president of the United States? Jackson was a prominent Tennessee Mason, and he once served as the grand master of the Tennessee Masons.[61]

The parallels to Masonry appear too numerous and specific to be mere coincidence. Ingram was a longstanding Freemason who was buried in 1909 "under Masonic auspices."[62] There is also evidence that Ingram wrote the narrative attributed to Bell, as *Our Family Trouble* has no proven existence before the 1890s. Curiously, the "Bell" narrative—which was purportedly written in 1846 "from memory"—contains anachronisms: words, objects, or events that are mistakenly placed in the wrong time sequence. For example, the diary seems written in the context of modern spiritualism—which did not flourish until the decades after 1848 when the Fox Sisters sparked new interest in spirit communication. There are references to private detectives, as in "a professional detective" and "the detective business."[63] The word *detective* did not originate until about 1840 and then in England as an adjective; the earliest known use of the *noun* in America is 1853. It was not until 1852 that Alan Pinkerton, a Chicago deputy sheriff, created America's first agency of private detectives, called the Pinkerton Detective Agency.[64] This suggests that the "Bell" narrative is of later vintage.

Ingram as "Bell"

Joe Nickell holds a doctorate in English literature and has compared Bell's supposed diary with Ingram's writing; he concludes that Ingram is the author of *Our Family Trouble,* not Richard Bell.[65] He notes that Bell and Ingram use the same distinctive expressions—such as referring to the events as "high carnivals."[66] "Bell" refers to the occurrences as representing "the greatest of all secrets,"[67] and Ingram calls it "this greatest of all mysteries" and "the greatest mystery."[68] Both refer to facial features as "physiognomy" and characterize the elder John Bell in the same words. For instance, the "Bell" text states that he "was always forehanded, paid as he went."[69] Ingram writes, "He paid as he went. . . . He was always forehanded."[70] Both "Bell" and Ingram have a penchant for being long-winded and use *multi-page* paragraphs[71] and sentences of more than a hundred words.[72] These are certainly not common features of most writers. While Bell was a farmer, the text attributed to him is filled with learned words like *personation, declamation, vociferator, beneficence,* and *felicity,*[73] just like Ingram, who uses *lodgement, unregenerated, indomitable, mordacity,* and *alacrity.*[74]

"Bell" frequently promotes the bible and Christianity,[75] as does Ingram.[76] Both use literary allusions. For instance, "Bell" refers to evil spirits driven "out of the man into the swine"—a reference to Mark 5:13.[77] Ingram refers to a spirit "from the vasty deep"—an allusion to Shakespeare's *Henry IV.*[78] "Bell" writes about old John Bell, "[I]f there was any hidden or unknown cause why he should have thus suffered,"[79] evoking the Book of Job (Job 10: 2–18). Ingram's imperative to "observe the warning on the wall, whether it be written by the hand of the spectre, or indicted by the finger of conscience"[80] clearly alludes to Belshazzar's feast and the famous story of the handwriting on the wall, from the biblical passage Daniel 5.

When we apply a standard readability formula to both texts, it shows that "Bell" and Ingram had nearly identical reading levels: 14.3 and 14.4, indicating the number of years of education required to read the passage easily and presumably to write it.[81] The levels are high, placing each at the sophomore level of college. This is not surprising for journalist Ingram, but for rural farmer Bell, it would seem unlikely. There are many similarities, suggesting that the same person wrote both texts. Both occasionally use *myself* for *I*[82] and *that* for *who*[83] and are guilty of comma-splicing[84] and incorrect use of the question mark[85] and the semicolon.[86] Both also commit subject-verb agreement errors.[87]

Another English scholar, Jesse Glass, believes that it is unlikely that Ingram was the sole author of *Our Family Trouble*. He says that Nickell's work lacks a clearly identifiable, extended sample of Ingram's text in order to get an accurate baseline and that Nickell mistakenly assumes that Ingram wrote the Bell diary. Glass speculates that two of Ingram's colleagues collaborated on *The Authenticated History of the Bell Witch*, including the supposed diary, *Our Family Trouble*. The first suspect is Henry Melville Doak, who wrote with Ingram on the *Tobacco Leaf*. Glass found that Ingram and Doak wrote a supernatural serial in 1874, "The Spirit of Croly Place," which contained key themes that coincidentally would appear in Ingram's book. Glass observes that "The Spirit of Croly Place" involves a thwarted romance and the family patriarch's death by a vengeful spirit. Another suspect is James Rice, a city reporter for the *Tobacco Leaf* during the early 1890s. Glass says the writing style is overblown and emotive and borrows heavily from yellow journalism and the sensational dime novel genre of the time. This is the very same style of *Our Family Trouble*, and it stands in sharp contrast with Ingram's sober style.[88]

Nickell rejects Glass's argument, noting that "writers write in different styles" and that themes, of which all authors have several, are not linguistic evidence. He finds Glass's approach to be subjective, vague, and unnecessarily complicated—a violation of the principle of Occam's razor, which holds that the hypothesis with the fewest assumptions is to be preferred as most likely correct. Using Glass's approach, Nickell says, one could find any number of "suspects," when Ingram alone is clearly capable of having written every word of the Bell diary. Nickell, an accomplished literary detective and author of the book *Detecting*

Forgery, has uncovered a series of similar Masonic tall tales written during the nineteenth and twentieth centuries. Doing so appears to have been a common pastime of Masons during the period.[89]

Folklore or Fakelore?

Let us look more closely on the one known published account of the Bell Witch prior to the appearance of Ingram's book in 1894 and at a few press reports heralding its imminent release the previous year. That reference is Goodspeed's 1886 *History of Tennessee.* It states the following:

> A remarkable occurrence, which attracted wide-spread interest, was connected with the family of John Bell, who settled near what is now Adams Station about 1804. So great was the excitement that people came from hundreds of miles around to witness the manifestations of what was popularly known as the "Bell Witch." This witch was supposed to be some spiritual being having the voice and attributes of a woman. It was invisible to the eye, yet it would hold conversation and even shake hands with certain individuals. The freaks it performed were wonderful and seemingly designed to annoy the family. It would take the sugar from the bowls, spill the milk, take the quilts from beds, slap and pinch the children, and then laugh at the discomfiture of its victims. At first it was supposed to be a good spirit, but its subsequent acts, together with the curses with which it supplemented its remarks, proved the contrary.[90]

This passage seems to validate Ingram's story, yet there are red flags. Two of the most significant elements of the story do not appear in Goodspeed's account: the poisoning of John Bell and the visit by Andrew Jackson. Imagine—a soon-to-be president of the United States investigates a spirit haunting, and a prominent community figure is poisoned, yet these key events do not appear in a story produced by local historians. For a supposedly well-known event that persisted over years, there is not one additional reference to it predating the influence of Ingram's book. If, as Goodspeed asserts, excitement was so great that "people came from hundreds of miles around to witness the manifestations," there should be numerous newspaper references. Even after Ingram's book appeared in 1894, not a single local letter to a newspaper editor affirming the events is known to have appeared, yet Ingram claims that he was deluged by letters after mentioning that his book was forthcoming. A search of Tennessee newspapers prior to 1893, when Bell began promoting his forthcoming book, failed to turn up any mention of the Bell Witch.[91] This is puzzling, as it was common for nineteenth-century papers to reprint articles from other papers, so long as they gave credit. Books on the history of Tennessee are also devoid of references to the Witch.[92] While Ingram claims that an 1849 issue of *The Saturday Evening Post* contains a lengthy article on the Witch, no one can locate a copy. Microfilm for this year no longer exists, but searches for the years before and after 1849 failed to turn up any reference to the article.[93] If the article existed, it almost certainly would have been reprinted in the American press, given its sensational nature.[94] Ingram writes that the article in the *Post* resulted in a lawsuit against the magazine by Betsy Bell (then Betsy Powell). Ingram says that the issue was settled out of court, "the paper retracting the charges" in a later edition.[95] There is no record of any retraction in the magazine, nor are there any press reports discussing what likely would have been a newsworthy story: a threatened lawsuit involving a poltergeist.

Creating History

Given that the only reference to the Witch before Ingram's book is the Goodspeed passage, it should be treated with great skepticism. It is worth examining how many nineteenth-century county histories were created. Goodspeed was essentially a vanity publication, where people paid to have material inserted and contributors like Ingram could pay their way into its pages. During the late nineteenth and early twentieth centuries, many county history books were published by subscription. This is why there are more histories of northern U.S. counties than those in southern states, as during this period, the North was more affluent and urban. While useful and comprehensive in documenting local people and events, county histories were also business ventures by publishers who relied on subscribers, who were known to influence the content.[96] "Mug book" publishing coexisted with subscription sales, where publishers offered biographical sketches with line drawings and photos of "noteworthy residents" who just so happened to be early subscribers to the book. Once a guaranteed subscription level was achieved, the history would go to press.[97] It is for this reason that historian Harold Way cautions that the use of "county histories for research needs to be taken with a grain of salt"; and they were often filled with misspelled names, incorrect dates, and misinformation about local indigenous people. Way writes that other issues included "population errors (possibly done on purpose to exaggerate and aggrandize an area or region), causes of death (lack of information that could negatively affect the impression of an area, especially information on communicable disease outbreaks), boundary demarcation errors and land ownership misstatements have been found to exist in several county histories."[98]

Ingram was a respected newspaperman in Robertson County during the 1880s and could have presented the Bell Witch story to those involved in compiling the various town histories. Given the sheer size of the task of creating a county history, there would certainly be a reliance on prominent local figures in recounting tales from each community. The compilers would be none the wiser. Tennessee resident Jack Cook, who has researched the Bell Witch legend for decades, observes that "it would not be uncommon for a man of Ingram's influence to relate the entire county history under his own pen. There was certainly a big push to bring the South back into national prominence at the end of the 1800's. Something like this might have been perceived as a means of attracting attention or business for Robertson or Montgomery County."[99] Historian Fred Rolater has studied the Goodspeed county histories, and he notes that they continued to be compiled by local citizens, with little editing.[100] This means that Ingram easily could have planted the information on the Bell Witch with minimal suspicion. As he was a journalist, there would be little reason to edit his submission or question its veracity. Ingram was well known in the area. In 1866, he cofounded *The Robertson Register*.[101] Rolater writes that when local records are missing, county histories are very useful, but "the veracity of the stories contained in the histories depends entirely on the author and his intentions . . . Sometimes they are correct. Often they are wrong. To your specific question, could Martin Ingram have included a story that he . . . had enhanced for the reader? Yes, that is entirely possible. It certainly happened often in these histories."[102] While we cannot say with certainty whether the Goodspeed passage was planted by Ingram, it is worth asking what is more probable—that the Goodspeed reference is fictional, or that there is not one reference to the Bell Witch in print prior to 1886? This situation is even more far-fetched if we consider that people were supposedly flocking from hundreds of miles away to visit the house and that the events supposedly endured over several years.

What Really Happened?

Ingram's manuscript on the Bell Witch is undoubtedly a hoax, but what is not known is whether it is based on a preexisting legend. In his book,

Ingram presents numerous "Citizens Whose Statements Authenticate the History of the Bell Witch." But the 43 signers from Cedar Hill are only stating that several men mentioned by Ingram were trustworthy early settlers; their collective statement makes no mention of the Bell Witch claims.[103] It is curious that Ingram would cite such a list to give credence to the Witch if it was so well known. Also, not one of the accounts given in this section of the book is from a direct witness to the events; everyone is conveniently dead. Ingram cites letters from numerous persons, supposedly between 1891 and 1894, all claiming to have heard stories about the Bell Witch directly from reliable persons now deceased.[104] At least one, John A. Gunn, claims to have recently seen the alleged Richard Williams Bell manuscript, *Our Family Trouble*; others relate incidents that supposedly confirm the accuracy of the manuscript. However, Ingram has never produced any of these letters for examination.

In his testimonials, Ingram cites real people who say that they heard about the legend from their ancestors. If so many residents were involved in the conspiracy, it seems implausible that no one ever tattled to the papers or to others. Given the absence of confirming evidence, we cannot be sure if Ingram's story has a historical foundation, but recent research by Dr. Glass sheds new light on this part of the mystery.[105] Glass has painstakingly examined every reel of newspaper microfilm held by the Tennessee State Archives for Clarksville, the city closest to the Bell homestead, up to the year 1896. He could not find a single reference to the Witch prior to the 1890s.[106] He believes that the story is a hoax concocted by Ingram, who followed a tradition of Clarksville newspaper editors and journalists who took delight in fabricating and embellishing claims. He believes that readers would have immediately recognized the story for what it was.

Glass found the local papers of the period filled with accounts of the marvelous and the supernatural yet silent on the Witch. Why, he asks, "would the Bell Witch have escaped all historical references when even the smallest and most oblique references survive to attest to similar 'unexplained' sensations like the Cock Lane Ghost, and the Fox Sisters at Hydesville, New York?" One story to receive heavy local press coverage was a poltergeist outbreak on the John Livingston farmstead in Smithfield, West Virginia, during the 1890s. Glass believes that it served as the foundation for the Bell Witch story. He summarizes the parallels: "A disembodied voice begins to talk to Mr. Livingston and his wife while poltergeistic activity happens in the house. Hundreds of people visit the Livingston home to 'test' the spirit. . . . One feature of the haunting is an 'invisible rope' stretched across the road in front of Livingston's house that keeps horse and wagons standing still."[107] He believes that a second element of the Bell Witch story, that of the poisoning "witch" Katy Batts, was likely taken from the most sensational murder trial in the region of that period, in 1890, when George Avant poisoned his wife Kate with a strychnine-laced toddy. (A toddy was a common drink of the period and contained a mixture of liquor, sugar and spices.) The murder trial received intense press coverage. Sensationally, Avant was freed after a hung jury.[108]

Glass found that Ingram was a well-known skeptic on spiritualist matters and had even waged an anti-spiritualism campaign in his newspaper during the 1870s. During autumn 1874, Ingram even investigated a poltergeist outbreak at the W. B. Settle residence in Clarksville involving the mysterious movement of crockery and a butter stand. The episode caused a stir among the local spiritualist community. The brief bubble of excitement soon burst when the cause was discovered to have been "a beetle of unusual strength under the stand."[109] Ingram used the opportunity to ridicule spiritualists.[110]

Glass found that Clarksville newspapers of the late nineteenth century had developed their own literary style, especially Ingram's *Tobacco Leaf*, and that readers had become accustomed to his tongue-in-cheek stories. He is certain that locals would have recognized these stories as tall tales encouraged by the existence of the local Liar's Club.[111] The influence of such clubs has received scant attention from academics, yet they were pervasive in parts of rural America as popular entertainment in an era without TV or radio, and no doubt they were responsible for some famous hoaxes of the period. Glass observes, "To modern readers, the most puzzling part of these hoaxes was the apparent willingness of judges, preachers, professors and other people of note in the community to participate by giving testimonials vouching for the reality of the hoax." As an example, he cites the claims made in 1897 by a Kansas farmer, who reported that one of his cows had been snatched by a mysterious airship. The Kansas cow-napping caper took place during a wave of airship sightings, amid rumors that an American had perfected the world's first heavier-than-air flying machine.[112] Many prominent citizens of Woodson County signed an affidavit attesting to having witnessed the incident, which was later uncovered as a tall tale created by a local Liar's Club.[113] In a similar vein, Bell Witch researchers have long been baffled by the lack of historical documentation for the Witch, outside of the testimonials written by leading citizens from the greater Adams-Clarksville region, which appeared in Ingram's book. The key point is that none of Ingram's testimonials existed prior to the early 1890s. Glass's hypothesis could explain Ingram's many letters from locals, the existence of which has been challenged by Bell Witch researchers for decades. If correct, contemporary researchers have been guilty of viewing latter-nineteenth-century events using an early-twenty-first-century prism.

Ingram's book appeared at a time when sensationalist or yellow journalism was at its peak. Is it possible that the community played along in perpetrating a collective deception? Adams was a small, isolated, close-knit community in the early nineteenth century. In 1820, less than ten thousand people resided in Robertson County. Is it possible the locals were in on the deception in order to draw visitors to the area or as a joke? After all, the 1890s were the heyday of spiritualism, with an estimated eight million adherents in the United States and Europe.[114] At the same time, yellow journalism was being used to boost newspaper circulation by exaggerating or fabricating stories. After all, if Ingram and "Bell" are one and the same, the entire story is a fabrication weaved into a real historical backdrop. In 1887, Matthew Arnold coined the term "new journalism" to describe the novel approach that many papers were taking in describing the news by blending fact and fiction. Newspaper historian Karen Roggenkamp states that this journalism "was much more closely tied to American fiction than scholars have traditionally recognized or than most readers would assume today. The dramatic presentation of news defined the industry" and focused on selling a story around a central plot.[115] Roggenkamp writes that the new journalism created a unique atmosphere in which fictions and hoaxes were perpetrated. "Reporters and editors rewrote current events into stories laced with the familiar motifs of hoaxes, scientific and travel adventures, mystery and detective tales . . . resurrecting these popular fictional forms as news items." The result of these manufactured news items "was something that looked a lot like fiction, read like fiction, and entertained like fiction but was ultimately, they argued, better than fiction, because it was, after all, 'real.'"[116] Not surprisingly, the 1890s featured many literary hoaxes. In 1895, *Scientific American* even published a picture of a man in Loveland, Colorado, holding a potato weighing 86 pounds, 10 ounces. In reality, the prestigious magazine had been duped. The giant spud was a hoax created by the editor of the local *Loveland Reporter*, W. L. Thorndyke.[117]

Jack Cook believes that a community deception is a possibility. "The simplest explanation is that everyone knew what he (Ingram) was doing and supported the effort for whatever reasons, giving him the freedom to use real names and situations with no consequence to his good reputation." Cook points out several possible motives, the root of which was money. "Ingram was in need of the money—the community of Adams needed the publicity" for both their railroad and the promotion of local businesses.[118]

It cannot be overemphasized that Ingram's book, "Bell's" diary, and the Goodspeed reference each notes that the haunting attracted a considerable audience, yet there is not one early mention of these crowds. Even the Jackson visit cannot be corroborated. While the Witch narrative contains many classic poltergeist elements, from mysterious rapping and stones flying through the air to the strange happenings following Betsy Bell when she stayed with neighbors, the story as told by Ingram and "Bell" lacks logical consistency. Why is there no attempt by clergy to exorcise the Witch? Where are the visits by learned people or journalists? Where are the accounts that were said to have been written in the papers of the time or in *The Saturday Evening Post?* Where are the church records, court documents, letters, and diaries? The story of the Bell Witch defies logic and common sense. A restless spirit attacks a family over several years, pinching, slapping, pulling hair, disturbing sleep, pelting them with pieces of wood and stones, and even poisoning the patriarch of the family, yet they remain in the house! The scenario is absurd, especially if we consider that a young girl was the subject of the Witch's wrath. If, as was asserted, the spirit followed Betsy wherever she went, why not take her to a university and have doctors examine her—or to a church and attempt to have her exorcised? Where are the accounts from the families with whom Betsy had supposedly taken refuge in hope of getting away from the Witch, only to be followed wherever she went? Both the "Bell" diary and the Goodspeed passage report that numerous visitors heard and sometimes conversed with the Witch. If the haunting persisted for years and was as widely known at the time as we are led to believe, it certainly would have attracted scientists. After all, the documentation of these happenings would be considered one of the greatest events in the history of science: studying and proving the existence of a disembodied voice and proof of life after death.[119]

Conclusion: A Legend in Search of a History

Time and again, Ingram teases readers by bringing them tantalizingly close to confirmation that the original story as reported by Richard Bell was a real historical event. He tells of a lengthy article on the Witch in an 1849 issue of *The Saturday Evening Post* yet fails to mention the author, and the issue cannot be located. Even the vial of poison that was supposedly used to kill John Bell could have been examined for toxins, but it was tossed into a fire. Richard Bell's original handwritten diary, *Our Family Trouble*, cannot be found despite being a precious family heirloom.

When taken as a whole, the absence of documentation for the Bell Witch is just too incredible. All of the letters confirming the story come from Ingram, supposedly in response to the impending publication of his book on the Bell Witch.[120] Yet many of the names in the letters that Ingram cites *were* real people. This is a conundrum, unless we are dealing with collusion among the letter writers. The answer may lie in a recent find by Dr. Glass. On July 15, 1892, a year and a half before Ingram's book was published, a curious article appeared in the *Tobacco Leaf*, describing a series of visits by Ingram to several county residents, who were interviewed about "intensely thrilling events" from seventy-five years earlier. The events, we are told, had created "a wide-spread sensation which continued for several years, and induced people to travel hundreds of miles to witness the strange freaks that were then of daily occurrence."[121] A week later, in a second article, he again mentioned "the stirring events of that vicinity seventy-five years ago."[122] He is clearly referring to the Witch. Even more intriguing, several of those interviewed would later give testimonials in Ingram's book, including Mahalia Darden, Nancy Ayers, Joshua W. Featherston, and John Allen Gunn. Ingram knew these people well. He grew up with them, and he appears to have stayed with them during his extended visit. Could these testimonials have come from residents who had subscribed to Ingram's book in exchange for including their names?[123] Was it an attempt to boost tourism or to have some fun by being part of a local conspiracy? Soon after the book appeared, it did not seem to be taken too seriously. A reference to it in the *Hopkinsville News* of March 12, 1895, is buried near the end of a local news column; it says, "Reading 'The Bell Witch' is quite the custom here now and the whole community is full of witches, two-headed dogs and graveyard rabbits after dark."[124]

In the final analysis, the story of the Bell Witch is best viewed as historical fiction, because it is an event without a history. Much of the online literature is written by people with emotional investments, to the point where their position is no longer an objective research project intending to locate new discoveries but instead an ideology to be defended. All sorts of unsubstantiated claims have been spread in books and on the Internet, causing some people to think they are dealing with a real event. For instance, in December 1937, a journalist for the *Arizona Independent Republican* reported the standard tale of the Witch and then noted, "The intensity with which the Bell Witch story gripped Robertson

County is indicated by the fact that in 1875—many years after the specter's disappearance—two men residing near Cedar Hill, Tenn., murdered a farmhand named Smith and were freed by a jury on their plea that they thought Smith was a reincarnation of the Bell Witch."[125] Not surprisingly, there is no evidence of such a trial.[126]

In December 1955, a reporter for the *Rocky Mount Evening Telegram* in South Carolina recounted the story of "The Old Bell Witch" by writing that he was "prepared to submit a list of at least ten printed sources to support the account that follows."[127] One would feel confident in presuming that none of these unnamed sources appeared prior to the 1890s. In 1986, the Maryland-based *Frederick Post* reported on modern-day encounters with the Bell spirit: "Many visitors to the cave have reported seeing the figure of a dark-haired woman floating through the cave's passageways. Several people have said they were touched by something. Others have heard footsteps, and sounds like chains dragging along the cave floor. One boy had a cap snatched from his head and deposited on a ledge 30 ft. up."[128] But compared to the mayhem of the early nineteenth century, these shenanigans are tame and could easily have a naturalistic explanation, including the hat, which could have been thrown there by a mischievous young boy! If the original Bell Witch story is fiction, the happenings at the Witch Cave stand as a testament to the human imagination and our propensity for self-deception. The *Frederick Post* article also included an interview with a resident of Adams, Tennessee, "Bims" Eden, who said that he'd had several run-ins with the Witch. In one incident, he stated, "I heard somebody knocking at my front door. I looked through the window and saw the image of a figure I didn't recognize walking away from the house. I saw it walk behind a tree, but it didn't come out on the other side of the tree. I got my shotgun . . . but when I got to the tree, there was no one there. There were no footprints in that fresh snow either."[129] As it turns out, Mr. Eden had a vested interest in perpetuating the story: he was part owner of the old Bell Farmland where the Bell Cave is situated. It is the same cave that draws over one hundred thousand tourists annually. At the end of this full-length article on the Witch were the following words: "Story and pictures provided by the Tennessee Tourist Development."[130] The story appeared in the travel section and was essentially an advertisement.

The Bell Witch legend serves many functions. For locals, it is a source of regional identity and pride, as community members gather each year to watch theatrical performances that form a part of their shared history. For believers in the paranormal, it is evidence for life after death. For area shop owners and businesspeople, it is a means of attracting tourists and boosting the regional economy. To those who adhere to scientific principles and rules of evidence, the story is almost certainly a hoax. Whether it was based on an existing legend, we cannot say, but there is no evidence that it was. This is why it is best described as a legend in search of a history. In either case, while there is no evidence that anything of a paranormal nature took place, it is a formidable detective story.

CHAPTER 2

The Exorcist: Diary of a Demonic Possession

"My dear fellow," said Sherlock Holmes . . . "life is infinitely stranger than anything which the mind of man could invent."
—Arthur Conan Doyle[1]

Few films have left such a lasting impression on American popular culture as *The Exorcist*, which tells the story of twelve-year-old Regan Mac-Neil (played by Linda Blair), who becomes possessed by a demon. Set in Georgetown in northwest Washington, D.C., the story centers on elderly archeologist and exorcist Father Lankester Merrin (Max von Sydow) and his attempts to free Regan of the evil force controlling her. For decades *The Exorcist* has been the standard by which all other "based on a true story" supernatural thrillers have been compared. At the time of its release in December 1973, some theater-goers became so distressed that they either vomited or fainted; several suffered psychotic breakdowns. Writing in the *Journal of Nervous and Mental Disease*, Dr. James Buzzuto of the Cincinnati General Hospital reported on four cases of psychosis triggered by the film.[2] Psychiatrist Louis Schlan treated two cases in the Chicago suburb of Forest Park.[3] Similar reactions were recorded across the country.[4] Most of those who exhibited psychotic reactions were devout Christians with preexisting psychiatric conditions that were aggravated by the stress of watching the film and the recent loss of a loved one. Psychiatrists have even come up with a term for such trauma: cinematic neurosis. Claims that the film was based on a true story and that people can become possessed by demonic entities gave the storyline a powerful backdrop. Based on William Peter Blatty's best-selling book by the same name, the story was widely claimed to have been inspired by the real-life diary of Father Frank Bishop, who documented the exorcism of a boy in St. Louis, Missouri, in 1949.[5] It would become one of the most-watched horror films of its generation. The original release in 1973 earned two Academy Awards and over $300 million in box office receipts—an enormous sum for its time. When it was rereleased in 2000 with eleven extra minutes and billed as "The Version You've Never Seen," it ranked among the highest grossing reissues of all time.[6]

But just how accurate is the real-life story that gave inspiration to *The Exorcist*? To be able to make this assessment, we need to examine the events of 1949 as recorded by the people who were there. On Friday, August 20, 1949, an unusual article appeared on the front page of the *Washington Post*. Written by reporter Bill Brinkley under the title "Ritual of Exorcism Repeated: Priest Frees Mount Rainier Boy Reported Held in Devil's Grip," it caught the eye of a young student at Georgetown University: William Peter Blatty, who became fascinated by the case.

> In what is perhaps one of the most remarkable experiences of its kind in recent religious history, a 14-year-old Mount Rainier boy has been freed by a Catholic priest of possession by the devil, Catholic sources reported yesterday. Only after between 20 and 30 performances of the ancient ritual of exorcism, here and in St. Louis, was the devil finally cast out of the boy, it was said. In all except the last of these, the boy broke into a violent tantrum of screaming, cursing and voicing of Latin phrases—a language he had never studied—whenever the priest reached the climactic point of the ritual, "In the name of the Father, the Son and the Holy Ghost, I cast thee (the devil) out."

The article stated that the priest remained with the boy for two months and witnessed several strange happenings, including "the bed in which the boy was sleeping suddenly moving across the room."[7] Blatty wrote to the priest who had performed the exorcism, Father William Bowdern, in hopes of gaining greater detail about his ordeal. Bowdern declined, saying that he had been ordered by the archbishop to keep the case secret. But he disclosed that an assisting priest, Father Raymond Bishop, had kept a diary of the episode. While the novel that Blatty would go on to write, *The Exorcist*, was fictional, it was inspired by the events in St. Louis. Writer Thomas Allen eventually obtained a copy of the diary and used it to write his book *Possessed*, which was published in 1993.

The diary also forms the crux of a documentary by the same name. Its authenticity has been verified by Father Walter Halloran, an eyewitness to the strange events.[8]

Blatty's novel chronicles the possession of a young girl and the attempts by Catholic priests to exorcise her. In real life, the possessed subject was a boy. The "true story" aspect is a major reason for the remarkable success of both the film and book. English professor and paranormal expert Alan Brown observes that *The Exorcist* "is not only one of the most frightening films ever made, but it is generally considered to be a fairly accurate depiction of an actual exorcism."[9] The late Father Francis Cleary, a bible scholar at St. Louis University, also praised the realism of the story, telling the *National Catholic Register*, "This is the one case of which we have the best record."[10] The exorcism not only was witnessed by doctors and nurses but also by Frank Bubb Sr., who worked on the top-secret Manhattan Project, which culminated in the creation of the world's first atomic bomb. At the time of the exorcism, he was a professor of physics and mathematics at Washington University in St. Louis. Bubb was left shaken when a small table in the boy's room appeared to levitate, leading him to comment later that "there is much we have yet to discover concerning the nature of electromagnetism."[11]

In the diary, the possessed boy is identified only as "R," to protect his privacy. In his book, Allen refers to him as "Robbie," which is a pseudonym. Robbie was born in 1935, into a struggling family in Cottage City, Maryland, near Washington, D.C. A single child, he was raised as an Evangelical Lutheran. Evangelicals emphasize the teachings of the four gospels (Matthew, Mark, Luke, and John) in the New Testament—the biblical scriptures that Christians believe were written after the birth of Jesus of Nazareth. Robbie shared the house with his parents and maternal grandmother.[12] He also had a beloved aunt in St. Louis who often visited. She was a devoted spiritualist, believing that spirits of the dead exist in another plane of reality and can be contacted through psychic mediums. She introduced him to the Ouija board, and the two would use it to contact what they believed were spirits of the dead from "the other side." Ouija boards are also referred to as "spirit talking boards"; they have many numbers and letters printed on the surface and the words "yes" and "no." Players place their fingertips on a small heart-shaped piece of wood (known as a *planchette*), which they move about in response to questions they have supposedly asked the spirits, thus spelling out a response. His aunt explained how, even without a Ouija board, "spirits could try to get through to this world by rapping on walls."[13] This was a well-known phenomenon among spiritualists of the time, who would try to develop a code by asking questions and counting the number of raps.[14]

The Possession Begins

It was a Saturday evening in the dead of winter 1949 when strange things began to happen. It was January 15. Thirteen-year-old Robbie was at home with his grandmother when she heard a mysterious dripping sound, and a painting of Christ appeared to shake. Over the next eleven days, the house was plagued by peculiar rapping and scratching sounds, which were attributed to rodents. On January 26, the family received devastating news: Robbie's aunt had died in St. Louis. Emotionally shattered, Robbie began to withdraw and obsess over the Ouija board, experimenting with it for hours a day. He may have been trying to contact his aunt.[15] Over the next several days, Robbie said he heard a mysterious squeaking like that made by shoes, as if someone were walking by his bed. Six nights later, his mother and grandmothers lay next to Robbie in bed in an effort to comfort him, when they all heard the squeaking. His mother called out to the dead aunt, "Is that you?" She asked the spirit aloud to knock three times if it was the aunt. Father Bishop's diary records that the trio felt "waves of air" on their skin and heard distinct knocks followed by "claw scratchings on the mattress." One possibility is that the squeaking was caused by the contracting bedsprings, because the sound "was heard only at night when the boy went to bed." As his mother and grandmother continued to lie with Robbie on his bed, Father Bishop wrote, they "heard something coming toward them similar to the rhythm of marching feet and the beat of drums." The sound appeared to "travel the length of the mattress and back again" repeatedly. A similar effect could have been created by tapping one's toes against the footboard of the bed.[16] Had Robbie caused the noises—or was his aunt trying to communicate from the afterlife?

Over the next four nights, strange markings appeared on Robbie's body. They would soon take the form of bloody messages scratched into his skin. Whenever the scratching noises were ignored, the mattress would shake. In one instance, it shook so violently that a bedspread was pulled loose.[17] Over the ensuing days and weeks, the disturbances intensified. They shared one common feature: Robbie was always nearby, whether they happened at home or in school. For instance, Father Bishop writes that fruit, such as a pear and an orange, flew across the room. "Milk and food were thrown off the table and stove. The bread-board was thrown on to the floor. Outside the kitchen a coat on its hanger flew across the room; a comb flew violently through the air and extinguished blessed candles; a Bible was thrown directly at the feet of R, but did not injure him in any way." When Robbie's desk at school mysteriously slid across the floor, he reportedly decided not to attend, to avoid further embarrassment. It also provided a convenient excuse to get out of school, which he loathed.[18]

Robbie began acting strangely and was unruly. His parents consulted a physician, a psychiatrist, and a psychologist. The doctor found Robbie to be in good health, with the exception of being "high-strung." The psychiatrist gave him a clean bill of health, declaring that he appeared to be "normal." The opinions of the psychologist were not recorded. His parents also sought the views of a spiritualist and of Lutheran clergy.[19] The Reverend Luther Schulze of the nearby St. Stephen's Evangelical Lutheran Church made several visits to the home to counsel the family on how best to help Robbie. They told him that they feared he was possessed by an evil ghost. His mother wondered if the "ghost" was his recently deceased aunt. While at the house, the Reverend Schulze reported seeing moving furniture and flying crockery. Robbie's parents grew increasingly alarmed and noted that his personality was changing. He appeared sad and withdrawn, and one night, apparently in his sleep, they heard him cursing. Starting in early February, the boy seemed tormented by nightmares, thrashing about in his sleep for hours at a time.[20]

Thinking that a change of scenery might help Robbie's deteriorating condition, the Reverend Schulze got his parents to agree to let him stay overnight with him and his wife. At about midnight, Schulze reported, he was awakened by a strange vibrating sound. Checking on Robbie, he found that the boy's bed was shaking "like one of those motel vibrator beds, but much faster." He said that as the bed vibrated, Robbie was awake and lying "perfectly still." Other disturbances broke out: a chair Robbie was sitting in began to move and eventually tipped over. At about 3:00 AM, the boy appeared to move across the floor while covered with blankets. At times he seemed to be in a trance.[21] Eventually Schulze suggested that the parents consult a Catholic priest, saying that they had more experience with such matters.[22] Robbie was examined twice more by a psychiatrist but failed to show for a third appointment, his parents opting for the services of a priest to exorcise him. While the decision to seek an exorcist may seem like an extreme measure so early in the case, psychiatrist Elizabeth Bowman believes that it may relate to a series of press reports about the deplorable conditions of Maryland mental hospitals. This was a huge scandal at the time, with conditions so poor that a headline in the *Baltimore Sun* proclaimed them a "Maryland

Shame" and described the story as "The Worst Story Ever Told by the Sun Papers."[23] Mental illness was a huge stigma at the time.[24] Given Reverend Schulze's recommendation and the family's religious beliefs, they decided to heed his advice, and they sought out Father E. Albert Hughes of St. James Catholic Church in nearby Mount Rainier.

Father Hughes was summoned to perform the exorcism, but with the boy's condition steadily worsening, he was admitted to a Georgetown hospital between late February and early March, as it was a Jesuit facility and seemed better equipped to deal with his condition on a spiritual level.[25] Father Hughes continued his preparation to exorcise Robbie. As the boy called out in a strange language, mysterious scratches began to appear on his chest. The attending nuns also struggled without success to "keep the bed still." As Father Hughes began his exorcism, Robbie, who was restrained to a bed, managed to free one of his hands. Snapping off a steel bedspring, he used it as a weapon, ripping into the priest's flesh, slashing his arm from his shoulder to his wrist. It required over one hundred stiches to close. Deeply affected by the attack and reeling from the trauma, Father Hughes withdrew from the case, feeling that he was dealing with a power beyond his capacity.[26]

Upon returning home from the hospital, the family discussed the possibility of making a temporary move to St. Louis to be with relatives. Shortly after, Robbie's mother heard screams from the bathroom. Rushing in, she found him with the letters *LOUIS* scratched across his ribs, oozing blood. When she asked him if it referred to St. Louis, he soon found and revealed the word *YES* scratched into another part of his trunk. When the question arose as to when to go, the word *SATUR-DAY* was found scratched into his hip. As to how long they should stay, *3 WEEKS* soon appeared on his chest.[27] The likelihood that Robbie had produced the scratches was dismissed on the grounds that his mother "was keeping him under close supervision."[28] However, Robbie easily could have made the letters earlier and revealed them when he deemed the time was appropriate. According to Father Bishop's diary, "The markings could not have been done by the boy for the added reason that on one occasion there was writing on his back."[29] This view seems naive; such feats are well within the realm of possibility by a determined youth—with or without a wall mirror. This was the only time when the scratched messages appeared on a difficult-to-reach part of Robbie's body.

After the family boarded a train and arrived in Missouri, the strange happenings followed. In St. Louis, there were more poltergeist outbreaks, whereupon Father Bishop was drawn to the case. There the priest would

meet the boy and write his now-famous diary. When he placed a bottle of holy water in Robbie's bedroom while the boy was supposedly
asleep, it soon went flying across the room. Another time, the entrance
to Robbie's room was mysteriously blocked by a fifty-pound bookcase.
Furniture also inexplicably tumbled over. Despite these occurrences,
both Father Bishop and Father Bowdern were unconvinced that something supernatural was taking place. They believed that Robbie could
have produced each of the disturbances in St. Louis.[30] Bowdern eventually changed his mind and was instructed by Archbishop Joseph Ritter
to perform an exorcism on the boy, accompanied by Father Bishop and
Jesuit graduate student Walter Halloran.

Father Bowdern went to the boy's room and began the formidable
task of exorcising him. Soon, eerie scratches were observed on Robbie's
body. The word *HELL* in capital letters appeared across his chest "in
such a way that R [Robbie] could look down upon his chest and read
the letters plainly." Father Bishop's diary also noted that "a picture of
the devil" appeared on the boy's leg, leading him to speculate that "the
exorcism prayers had stirred up the devil." The boy then appeared to
fall asleep, only to awaken and start "punching the pillow with more
than ordinary force."[31] With his only weapons being faith in God and
an ancient ritual that had been used many times in the history of the
Church, Father Bowdern felt certain that he was in an epic struggle
against Satan. On Thursday, March 17, the boy became violent and
began to thrash about wildly, spitting in the faces of the priests and even
at his own mother. He even urinated. Walter Halloran noted that the boy
would say things like "I got you a good one there" and "How do you
like that?" Later Robbie claimed to have no recollection of spitting.[32]
At one point Robbie exhibited such strength that two men were needed
to hold him down. Robbie "shouted threats of violence" and at times
struck out at the men who were trying to help him. The diary reports,
"He used a strong arm whenever he could free himself, and his blows
were beyond the ordinary strength of the boy."[33]

As the exorcism continued on and off in the coming days, the boy
would occasionally scream in a "diabolical, high-pitched voice." Other
times he would strike out with closed fists at those around him. One blow
landed on Halloran's nose, breaking it. At times, the scene appeared to
be surreal, as Robbie would sit up and begin to sing songs such as "The
Old Rugged Cross," "The Blue Danube" and "Swanee." He would weep,
curse, and bite his caretakers. At times his antics put the attending priests
on an emotional roller coaster. At one point, on March 18, he appeared
to free himself of the Devil, calling out, "He's going, he's going" and

"There he goes." His body went limp. He appeared to be normal and said that he had seen a vision of a black-robed figure walking away from him in a black cloud.[34] However, there was little respite for the priests; before long, he began to cry out, "He's coming back! He's coming back!" Soon after, the priests were again trying to drive the Devil from Robbie. At times it appeared that Satan was speaking and writing through him. In one instance, he wrote, "In 10 days I will give a sign on his chest . . . he will have to have it covered to show my power." Another time he wrote, "Dead bishop."[35] On April 1, the boy was taken to the rectory and baptized.

The priests were convinced that they were in a desperate struggle to save Robbie's corrupted soul. Despite the gravity of the situation, in hindsight, some of Robbie's actions bordered on comical. For instance, as the priests tried desperately to exorcise the boy through the remainder of March, random scratches and words continued to appear on his body. When there was a discussion of Robbie attending school once the ordeal was over, he grimaced, opened his shirt, and revealed two words clearly scratched onto his chest: *NO SCHOOL*. Apparently Satan has an aversion to education.[36] If there was any question that Robbie was responsible for the origin of the letters that mysteriously appeared on his body, it was seemingly answered on one occasion, when Jesuit priest William Van Roo watched him scratch out words on his chest. It is unclear whether he realized he was being observed: "Robbie's right hand began moving on his chest. Van Roo looked down. Blood. He had not noticed the length of Robbie's fingernails. With one of those fingernails Robbie was scratching two bloody words on his chest in large capital letters: HELL and CHRIST."[37] During an earlier incident, priests looked on in amazement as they reported seeing "a new scratch slowly moving down his leg."[38] While this may seem mysterious, Robbie could have made a quick scratch just before the priests looked at his leg. He had let out a yelp just before noticing the scratch appear, which suddenly drew their attention to his leg. What they witnessed may have been the immediate aftereffect of the scratch as the skin responded to the injury. Joe Nickell has produced similar scratches while experimenting on his own body.

On April 4, the family returned home to Maryland due to Robbie's father's need to work and because of the strain that the family's presence had placed on relatives in St. Louis. Within five days, the boy's condition worsened, and he was sent back to St. Louis, where he was admitted to a hospital operated by an order of monks. Due to his violent past, he was strapped onto a bed in a high-security room with iron bars across the window. During the day, he was well enough to receive religious education classes and go on short outings; at night the exorcism continued. There were several attempts to give him Holy Communion, but each time he spit out the blessed wafer of bread. Robbie said that the Devil would not allow it.[39]

The ordeal finally ended on April 18, when Robbie proclaimed, "He's gone!" He said he had seen a vision of "a very beautiful man wearing a white robe and holding a fiery sword." The figure, presumably Jesus, took the sword and drove the Devil into a pit. Two years later, on August 15, 1951, Father Bishop recorded that the boy and his parents had visited the brothers who had cared for him; he observed, "R, now 16, is a fine young man." He also wrote that Robbie's parents were now Catholics, "having received their first Holy Communion on Christmas Day, 1950."[40]

Seeking Answers

The case of Robbie appears to involve superstition masking a troubled boy's problems, prompting him to engage in elaborate role-playing. Bishop Ritter was curious about the case and appointed a Jesuit philosophy professor to determine the nature of the boy's disturbances. He concluded that Robbie had not been demonically possessed,[41] as nothing was beyond the abilities of a teenager to produce: moving furniture, flying objects, tantrums, or even his "trance state." It is also clear that the boy was writing the letters on his body, as witnessed by one of the Jesuits. These factors point to role-playing and trickery. In 1999, the case took an unexpected turn when Maryland historian Mark Opsasnick conducted an investigation into Robbie's early life, interviewing over one hundred people, including former neighbors and classmates. The more he looked into the case, the more his suspicions were aroused. For instance, both the book *Possessed* and the documentary on the case, *In the Grip of Evil*, claimed that the family's home was in Mount Rainier, Maryland, when clearly it was not: they lived in nearby Cottage City. This discrepancy titillated his interest, prompting him to delve deeper, reasoning that if such basic information was flawed, what else might be untrue? He told the *Washington Post* that the boy had been a clever trickster who relished pulling pranks to frighten children and even his own mother.[42] In his final report on the case in 2000, he disclosed that some of Robbie's childhood pranks closely resembled the poltergeist activities that centered on him. For instance, his childhood best friend describes the following incident that took place during the 1948–49 school year: "We were in eighth grade . . . and we were in class together at Bladensburg Junior High. He was sitting in a chair and it was one of those deals with one arm attached and it looked like he was shaking the desk—the desk was shaking and vibrating extremely fast and I remember the teacher yelling at him to stop it and . . . he . . . yelled 'I'm not doing it' and they took him out of class."[43]

In the Grip of Evil shows one of the priests commenting on Robbie's uncanny ability to spit on the faces of the clergymen with remarkable accuracy from several feet away. He seems to imply that it was of supernatural origin. Yet one of the boy's schoolmates and neighbors said that parts of the documentary were exaggerated, especially Robbie's spitting, as Robbie and his close friend had a habit of spitting in an unusual way. He said they had the ability to "spit with great accuracy up to ten feet. It was a common thing. They'd keep their mouths closed and raise their lips and spit through their teeth and they somehow developed a way to do that. I saw them do that all the time."[44]

As for the boy's moving bed, this schoolmate said that he had been in Robbie's house and seen the bed and that the movement was no mystery. "In those days the beds had wire springs and were on wheels and it was not too hard at all to make the bed bounce and move about—it was harder to keep it in one place and his bed was like that. A lot of these things can be exaggerated to make a story and that is exactly what happened."[45] Opsasnick concludes that the boy, to whom he refers as "Rob Doe," was a seriously disturbed child who was adept at manipulating those around him. He writes, "[T]here is no question there was something wrong with Rob Doe prior to January 1949, something that modern-era psychiatry might have best addressed. Rob Doe was not just another normal teenage boy."[46] He says that Rob exhibited emotional problems stemming from a poor home life. "The facts show that he was a spoiled and disturbed only child with a very overprotective mother and an unresponsive father. To me, his behavior was indicative of an outcast youth who desperately wanted out of Bladensburg Junior High School at any cost. He wanted attention, and he wanted to leave the area and go to St. Louis. Throwing tantrums was the answer. He began to play his concocted game. For his efforts he got a collection of priests . . . who doted over him."[47]

The Power of an Idea

The lesson from *The Exorcist* is that of the power of belief on the human mind. As Chicago sociologist William Isaac Thomas once famously wrote, "If men define situations as real, they are real in their consequences."[48]

While the film is likely based on a hoax, marketing it as "based on real events" enhances the power of the story. Considering the mere possibility that the story has a kernel of truth is likely to increase its emotional impact, as it could be seen as potentially happening in real life. This is exactly what occurred when it was released. Watching these events on the big screen was overwhelming for some viewers, who suffered traumatic neurosis and psychotic episodes.

The case of "Robbie" is a fascinating example of a supposed paranormal disturbance that began as a poltergeist outbreak, advanced to one of alleged spirit communication, and finally escalated to diabolic possession. The annals of the supernatural are replete with cases involving young men and women who were able to fool the adults around them, in part because the adults did not believe it was possible for someone so young to successfully deceive them. Two famous examples are the Fox Sisters and the Davenport Brothers. The modern spiritualist movement was launched in 1848, after poltergeist disturbances centering on the Fox Sisters in Hydesville, New York. It was essentially founded on the mischievous pranks of children. It was not until 1888 that Maggie Fox publicly confessed to having faked communication with the spirits of the dead.[49] Margaret Fox said that their shenanigans began as an effort "to terrify our dear mother, who was . . . easily frightened." She noted that her mother "did not suspect us of being capable of a trick because we were so young." Among their antics, which went undetected for decades, they shook the dinner table, threw slippers at a disliked relative, and produced noises by knocking on a bed frame and by bumping the floor with an apple tied to a string.[50]

In 1854, two schoolboys in Buffalo, New York, Ira and William Davenport, fooled many people into believing they possessed paranormal powers. The sons of a local police officer, the pair was responsible for cutlery dancing around the family's kitchen table and other oddities. Ira claimed that spirits would occasionally take him to faraway places. The boys soon advanced to spirit rapping, communication with the dead, and trance writing. Ira later confessed to magician Harry Houdini.[51] In recalling the saga of spiritualism and modern-day claims of otherworldly spirits in films like *The Exorcist*, it is perhaps appropriate to recall the words of philosopher George Santayana: "Those who cannot remember the past are condemned to repeat it."

CHAPTER 3

Poltergeist: The Inspiration for the Film

You know my method. It is founded upon the observation of trifles.
—Sherlock Holmes[1]

In 1982, Steven Spielberg's *Poltergeist* enthralled audiences with the story of the Freeling family of suburban Cuesta Verde, California. Their life is turned upside down when the youngest daughter, Carol Anne (Heather O'Rourke), strikes up a relationship with a mysterious force that soon enters the house through their television. Eventually the little girl is abducted through her bedroom closet, which is a portal to another dimension. The film earned just under $122 million at the box office: a smashing success, as it cost just $10.7 million to make.[2] While containing several incidents that are commonly attributed to poltergeists, the storyline soon grows increasingly fantastic and bears little resemblance to alleged real encounters, as bodies and coffins explode out of the ground before the house implodes and is sucked into another reality. The inspiration for the film is said to be based on a much more light-hearted outbreak 24 years earlier in suburban New York City.[3]

Beginning in early February 1958 and persisting for five weeks, Americans were captivated by a series of strange occurrences that were reported at a house in the town of Seaford, on eastern Long Island (pop. 14,718 in 1960). Visitors arrived in droves, hoping to glimpse the mysterious happenings, until they stopped in mid-March, as suddenly as they had begun. The poltergeist was affectionately dubbed "Popper" in the press, for its propensity to pop open bottle tops before tipping them over. But its antics were by no means confined to bottles, and they included everything from toppling bookcases and furniture to sending plates, bowls, and religious statues flying through the air. It just as easily could have been dubbed "Tipper" or "Tosser." More mischievous than malevolent, Popper the Poltergeist seemed more akin to Casper the Friendly Ghost than the evil force that typifies many hauntings today. It quickly became a media darling. Many notable journalists reported on the haunting and got to know the family on a first-name basis. Among them were the editor of the influential Catholic magazine *America* and Robert Wallace of *Life*; both spent time at the home and wrote features on the outbreak. Legendary broadcaster Edward R. Murrow was given a tour of the house. *The New York Times* covered the strange goings-on, and wire services brought the case to the attention of people around the world. It seemed as though Popper was popping up everywhere—from the *New Yorker* to *Reader's Digest*. Later that year, just before Halloween, Popper's exploits were shown to a national television audience on the popular CBS show *Armstrong Circle Theatre*. The hour-long program featured live interviews with witnesses and reenactments of the events by professional actors.[4]

The case of Popper has been viewed as a landmark in the history of poltergeist research, as it attracted scientists from the Duke University Parapsychology Laboratory.[5] They eventually concluded that the events were most likely a genuine example of telekinesis—the ability to move objects with one's mind.[6] As paranormal historian Rosemary Guiley observes, it represents "the first modern investigation by parapsychologists of poltergeist disturbances." She also writes that the episode "remains unsolved."[7] The investigators from Duke were baffled, and they ruled out human deception. Other researchers consider the case to represent some of the best evidence for the existence of a poltergeist. In his book on true suburban legends, Sam Stall states that no one has been able to "offer an explanation for the goings-on."[8] In *Haunted America*, Michael Norman and Beth Scott report "that neither the police nor the country's most prestigious parapsychologists were able to explain" the events.[9] In 2012, *Huffington Post* journalist David Moye wrote that "there was never any explanation for the events."[10] How accurate are these claims? Have any scientists been able to offer a plausible answer for these mysterious happenings? Curiously, if one were to travel from the site of the Seaford events at 1648 Redwood Path to 112 Ocean Avenue in Amityville, the scene of another famous haunting eighteen years later, it is just over five miles, or about twelve minutes in normal traffic.[11]

The Herrmanns seemed to be the typical American family, residing in a modest one-story, ranch-style home in the suburbs, amid rows of similar houses. A green three-bedroom home with white trim, immediately after it was built in 1953, the family moved into it. The couple oozed normalcy and level-headedness, two traits that lent credence to their story. A devout Catholic, James Herrmann, 43, lived with his wife Lucille, 38, and their two children: Lucille, 13, and James Jr., 12, also known as "Jimmy." The Herrmanns were well educated and financially successful—pillars of their community. James was a representative of Air France, serving as a Marine Corps sergeant in the Pacific theater during the Second World War. He was also a member of the Seaford Auxiliary Police, public volunteers who would assist the regular police with routine duties, such as traffic control at community events, and who had the power to make arrests. Lucille was a housewife and former head nurse at St. Luke's Hospital in Manhattan.[12] Perhaps the episode held widespread appeal because of the prankish nature of Popper's deeds or because people could identify with the Herrmanns, for it seemed that just as easily, it could have been one's own house that was infested. There is no doubting the impact of the affair, which briefly propelled the family to celebrity status and allowed them to meet a *Who's Who* list of luminaries of the day, from Jack Parr to Douglas Edwards, before fading back into obscurity.

Popper Is Born

Monday, February 3, 1958, was a typical winter's day on Long Island. It was clear and chilly with a high of 29 degrees; the relative humidity was nothing out of the ordinary: 43 percent. Then something extraordinary happened. According to press reports, Mrs. Herrmann was at home with her two children when suddenly, at about 3:30 p.m., loud noises could be heard echoing through the house, like champagne corks popping. As she went from room to room to investigate, she found that several different bottles containing a variety of liquids had popped their tops and fallen over. In the bedroom, the cap on a bottle of holy water had come unscrewed, and the container had tipped over and spilled out its contents. It was a similar scene in the bathroom cabinet, where two bottles were laying on their sides—one of shampoo, the other, medicine; their caps were also unscrewed. In the kitchen, a bottle of liquid starch had been the target, while in the cellar, it was a gallon container of bleach.[13] Each of the bottles had a screw top made of either metal or plastic. In Jimmy's bedroom, a ceramic doll had its neck snapped, while the model of a plastic ship had several small pieces broken off.[14] Mrs. Herrmann found the events to be eerie and mystifying, but she was not frightened.

At a loss to explain the strange sequence of events, Lucille rang her husband at his New York City office. James was equally perplexed, but since no one had been hurt and there was no major damage, he decided to keep to his normal routine and returned home that evening at seven o'clock on the Long Island Railway. During the 35-mile trip, he had time to think of possible explanations. Perhaps it was a rare chemical reaction? Yet none of the liquids were carbonated. The hypothesis was soon dismissed, as a variety of contents were involved, and the holy water was just plain water. He also considered the possibility that there might be a practical joker in the family.[15] The next three days passed uneventfully.

The afternoon of Thursday, February 6, it happened again, at nearly the same time: 3:30. Mrs. Herrmann and the children were startled by loud popping as half a dozen bottles in different parts of the house lost their caps and tumbled over. The following day at the same time, with the same trio on hand, there was a third series of incidents. The final straw came on Sunday morning at 10:15, when Mr. Herrmann experienced the phenomenon firsthand; he was so disturbed that he rang the police. While he stood in the bathroom doorway and chatted with Jimmy, who was brushing his teeth at the sink, two bottles near the sink tipped over at the same time.[16] Nassau County patrolman James Hughes responded to Mr. Herrmann's call. What follows is a report on the incident written by Nassau County detective Joseph Tozzi, who was later assigned to the case:

> On Sunday, Feb. 9th, 1958, at about 1015 hours, the whole family was in the dining room of the house. Noises were heard to come from different rooms, and on checking it was found that the holy water bottle on the dresser in the master bedroom had again opened and spilled, a new bottle of toilet water on another dresser in the master room had fallen, lost its screw cap and also a rubber stopper and the contents were spilled. . . . [A] bottle of shampoo and a bottle of Kaopectate [a popular antacid and anti-diarrhea medication] in the bathroom had lost their caps, fallen over and were spilling their contents. The starch in the kitchen was also opened and spilled again and a can of paint thinner in the cellar had opened, fallen and was spilling on the floor.

As Officer Hughes was interviewing the family in the living room, loud pops rang out from the bathroom. Investigating with the Herrmanns in tow, he found that the medicine and shampoo bottles had tipped over again.[17]

As the disturbances began to increase in frequency and magnitude, on Tuesday, February 11, Detective Tozzi was given the go-ahead to investigate the case full-time. Two days later, Tozzi gathered up five of the bottles that had popped their tops, spilling their contents, and sent them to the police lab in Mineola, New York, for analysis. The tests were unremarkable, and no foreign substances were found.[18] Several of the affected items were targeted more than once. For instance, on Saturday, February 15, a bottle of holy water on the couple's bedroom bureau was found tipped over for a fourth time. Mr. Herrmann noticed that it felt warm. Suddenly, he dashed through the house, touching as many bottles as he could find, hoping to identify a pattern, but none were warm.[19]

That evening in the living room, a dramatic incident took place involving Mr. Herrmann's adult aunt, Marie Murtha, while she was watching TV. Jimmy and young Lucille were also in the room, sitting on the sofa. Suddenly at 7:40, Marie said that a porcelain figurine began to wiggle and then flew through the air two to three feet before landing on the rug, undamaged. It was one of two figurines resting on a coffee table by the sofa. A closer examination of this incident is revealing. The figurines were located *near Jimmy.*[20] While Marie claims to have seen the statuette lift off and move through the air, the event happened quickly. When deception expert Milbourne Christopher looked at a report of the incident, he noted that a TV set was on in the room and observed, "It is logical to suppose that her attention was there. A quick movement by the occupant of the sofa could have jarred the small end table with enough impact to send the upright figurine falling to the floor the mere two feet away."[21]

Soon, two members of the famous Duke University Parapsychology Lab arrived on the scene: Dr. J. Gaither Pratt and William Roll. Both men interviewed Officer Hughes while the incident was fresh in his mind. He corrected the police report, saying that one bottle, not two, had fallen over in the bathroom while he was there.[22] He said he had inspected the bathroom before hearing the noise and was certain that the bottle had not been on its side. However, Roll wrote that when Hughes was questioned further, he had excluded "the possibility that someone had turned the bottle over after he had seen it as they were leaving the bathroom."[23] Roll and Pratt could not explain the events and eventually suggested the existence of RSPK: recurrent spontaneous psychokinesis, whereby one of the family members—most likely young Jimmy—had unconsciously created a psychic force. There is one major problem with this hypothesis: the existence of such a force has never been proven. Despite Pratt and Roll's trust in the Herrmann family and their confidence that the children were not consciously involved, about fifty of the sixty-seven recorded events they tallied centered on Jimmy.[24] They concluded that seventeen incidents could not, "if correctly reported, be explained as easily performed, single pranks."[25] The key words here are "if correctly reported" by the many visitors to the house. While Roll and Pratt were believers in the existence of psychic phenomena and poltergeists, forty-five years after the case had faded from the headlines, Roll admitted that he still "could not be certain" whether or not trickery was involved.[26]

One telling incident occurred on February 19 and is described in Detective Tozzi's police report. Tozzi was with the Herrmanns in the basement, while Jimmy was upstairs doing homework at the dining room table. A loud noise echoed out. Racing upstairs, Tozzi wrote that they found that a "porcelain figurine had left the end table at the south end of the sofa and flown through the air approximately 10 feet" before striking a desk and breaking off one of its arms. Tozzi eliminated Jimmy as a suspect, noting that "No one was in the living room at this time . . . it would have been impossible for James to have left the dining room, thrown the figurine and returned to the dining room" without going undetected by those in the basement, as the wooden floors were creaky and "every sound can be heard through them."[27] But Tozzi's report is just that—a report—and does not necessarily reflect what happened. He failed to consider a plausible alternative explanation. James Jr. easily could have obtained the object and hidden it where he was doing his homework. It was small enough to have been concealed under a book, pulled out, and thrown through the doorway leading to the living room. Magician Milbourne Christopher observes that both the Duke University parapsychologists and local police accepted the statements by little Jimmy. Yet, research into human perception shows that it can be easily mistaken. As Christopher explained, "Let us suppose that what the boy said was not true, that he was in one room when he said he was in another in some instances. Also let us suppose that what people thought they saw and what actually happened were not precisely the same." This has been shown to have occurred during the course of Tozzi's investigation, when we compare police interviews with those of the parapsychologists. Christopher says that according to police notes, "the boy and his mother 'actually saw' the bleach bottle leave a box and crash on the floor." Yet later, when Dr. Pratt conducted independent interviews, "neither witnessed the out-of-the-carton action." This led Christopher to comment, "Any trial lawyer will testify that witnesses often believe that they have seen things that did not occur. For example, a woman hears a loud noise, then sees a pistol. She may be confident she heard the pistol fire" even though the sound came from a different source—say, a passing car backfiring or a firecracker.[28]

Theories Abound

Speculation as to what was triggering the mysterious happenings soon became a national obsession; hundreds of letters from concerned citizens arrived for both the Herrmanns and Detective Tozzi, and 1648 Redwood Path became the most scrutinized house in America. Everyone seemed to have his or her own pet theory and wanted to test it. Some visitors offered spiritual solutions. On February 17, Father William McCloud of Seaford's Church of St. William the Abbot stopped in and blessed the house, amid discussion of seeking permission from the bishop to perform an official exorcism.[29] He walked through each of the six rooms, sprinkling holy water and urging the good spirits to expel the bad: "O heavenly Father, Almighty God . . . we humbly beseech thee to bless and sanctify this house . . . and may the angels of thy light dwell within the walls."[30]

On February 18, a dignified gentleman wearing a smart-looking blue wool suit walked through the house, carefully surveying the situation. He was presumed to be a journalist. Suddenly, he fell to his knees in the dining room, cried out that he was "a holy man" from Center Moriches, forty miles to the east, and proceeded to pray for the next ten minutes. He then got up and drove off, but not before proclaiming, "Everything is all right, you have been forgiven."[31] This incident was rather tame compared to other members of the fringe element. One person wrote, "Dear people, you are being visited by those from Space. Speak friendly to them. They come for America's good." Another wrote, in broken English, "Herman, I was read about your trouble in the paper. Sound like it could be ghostlys and ghostly don't like sulphur. Burn some in every room and if it ghostly it will go away."[32] One letter writer offered a similar solution and suggested waving a white handkerchief to drive out the spirits. Another optimistically instructed the Herrmanns to place a notepad and pencil in every room. On top of each pad was to be written, "Who are you?" to afford the ghost an opportunity to identify itself.[33]

Skeptics appeared to be in short supply. A resident of Cambridge, Ohio, suggested the likelihood of "a slick little trixter" in the form of one James Jr. who was "bored at school."[34] Arthur Matthews of Little Neck, New York, chastised *Life* magazine for devoting space to the supernatural when there were more pressing evils, such as communists.[35] A physician in Grand Rapids, Michigan, compared the events to an old-fashioned French stage play involving legerdemain (sleight of hand), where a member of the audience is invited to the stage to ensure that no trickery is going on—in this case, Detective Tozzi.[36]

Early in their investigation, police theorized that high-frequency radio waves could have been responsible for the strange events, and they even interviewed a neighbor who told them that he had not used his transmitter in several years. The Radio Corporation of America dispatched a test truck, complete with crew, to look for radio frequency waves outside the house. Nothing was found. Employees of the Long Island Lighting Company were called in and set up an oscillograph in the basement. While it was in use, three incidents were recorded in the house, yet no unusual floor vibrations were correlated with the events, even though one involved a bleach bottle popping its top in the same room as the device. Company employees also checked the fuse panels and wiring; everything was in working order.[37] On February 25, the Seaford Fire Department probed a nearby well, based on the theory that it might have become unstable and triggered earth tremors. It was stable and showed no radical changes in five years. Old maps were examined for possible hidden water sources, but none were found. The Town of Hempstead Building Department even checked the structure of the house for anomalies and gave it a clean bill of health.

One day physicist Robert Zider showed up from the prestigious Brookhaven National Laboratory in central Long Island. A specialist in high-energy particle acceleration, he surprised many by pulling out a Y-shaped willow dowsing stick and circled the house. His complex theory for the disturbances is perhaps best described by a *New York Times* journalist who noted that Zider claimed to chart unusual magnetic fields created by streams of water under the house. "He related this to the presence . . . of a recharge basin, or sump, recently heavily coated with ice. Mr. Zider felt that powerful vibrations, caused perhaps by a passing jet plane, might have so jolted the ice that the shock wave was transmitted by the underground water faults in such fashion as to 'back up' or strike hard directly under the Herrmann house."[38]

One of the more plausible explanations came from an elderly woman in Revere, Connecticut. Mrs. Helen Connolly wrote to say that she had experienced similar happenings in her home several years earlier, when household items began to move about. A building inspector eventually diagnosed the problem as a "downdraft of warm gasses" passing through the chimney. As soon as a cap was placed over her chimney, the strange activity stopped. A rotating turbine ventilator cap was placed over the Herrmanns' chimney. Hopes of an easy fix were soon dashed when a figurine flew through the air. On the bright side, the cap had only cost $9.[39]

A Poltergeist Named Jimmy

After getting to know the Herrmanns intimately over several weeks, *Life* magazine journalist Robert Wallace believed that a mysterious phenomenon had occurred in the house and that the Herrmann children were not pranking. Yet, despite his trusting nature, he made an astute observation: "In the poltergeist literature it is often pointed out that the phenomena cease when a great deal of attention is concentrated on them. Is it possible that the outburst of publicity . . . somehow changed the 'psychological atmosphere' of the household?"[40] Yet the presence of more people equals more scrutiny and a greater chance of detection. Hence there is an even more plausible explanation than the one advanced by Wallace, without recourse to the existence of unseen, hypothetical psychic forces that have not been proven to exist: little Jimmy did it.

If we follow basic detective protocol and evaluate the evidence, James Jr. had the means, motive, and opportunity. In every one of the 67 known incidents, he was in the house; and most suspiciously, whenever he stayed with relatives or was at school, the poltergeist was quiet. Jimmy may have felt more comfortable being on familiar turf, and he may have been targeting his parents. One psychologist who interviewed the family noted that Mr. Herrmann was a strict and uncompromising disciplinarian, a trait that likely fostered hostility in both children. He stated, "[I]t was impossible to avoid the noticeable impact of Mr. Herrmann's personality. In his interview with me he stated that he rules the family with an iron hand." The psychologist said that in his presence, the father treated the children abruptly, issuing commands as if he were still in the Marines. "They were told to come and go, when to speak, and when to remain quiet."[41]

Psychological tests were later released that revealed that Jimmy hated his father and exhibited "passive demandingness, hostility to father figures, impersonal violence, and isolation of affect [emotion]." When Jimmy was asked to create imaginary stories, in one account, he fights and murders his father; in another, he writes about a boy "living with a guardian whom he hates."[42] This fits the classic profile of the central figure in poltergeist cases throughout history: a disturbed adolescent. It is also curious where the incidents took place. William Roll would later observe, "Most of the disturbed things belonged to the parents and the events often happened in their living space."[43] It may be noteworthy that some of the objects targeted had religious significance—the bottles of holy water that were found tipped and spilled, over and over, and a statue of the Virgin Mary that was broken—which may reflect Jimmy's frustration with being raised in a strict Catholic family. Yet, instead of scrutinizing Jimmy for possible fraud, they assumed it was one more reason why he was disturbed, which—due to built-up psychic energy— resulted in the objects moving about the house.

Distorted Press Coverage

Throughout 1958, newspapers reported that the Duke University scientists were "baffled" by the case and could find no evidence of a hoax. A flurry of articles appeared, most quoting Pratt and Roll as having been mystified and saying that the outbreak appeared to be an authentic example of a psychic phenomenon.[44] Little space was given to two other investigators who drew diametrically opposite conclusions. The first was Dr. Karlis Osis (1917–1997), a psychologist from the New York-based Parapsychology Foundation. On Thursday, May 15, Osis announced his findings to the media, concluding that little Jimmy and the poltergeist were one and the same. "The presence of James Herrmann Jr. in all likelihood was a necessary condition for the occurrence of the phenomena. There was a close relationship between his activities, habits and whereabouts, and the distribution of the disturbances." Firstly, he observed that "Popper" never engaged in antics between one and six o'clock in the morning—the very time when the two children were likely to have been asleep. Second, when Jimmy was in bed, the disturbances occurred either in his room or nearby. Next, there was the odd incident of the bottle of holy water that Mr. Herrmann found was warm to the touch, along with many of the bottle caps that had seemingly popped off. Osis found that Jimmy was a member of the school science club, where he could have learned simple tricks to get container tops to pop, using chemical reactions. He also points to a suspicious incident in the basement, when a bookcase weighing 120 pounds moved two feet away and tumbled over. Jimmy was seen to be breathing heavily afterward. As for the boy's motivation, Osis noted that as Mr. Herrmann was a strict disciplinarian, Jimmy may have been rebelling or "blowing off steam."[45]

Media coverage of the skeptical conclusions drawn by Dr. Osis was somewhere between scant and anemic. A lengthy article on the case published by United Press International in June noted that Dr. Osis had concluded that little Jimmy used "sleight of hand" and knowledge of basic chemistry to create a belief in the poltergeist. Just two sentences were devoted to this view, while the remainder of the article discussed the like-lihood that the house really was haunted, citing Pratt, Detective Tozzi, and the Herrmanns. The headlines for the article, which would have been devised by the local papers carrying it, gave no hint of skepticism. An editor for the Santa Fe *New Mexican* used the title "'No Trick' Says Victim: Jumping Bottles Still Stump Scientists,"[46] while the Greenville, Mississippi *Delta Democrat-Times* (which also carried Osis's skepticism) headlined with "That House of Flying Objects Subject of Several New Reports."[47] Given the conclusions of Osis, perhaps a more appropriate title would have been "Psychologist Concludes Seaford Poltergeist Is a Hoax." Most papers completely ignored the findings of Dr. Osis. In August, the *New York Times* would proclaim, "L. I. 'Poltergeist' Stumps Duke Men," writing that the Duke team reported being "at a loss to explain the strange goings-on" involving the "puzzling disturbances."[48] Of that newspaper's four articles on the case, none even mentions the report by Osis. But why downplay the negative findings? It is likely because a story about scientists being baffled by a seemingly haunted house is more appealing and attention-grabbing than one that concludes that it was a hoax perpetrated by a little boy.

Writing on the case in 1964, Pratt would later claim that he and Roll had *not* determined the cause of the outbreak. "We reached—I repeat—no conclusion regarding the case," he said, noting that "it would be an improper application of scientific method to attempt to go further."[49] Yet in 1958, Pratt gave a very different impression to the press. Dr. Osis was clearly irritated by Pratt's proclamations to journalists in which he implied that Jimmy had special psychic powers. He saw Pratt as grandstanding and making claims that were scientifically unsubstantiated and therefore bad for the field of parapsychology. Pratt told the *New York Times* that experiments at Duke University had "led to the definite conclusion that there is some sort of influence of mind over matter." That was not true in 1958, and it is not true today. In 1958 he was quoted in the *New York Post* as saying "'thought waves' may have done it." He also told the United Press that "the mysterious happenings" were "not a hoax perpetrated by a member of the family."[50]

A closer inspection of the original incident that marked the beginning of the affair shows that it was inaccurately reported in the press. Virtually all press reports gave the impression that the outbreak began when Mrs. Herrmann and her two children were at home on the afternoon of February 3, heard bottles popping and tipping over, and quickly moved from room to room to investigate. Robert Wallace of *Life* magazine was typical, noting that "at about 3:30 a number of bottles containing various liquids, in various rooms of the house, suddenly began to 'pop' and to jump about. . . . As they hurried to investigate the sounds they discovered that the bottles had been freshly spilled and therefore could not have been tipped over earlier. . . . As to the noises that accompanied the uncapping . . . they were loudly audible throughout the house."[51] In reality, based on detailed interviews with the trio, the events were far less dramatic. Upon arriving home from school, Jimmy went to his room and reported finding that a ceramic Davy Crockett doll had been smashed into a model ship. Mrs. Herrmann then began checking other rooms for damage and found a bottle of holy water tipped on its side on her dresser, the cap removed and the water spilled. It was only at this juncture that she heard the first popping sound. Over the next 45 minutes, she would hear mysterious pops and find bottles tipped over.[52]

A Strange Ban on Magicians

A second skeptical investigator also entered the fray: one of the world's most acclaimed stage magicians, Milbourne Christopher (1914–1984). The former national president of the Society of American Magicians, Christopher contacted Detective Tozzi and asked to conduct his own investigation, but oddly, Mr. Herrmann refused, saying that he did not want a magician in the house. Christopher then gathered all the information on the case that he could from afar, and he claimed that he could duplicate each of the alleged poltergeist effects reported at the house. During an interview with reporter Jack Fox of the *New York Post*, Christopher was able to make several bottles with screw-on tops "explode" and even caused an object to sail through the air, all to the bafflement of the journalist, and all done through deception and magic. Over the ensuing day, he gave similar demonstrations to other journalists.[53] Remarkably, Christopher's conclusions received little media attention, both then and now.

Even today, numerous books on the paranormal are quick to cite the findings of Roll and Pratt, which support the position that a genuine anomalous event took place, while virtually ignoring the findings by Dr. Osis and Christopher—or in the rare instances that their skeptical views are mentioned, they are quickly dismissed. Prominent "ghost hunter" Hans Holzer briefly mentions the Osis study but then looks for more exotic answers and criticizes Osis for failing to see the obvious: spirits of the dead. Instead of investigating in order to draw conclusions, Holzer sought advice on the episode from a medium, who was able to "psychically" discern that the house had been built on a burial site—an action that had supposedly caused the haunting. But why did it take five years for the poltergeist to appear? She says there was no receptive medium in the house until Jimmy appeared and was approaching puberty, thus making his energies available to the infesting spirit.[54] It is not unusual for paranormal researchers to explain poltergeist disturbances by delving into the history of a suspected haunted house, in an attempt to dig up a traumatic event that had happened at the location. In Seaford, investigators had no such opportunity, since the house was only five years old and the Herrmanns were the first to move in. Plan B is to then use the standard "haunted Indian ground" or "unmarked pioneer cemetery" hypothesis.

A Comedy of Errors

During their investigation, Pratt and Roll said they considered the possibility that Jimmy had created the popping effect by adding an outside agent to the containers, so they tried to create the same effect themselves. They bought dry ice (frozen carbon dioxide) and placed pieces into containers before screwing on the caps. As the pressure increased, the gas was forced around the threads but did not loosen the caps. After a series of trial-and-error experiments, the pair drew the following conclusion: "In general, it became clear that pressure does not cause these types of caps to unscrew and come completely off. Either the gas escapes around the threads or the bottle explodes, the cap remaining in place. We found it made no difference if we oiled the threads of the glass."[55] *The problem was that neither Pratt nor Roll was a chemist or an expert in deception. Instead of contacting specialists in their fields and seeking their participation or advice, they chose to conduct their own amateurish experiments.*

Pratt and Roll concluded that it was not possible for Jimmy to have used skilled magic tricks to produce the disturbances. "We ascertained that the performance of magic is not known to be among James's hobbies, and it is improbable that a boy would be interested in magic without having the fact become known"—but even if he had, they said, the effects could not be explained with recourse to magic.[56] This was yet another example of their arrogance and loss of objectivity. These researchers and the Herrmanns ignored a golden opportunity to solve the mystery (or eliminate magic as a cause of some of the disturbances) when Milbourne Christopher not only offered to investigate but also reported that he could explain how someone could have caused *the same exact effects* as the poltergeist, through magic and deception. Pratt would later meet with Christopher that June, and as they talked, a figurine suddenly flew through the air from a bookcase, landing eight feet away—very similar to what had happened at the Herrmanns'. Pratt examined the room closely and had no clue as to how it was accomplished. Several days later, he wrote to Christopher, saying that he understood why the Herrmanns were apprehensive about allowing him to visit, as he had "prejudged the issue," and they had dismissed his demonstration as "magic."[57]

Early on, Detective Tozzi was suspicious of the children's involvement. He interviewed them and made it clear that if they were caught pranking, "it was a serious matter."[58] He interviewed them a second time, on February 20, when Tozzi's suspicions were rekindled following an incident that occurred as the pair had entered the basement. Suddenly, as Tozzi wrote in his report, "a small metal horse that was on the cellar stair shelf struck that floor at the writer's feet. . . . The writer accused James of having thrown this figure and interrogated him for quite some time." He denied having any involvement with the disturbances.[59] However, it is clear that the detective had broken one of the basic principles of police work: never become emotionally involved with your suspects. Tozzi had grown fond of the family. This was evident when police decided to "secretly" place fluorescent dust on some of the items that had been disturbed by the "poltergeist," in expectation of shedding light on the mystery. This was a clever strategy, as several of the affected items had been tossed or tipped multiple times. It was ingenious. Yet, inexplicably, *police told the family of their plan ahead of time*, even to the point of telling them which bottles had been dusted, and cautioned them not to touch them![60] Detective Tozzi clearly failed to exercise good judgment. How else can one explain announcing the use of the fluorescent powder *before* it was used? This was not good police work, and it could be recounted in a police manual on how *not* to conduct an investigation! Tozzi's actions fall somewhere between comical and absurd.

Even from afar, Jimmy appeared guilty—at least to some newspapers that were situated near the house and could send reporters there to check on the proceedings firsthand, such as the *Long Island Star-Journal*. Near the height of the antics, on February 25, they appeared to subtly point the finger of suspicion at the boy with the headline "Son's Favorite Victim of Seaford 'Ghosts.'" The article noted that the supernatural force at Seaford appeared to "have a penchant for . . . James Herrmann Jr. They do their best work when he's around."

At 4:40 p.m. a chest of drawers in young Jimmy's bedroom overturned with a loud rumble and crash—for the second time in 24 hours Jimmy got to the room first. When the chest went Sunday Jimmy was in the room asleep.

At 8:30 p.m. an ash tray in the living room flung itself five feet across the room . . . Nobody was around.

[. . .]

At 9 p.m. a world globe sitting on a 31-inch metal bookcase in Jimmy's room picked itself up, flew across the bed in which Jimmy was sleeping, gained altitude to clear a 38-inch chest of drawers on the other side of the bed and then curved through two doorways to plop at the feet of a reporter sitting in the living room.

At 9:15 p.m., with Jimmy again in bed, his metal bookcase went over with a thud.

THE "GHOSTS" completed activities at eight minutes after midnight by dropping the picture of a Wild West scene from a wall in Jimmy's bedroom.[61]

Despite recording 67 incidents, Roll and Pratt had not directly witnessed a single one. In concluding that psychic energy from James Jr. was most likely responsible, they were disregarding traditional views that such events were caused literally by noisy spirits or ghosts. Throughout all of recorded history, no one has provided definitive evidence for the existence of a ghost, noisy or otherwise; the same is true of claims that certain people can channel psychic energies in order to move objects. However, history is replete with examples of people who have been caught while claiming they could move objects using psychic energy. There is no reason to hypothesize the existence of unproven "psychic energies." Near the end of the investigations, the family grew protective of little Jimmy, after suggestions that he might have been responsible. Despite their unreliability in court, the Herrmanns agreed to take a lie detector test to eliminate themselves as suspects, but Mr. Herrmann later changed his mind at the last minute. The reason he gave was that he feared it would be used to implicate Jimmy as the culprit.[62] The disturbances came to an abrupt end on March 10.

An Epidemic of Poltergeists

By April 1958, publicity for "Popper" appeared to have triggered an epidemic of poltergeist reports across the country,—or, at the least, an epidemic of reports of recent cases, some predating Seaford. According to the *American Weekly* magazine, in a house in Clayton, California, a fountain pen was reported to float down a hallway, even turning corners, while rocks supposedly dropped from the ceiling. In Resthaven, Illinois, a refrigerator was said to whistle, walls rumble, and saucers fly through the air by means of a poltergeist with a fetish for propelling fruits and vegetables. At a farmhouse near Hartsville, Missouri, a comb was seen to fly off a dresser top, while in Tulsa, Oklahoma, an electric carpet sweeper was said to roam a house without being plugged in, as if guided by an invisible hand.[63] The Clayton and Tulsa outbreaks had begun the previous year, but the publicity associated with the Seaford case appears to have thrown more media attention to these and other reports, and in some instances it may have created new ones. It also drew more attention to the Duke University lab and the cases it was investigating.

The mayhem associated with the haunted vacuum cleaner in Tulsa was hypothesized to be a rare electrical anomaly.[64] The homeowner, Mr. C. A. Wilkinson, was adamant in his insistence that plugs were jumping out of the wall sockets, resulting in his fridge motor burning out—twice, no less—and damage to a $1,300 electric organ. A wall clock had fallen to the floor six times. Wilkinson went to great lengths to try to put an end to the pandemonium. "I thought maybe wire-mesh fence was picking up electricity somehow and sending it through the house," he said, "so I took the fence down. Then I dug up all the water pipes in the back yard, but that didn't help either."[65] One evening the inexplicable movement of tables and chairs had frightened the family. They fled the house and slept in their car. The most incredible incident was reported to have targeted the Wilkinsons' daughter Shirley, who one night burst into her parents' bedroom, claiming that while apparently fast asleep, she had awakened to find the carpet sweeper rolling across her stomach! The cavalry soon arrived in the form of a local group of parapsychologists, who suspected that the little girl was the poltergeist. She vehemently denied the claims: "They're just making it up," she said, bristling with defiance and indignation. "Grandpa did it. I know he did it, but they're blaming it on me." Her grandfather had died six years earlier.[66]

At Resthaven, a small village in northeast Illinois, fourteen-year-old Susan Wall was the center of activity. The girl was living with her grandparents. Walls were reported "to shake and rumble and whistling noises came from empty rooms." When the family moved to the house of a relative, the disturbances followed and intensified: a bar of soap flew across a room, furniture mysteriously tumbled over or broke, and a coffee pot supposedly floated above the stove and tipped over. A friend stopping in to check out the happenings became a victim when "from nowhere" an orange flew through the air, striking the back of his head. Another visitor was struck by an apple. Young Susan also took her knocks, having been plunked in the back of the head by a chunk of butter weighing a quarter of a pound and hit on the arm with a cabbage.[67] At the height of the disturbance, the Associated Press reported that journalists and photographers joined hundreds of visitors who were hoping to catch a glimpse of the phenomena, which quickly died down. This prompted one writer to remark that the poltergeist seemed to grow tired of the crowds.[68] Deputy Sheriff Chester Moberly had a different perspective and was suspicious that more mundane forces were involved. "Maybe they're all innocent . . . but I notice I haven't been getting any more reports after I threatened to use a lie detector on the whole batch of them."[69]

A Haunting in the Eye of the Beholder

All of these so-called haunted houses had common elements that were evident at Seaford: no one could verify the strange happenings in front of scientists or outside investigators, and the disturbances were associated with adolescents who seemed to attract the activity and were suspected of staging the events, although they were not caught in the act. In the end, the Seaford "poltergeist" turned out to be a split verdict: the final score was three to two; that is, of the five investigators, three concluded that there was no evidence of trickery and that the shenanigans by Popper were likely a real paranormal phenomenon. Both Christopher and Osis concluded, based on the same evidence, that Jimmy was the culprit. As one reexamines this case, it becomes clear that Pratt and Roll were out of their depth of expertise and should have accepted the offer of assistance from Christopher, as they were woefully untutored in the arts of basic chemistry, tomfoolery, and deception. Instead of spending their time trying to see if they could recreate the disturbances by experimenting with containers and their caps, they should have consulted experts. It was equally clear that Detective Tozzi had lost his objectivity. Even Robert Wallace, in his article in *Life* magazine, rushed to Jimmy's defense, writing that it was unfair to suggest Jimmy as the culprit, since Tozzi had "not seen fit to accuse the boy."[70] This was untrue. Tozzi had seriously suspected Jimmy on at least two occasions and subsequently grilled him with questions both times, but he never caught him in the act and eventually felt that he was innocent. Tozzi was far from impartial and had grown too fond of the family to be able to conduct an effective, impartial investigation. On March 6, after her prized coffee pot was found flipped upside down and damaged, Mrs. Herrmann said that she was willing to try anything if it would stop the disturbances. At this point, Tozzi phoned a local church to ask about the possibility of conducting an exorcism of the house. This option was not likely to have been found in the police detective handbook!

In the final analysis, if we track the key figure (Jimmy), focus on the disturbances and their nature, and consider the "clandestine effect," the finger of guilt points to Jimmy. If we follow his movements, it becomes clear, as Pratt concedes, that "the disturbances took place nearer to James, on the average, than to any other member of the family."[71] He was also commonly the first on the scene or the only one present when a disturbance occurred.[72] The "poltergeist" only acted up when Jimmy was in the house. The disturbances were not scattered randomly throughout the house but were, more often than not, linked to Jimmy. The highest concentration of disturbed objects was in his room. Further, if one looks at the types of objects that were disturbed, Pratt places them into two categories: bottles popping and "displacements of furniture and household objects."[73] In most instances, the movement of furniture is closely tied to Jimmy, and there are no other witnesses. A picture above his bed fell twice, and a lamp tumbled over once, both while he was in the room alone. In the basement, when a phonograph crashed to the floor, Jimmy was the sole person present. These objects would have been easy to toss without detection. As for the popping bottle tops for which Popper received its nickname, this could have been accomplished through simple misdirection, as Christopher demonstrated with reporters, pointing out that no one had seen a bottle cap pop. People heard a noise that they assumed was a pop, only to rush to the site of the sound to find the bottles open and on their sides. One way to accomplish the bottle "popping" would have been to have opened and overturned the bottles before making the noise. Such a trick could be accomplished easily, even by a young boy, as sound is the easiest of the five senses to fool. Pratt and Roll dismissed this possibility based on their examination of just one incident.[74]

But how does Christopher explain the incident involving the two bottles that moved in different directions in the bathroom as Mr. Herrmann stood in the doorway—a disturbance that baffled him so much that he called the police for the first time? Christopher says that he knows of two ways that a magician could have performed the exact movements. If Mr. Herrmann was not looking directly at the bottles, Jimmy easily could have pushed them with his free hand. It can also be accomplished, according to Christopher, using a piece of thread:

> Hold a bottle in your left hand near its base. With your left thumb press the end of the thread firmly to the side of the bottle near its

bottom and wind the thread around the bottle several times until, by friction, the end is held firmly. Place this bottle upright on a shelf close to the wall with the thread extending horizontally so that you can pull it taut. Take the second bottle, put it upright between the first container and yourself. Move it to the left so that it carries the thread with it. Drop your end of the thread until you are ready for action. To send the two bottles in different directions, grasp the end of the thread and give a quick sharp yank. The second bottle will be sent to the right, the first will come forward.[75]

Christopher notes that Jimmy would not even need to be looking directly at his father to accomplish the trick, as he could monitor his reflection in the mirror. As soon as he noticed his father look away, even for an instant, he could have subtly yanked the thread. Such a feat is not as complicated as it may sound, and it would not be difficult to master with practice, given that Jimmy had the element of surprise in his favor.

The antics of Popper ended with a fizz on March 10, under curious circumstances. Mr. Herrmann had turned down the request by Milbourne Christopher to investigate the case after making it clear "that he did not want a magician in the house" and characterizing magicians as being in the same category as charlatans, mystics, and mediums.[76] Clearly this was not a credible reason. Then there is the sudden flip-flop by Mr. Herrmann over taking a lie detector test. Initially, he had agreed to allow his entire family to be polygraphed, but then he rescinded the offer, specifically telling Dr. Pratt that it was because "the children had objected."[77] Had the "poltergeist" been caught in the act and was the "haunting" to be kept a household secret, or was the talk of polygraphs making certain family members nervous to the point of deciding to stop their antics? These explanations are far more plausible than creating a hypothetical condition—psychokinesis—the existence of which has yet to be proven.

It is noteworthy that just days before the disturbances ended, on March 5, Dr. Osis offered to end the speculation, once and for all, that any family members were engaged in pranking. He proposed to create a set of "foolproof conditions" by sealing up the most disturbed location—Jimmy's room—after placing in it the most desired objects that had been targeted by the "poltergeist" and adding monitoring devices. Osis said, "If the poltergeist were a real psi force, this would have offered a splendid opportunity. If it were not, the owner of the room . . . would be motivated to put an end to incidents" so as to avoid being caught. Soon after his proposal was made, the disturbances stopped, even though Mr. Herrmann had eventually rejected the plan.[78]

There are several instances where either Pratt or Roll was too trusting of the family and failed to follow fundamental rules of investigation. For instance, on March 9, a loud thud was heard from the direction of Jimmy's room, while he was supposedly in bed. An investigation found that no objects had been disturbed. Several minutes later, a louder thump echoed out, prompting a search of his room. Pratt writes, "Lucille, still in bed, said it came from James's wall just as if he had hit it with his fist or elbow. I asked James to do this and he was able to nearly get the same sound." Remarkably, instead of suspecting James of having thumped the wall, Pratt dismisses his involvement, noting that James said he was partly asleep during both thumps. Pratt takes Jimmy's word for this and downplays the two incidents as trivial: "These sounds are, of course, trivial in comparison with the other events and they would not be worth pointing out except for the sake of completing the record of what happened in the house while we were there." This incident shows the extent to which Pratt was biased, uncritical, and easily duped.[79] To label these sounds as trivial—and to fail to follow up on the suspicious thuds—explains why it was so easy for Jimmy to have fooled a house of adults. In another instance, Pratt observes that because several disturbances involved religious objects and because such acts constituted "a serious religious offense," it "seems unlikely that a family as devout as the Herrmanns would be party to such sacrilege."[80] On the contrary, if Jimmy was rebelling against his parents' restrictions, which would have included following certain Catholic protocols, the targeting of such objects in order to vent his anger and frustrations would not be out of the question. Pratt was also prone to embellishment. For instance, in recounting the case several years later in his book on parapsychology, Pratt describes an incident in which he hears "a series of explosive sounds," one of which "literally shook the house." Later in the book, these same events are described as "dull thumps" coming from the direction of Jimmy's room and the "explosion" of a cap popping off a container of bleach sitting in the basement. It is difficult to imagine the latter disturbance shaking the house.[81]

Pratt and Roll's study on the Seaford outbreak was published in the June issue of the *Journal of Parapsychology*, with great fanfare within the parapsychological community. It has been widely touted as the first scientific study of a poltergeist. However, it is far from scientific, and it is remarkably flawed. Dr. Pratt would later caution critics that the study was "inconclusive," yet Pratt and Roll clearly conclude that the most likely explanation was that Jimmy was able to move objects with his mind. They also state that numerous laboratory tests since the 1940s had demonstrated that psychokinesis (PK) "has been widely confirmed."[82] Hogwash. Their article is a study in wishful thinking and amateur detective work involving two scientists who were pranked and outwitted by a little boy. The evidence that Jimmy was the poltergeist was everywhere, yet they failed to see it. Time and again, Dr. Pratt's words were incongruent with his claims. It is a testament to their pro-poltergeist bias that Pratt and Roll's study failed to even cite the research findings of Christopher and Osis.

While several of the "popped" bottles were taken to the Nassau County police lab for a chemical analysis, and while nothing suspicious was detected, lab inspector Frank Pribyl observed that the tests were far from exhaustive. For instance, he said, "[I]f the bottles had been 'popped' by some chemical which dissolves in a gaseous form, it would not have been detectable by the reagents used."[83] ("Reagent" is a chemistry term that refers to a substance that is used to produce a chemical reaction in order to detect the presence of another substance.)

Popper did not appear to feel comfortable around scientists. Dr. Pratt said that his first visit at the Herrmann household lasted four and a half days. Curiously, there were two disturbances within thirty minutes of his arrival, while the next four days "had no unexplained occurrences." Suspiciously, the day after Pratt left, the poltergeist went into a frenzy, with no less than seven disturbances! A glass bowl mysteriously upended, a lamp fell over, a world globe was found to have moved, a picture had fallen to the floor, loud noises were heard, and a night table fell down.[84] Pratt returned to the house on March 7, accompanied by Dr. Roll, and the two spent over a week investigating. During this time there were just three incidents—two thumps appeared to come from Jimmy's room (March 9), and the last incident involved a bottle of bleach that had tipped over in the basement with its cap off. Once again, the poltergeist had proven to be very shy around scientists who were staying in the house.[85] If Pratt and Roll had examined their own evidence objectively, they would have concluded, as had Dr. Osis and Milbourne Christopher, that Jimmy was responsible. Here is an excerpt from their own report: "Nothing ever happened while all the family were out of the house, when they were fast asleep, or while the children were both at school. In all but one case, James was known to be in the house during the disturbances, and he may have been home during that one as well (Event 55). Other members of the family were frequently absent. Also, the disturbances took place nearer to James, on the average, than to any other members of the family."[86]

As for "Event 55," on Sunday, March 2, James Jr. was actually present. According to the report, at 7:30 p.m., Jimmy went to the store with Mr. Herrmann and his brother. Mrs. Herrmann remembered tidying up the house just prior to their leaving. Upon returning, Jimmy and his father found that the boy's globe had been moved from his bookcase to the center of his bed. The only people in the house at the time had been Mrs. Herrmann and her daughter. Had Jimmy snuck into his room upon their return and moved the globe? It is certainly more plausible than the alternative hypothesis—supernatural powers from a twelve-year-old boy.

In examining the case of Popper and how shoddily it was investigated by a professional detective and two doctorate holders, we would be wise to recall the words of magician Alex Stone: "Magic makes us more aware of how prone and vulnerable the mind is to deception. The human mind is wonderfully efficient and capable of noticing patterns and executing complex tasks, as well as focusing on narrow tasks for a long time. But with this virtue comes the flip side: We tend to miss peripheral distractions."[87] This is why texting and talking on mobile phones while driving is so dangerous. The same process renders us vulnerable to believing in poltergeists. Having passed a detective training course or attained a PhD in psychology does not render one immune from deception.

The Seaford "poltergeist" is a case study in lost objectivity and missed opportunity. The failure of Mr. Herrmann to allow a respected magician into the house should have raised a giant red flag in the camp of Roll and Pratt. Instead of insisting that Milbourne Christopher be allowed to visit the house, they too downplayed Christopher's claims. It is also a study in selective media coverage, as journalists latched onto the dramatic comments by Roll and Pratt about the baffling nature of the case, while downplaying Dr. Osis's conclusion that the case was a hoax. The media afforded little coverage to Christopher, who was able to duplicate each of the poltergeist's antics. This is because the media is a business that gravitates toward the sensational, which is usually better for business when compared to reporting on the mundane. Which is more exciting: that a little boy, with possible accomplices, fooled experts from around the country, including psychologists and a police detective, or that the same boy appears to have the ability to move objects with his mind? The story of the Seaford poltergeist is remarkable not because there were mysterious paranormal phenomena going on, but instead because a twelve-year-old boy was able to outwit a seasoned detective and two psychologists with PhDs, all because they grew too close to their subjects and ignored basic principles of investigation.

While Steven Spielberg's film *Poltergeist* has been credited with inspiring the movie, to their credit, those promoting it never claimed that it depicted real events.[88] There are initial parallels with the Herrmanns—a young suburban family harassed by a poltergeist that centers on an adolescent, a house built on an apparent burial ground—but that is where the similarities end. Matters soon turn dire, as the young girl is kidnapped and taken to another dimension through a portal in her closet. With the aid of several parapsychologists and a medium, the little girl is retrieved. It is revealed that the spirits were angry because the house was built over a cemetery. At the end, the family manages to escape as the house collapses and is sucked into another dimension. Apparently, popping bottle tops and flying statues were not exciting enough.

CHAPTER 4

The Conjuring: What Possessed the Perron Family?

Talk of the devil and he is bound to appear.

—English proverb[1]

In July 2013, the supernatural thriller *The Conjuring* premiered in movie theaters across the United States; by December it had grossed over $318 million worldwide.[2] The film's success and high test screenings before it was even released have spawned talk of a franchise of similar projects—all based on the investigations of Connecticut medium Lorraine Warren and her late husband, Ed.[3] The film has been marketed as based on true events—the story of Roger and Carolyn Perron (pronounced *pear-in*) and their five daughters, who moved into a "haunted" Rhode Island farmhouse in 1971, in the tiny, rural village of Harrisville (pop. 1,605 in 2010). Much of what we know about the case comes from the eldest Perron daughter, Andrea, whose books are based on interviews with family members.[4] But how close to real life are her claims, and how accurate is the film? Many researchers have viewed the case of the Perron family as genuinely unexplainable. The screenwriters for *The Conjuring*, Chad and Carey Hayes, claim that 80 percent of the film is true to life.[5] A closer examination reveals it to be loosely based on events that were claimed by the Perrons, claims that appear to have been accurately reported as the family perceived them. However, this does not necessarily mean that their experiences were grounded in reality.

Prelude to a Haunting

The summer of 1971 was both brutal and deflating for Roger and Carolyn Perron, who were living with their five daughters in the quiet, sleepy community of Cumberland, a suburb of Providence, Rhode Island. A series of traumatic events would soon leave them emotionally distraught and moving to more remote, greener pastures. One day their pet dog Bathsheba was struck and killed by a car as several of the girls watched in horror. Adding to the anguish, the tragedy was entirely preventable and had been triggered by a speeding teenager barreling down a nearby street. Local gangs became active in the neighborhood; bullying grew common. Then one day, returning from a short vacation, they found that their house had been ransacked, and three of their prized cats lay dead. When their daughter Andrea thought she knew the name of the boy behind the break-in, she stalked him, waited for the right moment, and beat him senseless, resulting in her being hauled into court. The charges were dropped eventually, but misfortune kept dogging the Perrons that summer. Then one day, from out of the blue, a neighbor had a heart attack at the wheel of his truck and crashed on their lawn. Andrea later would write that the neighbor's wife "blatantly accused Carolyn of being a witch" and causing the man's death.[6]

By January 1971, the traumatized family moved into their new home, a majestic eighteenth-century colonial farmhouse situated in the tranquil, rustic Rhode Island countryside. The first sign that something was amiss was a cryptic remark made by the previous owner, a Mr. Kenyon, who told Roger, "For the sake of your family, leave the lights on at night!"[7] Soon, strange noises were heard in the house, followed by a series of mysterious happenings. Gradually the family came to realize that the house was haunted—except Roger, the skeptic of the family, who was often absent because of work.

In telling the story of the haunting on behalf of her parents and siblings, Andrea's writing gives no indication that any of the events they experienced were the result of the family perpetrating a collective hoax; they appear to have been genuinely frightened. However, at least one of the girls—Cindy—may have been responsible for several poltergeist claims that may have scared her mother and siblings even more. In the book, Andrea boasts that her recounting of the events "contains no embellishment" and that her "intention is not to entertain but rather to inform."[8] While well-intentioned, this is certainly not true. In fact, it soon becomes evident that Andrea and her family have a penchant for exaggeration and for transforming relatively benign, mundane events and circumstances into threatening, supernatural ones. These events were magnified by Roger being away at work for days at a time, leaving Mrs. Perron to fend for herself as the lone adult overseeing five girls in their remote farmhouse. It was an ideal recipe for a haunting. An example of Andrea's proclivity for drama and for making mountains out of molehills was evident even before they realized the house was haunted, when an antique clock stopped. She described the event by turning it into a great mystery, noting that "its pendulum [was] stilled by some unknown force."[9] In fact, clocks stop ticking every day. Such events do not necessarily indicate that supernatural forces are at work. The haunting began with relatively minor incidents, such as the stopped clock, distant voices, hearing a possible intruder, and young April reporting that someone had shaken her while she was asleep. Events soon graduated to the family interacting with "spirits." As the incidents accumulated, Mrs. Perron felt that she was being watched—a feeling that "severely rattled" her.[10] She was soon convinced that there was a supernatural presence in the house. Eventually, the flames of hysteria were fanned by two self-proclaimed ghost hunters, who set into motion a series of events that culminated in a bizarre séance.

The Cast of Characters

Roger Perron was married in 1957. His work as a traveling salesman (not a long-haul truck driver, as claimed in the movie) strained his marriage. The couple eventually divorced, keeping him largely a stranger to his children.[11] He was skeptical of most of the occult phenomena reported by the others. His daughter Andrea characterizes Roger's skepticism as being a continual challenge to her mother's integrity and making her feel "as though her opinion was entirely irrelevant, her recounting of events fraudulent."[12] The girls were squarely in their mother's camp. At times, Roger expressed openness to the possibility that there really were spirits in the house, possibly to promote domestic harmony.

Carolyn Perron was impulsive. When she saw an ad for a colonial farmhouse in Harrisville, Rhode Island, in 1971, she viewed the property and, without consulting Roger, made a down payment, even though they were strapped for cash. A lapsed Catholic, she "felt" and "sensed" various "presences,"[13] practiced dowsing for water,[14] saw apparitions, and on one occasion appeared to be "possessed."[15] Carolyn was deeply spiritual and had a tendency to redefine mundane events and reinterpret them within a supernatural context. She seemed prone to psychosomatic ailments and experienced fainting spells, typically in front of the fireplace and in Roger's presence. Occasionally, he would have to rush in dramatically to save her from the fire.[16] Carolyn firmly believed that the various paranormal manifestations reported in the house were the spirits of dead people who had once lived there. Andrea wrote about her mother, "It was not happenstance. They were not some random spirits passing through; floating in on a lark. Of this, she was certain. They were a sudden chill in the air, recognizable figures; familiar characters by the time any attempt was made to identify them. Her children had given them names, as if they'd been pets: Manny. Oliver."[17] Mrs. Perron's beliefs and "encounters" were significant in that they created a "haunted house" mindset in her daughters—which was made all the more chilling with their father away so much of the time. The absence of Roger, who tended to downplay the incidents when he was around, further enhanced the eerie ambience and tension within the house. What could be spookier than a mother and her daughters living in an isolated farmhouse that is supposedly haunted, without the presence of a father figure?

Like Mother, Like Daughters

"Each of the girls developed a *real* emotional attachment to the spirits in the house," Andrea says casually, "while bonding between dimensions."[18] The scribe of the family, she later wrote down their experiences. Andrea (sometimes called Annie) was the Perrons' first child, born in 1958. No wallflower, she was assertive and confident, as evidenced by her confrontation with the boy who allegedly vandalized their house, when she pummeled him. About three years later, she was dismissed from a confirmation class when she had an "altercation" with the priest, challenging him about such subjects as homosexuality.[19] Andrea sometimes saw "shadows" and heard voices.[20]

Nancy, the second daughter, was a spunky, spirited, "nine-year-old spitfire," explains Andrea.[21] When "spirits" began to appear to the new residents, Andrea says of her sister, "Competitive in every way, Nancy *had* to claim credit for the first official sighting."[22] A girlfriend once accused her of faking poltergeist occurrences in her presence, but friendship prevailed, and the girl reconsidered.[23] Odd things happened to Nancy. For example, when she took an unfamiliar trail and became lost on the way home, she reported encountering an apparitional family.[24] She and a girlfriend played with a Ouija board, and she claimed, "The spirits talk to us through it."[25]

The middle-born daughters of the family were Christine and Cynthia. Christine (aka Chrissy) had supposedly "developed supernatural skills acquired only through the use of a sixth sense."[26] Andrea writes that on one occasion, an evil force or being "had rudely awakened Christine in the middle of the night." For months at a time, however, Chrissy would sleep undisturbed by "the presence."[27] The fourth child, Cynthia (or Cindy), "attracted supernatural activity unlike any of her siblings" and had "passive/aggressive tendencies."[28] She reported multiple encounters with apparitions[29] and claimed to receive "telepathic messages."[30] On one occasion she described how an invisible entity came to her aid.[31] Another time she reported entering "another dimension."[32] Her bed, she said, vibrated at times and, when she was thirteen, "levitated," or at least rocked wildly once, while she screamed incessantly—although the rest of the family, downstairs, heard none of this.[33] Cindy exhibited many classic symptoms of a fantasy-prone personality.

April, the youngest child, was only five and a preschooler when the Perrons moved into the old farmhouse. April had an imaginary friend, "Oliver," who became her frequent playmate. Their communication was "telepathic."[34] The "baby" of the family, April watched "as her sisters begged for the same type of attention she received all day, every day."[35] When she did go to school, her behavior landed her in detention from time to time. While Mrs. Perron believed that "Oliver" was from the spirit world, a more mundane explanation can account for the little girl's actions. Imaginary companions in childhood are common. One survey of eighteen hundred children between ages five and twelve found that 46 percent of them had an imaginary friend at some point. The reported incidence declines dramatically in adulthood.[36] Far from being an indicator of mental disturbance, invisible friends are widely viewed by psychologists as normal and healthy. Research shows that they can provide friendship and entertainment to children in times of loneliness and boredom.[37]

Finally, there were Ed and Lorraine Warren, the demon-hunting duo who visited the home several times. They were *not* sought out by the Perrons, as portrayed in *The Conjuring*; instead, they just showed up on a night soon before Halloween.[38] Their modus operandi was to arrive at a "haunted" house, which they soon transformed into a "demonic" one, in keeping with their own medieval-style Catholic beliefs.

Carolyn Perron: The Power of One

Mrs. Perron, with her status as the only adult in the house for much of the time, was a powerful influence on her daughters. Her interpretations of various incidents as ghostly encounters shaped the girls to perceive numerous events within the house in a supernatural light. Apparitions and pranks reportedly assailed the Perrons from the outset, sparing only Roger. It is perhaps no coincidence that he was the most skeptical. Many of the accounts described by Carolyn are so incredible that they could be readily dismissed as the figment of a fertile imagination, signs of a mental disturbance, or a hoax, yet a fourth possibility is far more likely. A survey of the many seemingly supernatural experiences encountered by the family, as recounted by Andrea Perron in her voluminous books, is revealing. It is evident that several family members experienced an array of psychological conditions that were being redefined as supernatural in origin. For instance, during one early experience when Carolyn was lying in bed, she described seeing her dresser erupt in flames! Trying to react, she could not move.

On the night in question, before retiring for the night, Carolyn, who had a fear of fires, checked the fireplace and noticed a few dying embers. She then got under the quilt and tried to fall asleep. Suddenly there was a "swoosh" as if from an igniting fire. She got out of bed and checked the nearby fireplace, but the fire had gone out completely. Then she heard crackling from behind; it was from inside her bedroom, where her dresser was ablaze. It was a frightening and vivid scene; she could see "sparks jumping from a fireball, the core of which burned so brightly she could barely gaze into it. Off-shoots sprung from its center, appearing like wild sparklers out-of-control, pinging then popping in every direction."[39] Carolyn said that her body would not react, as all she could think of was the fire and her sleeping girls. Then suddenly, "in a mere fraction of a second, it was gone." After falling to the floor, she eventually collected herself and checked the room for evidence of the fire, but there was no smoke, no singe marks, no smell—nothing. She was terrified and baffled.[40]

Carolyn's description of the strange events in her bedroom that night is a textbook example of a waking dream accompanied by sleep paralysis. During such dreams, the subject has partial or total awareness while in a dream state. These states often occur during the twilight period as they are dozing off or waking up. In this instance, Carolyn was falling asleep. The events during these dreams are often described as having extreme clarity and bright, vivid colors. They are commonly accompanied by sleep paralysis, because the body is still in sleep mode.[41] If the content of the dream is harrowing, such as one's house being on fire, then being unable to move can be a terrifying experience. It is common for preoccupations to be reflected in the content of the dream; in this instance, Mrs. Perron had been concerned over the possibility of a fire just prior to retiring. Sleep researchers are increasingly realizing that many reported encounters with the paranormal are actually dreams. Paul Davies writes that because some dreams appear "real, it is quite possible for someone to remember one as a real experience, and report it as such."[42]

Carolyn had another waking dream in which, stirring from sleep and "sensing a presence," she opened her eyes and saw the figure of a grotesque-looking woman hovering over her. As with her earlier experience with the "fire," she was unable to move, while perceiving intense, brilliant images. "The image of it leapt through her eyes into her mind, impaling her memory with a spectral wonder so vivid and compelling, it had to be processed in tiny patterns and fragments . . . slicing into her consciousness . . . bombarding the senses."[43] As the repulsive figure moved closer, she was unable to move or speak. Desperate, Carolyn said she was able to kick Roger, who lay next to her asleep. She then "jerked Roger's head severely back and forth." When there was no response, she thought he was dead. Soon after, the entity suddenly vanished into the night. She eventually awoke to realize that Roger was unharmed. It is probable that she had never forcefully shoved his head back and forth—it had happened in her dream. But to Mrs. Perron, *it had* really happened, reinforcing her belief that the house was haunted—a belief that she conveyed to her daughters.[44] Let's compare this incident to the experience of a medical student in the state of Pennsylvania:

> I was lying on my back just kinda looking up. And the door slammed, and I . . . opened my eyes. I was awake. Everything was light in the room. . . . I couldn't move. . . . [T]his grayish, brownish murky presence was there. And it kind of swept down over the bed and I was terrified! . . . I felt this pressing down all over me. I couldn't breathe. . . . I was helpless . . . I was really scared . . . This was *evil!* . . . I struggled to move and get out. . . . [Later] the whole thing just kind of dissipated away.[45]

He emphasized the reality of the scene, saying, "This thing was *there!*" The nebulous presence floating from above; the bright, vivid detail; the inability to move; the sense of evil; the difficulty breathing—this account parallels Carolyn Perron's experiences and many others in the annals of folklore.

Carolyn was quick to use these "encounters" to reinforce her belief that spirits of the dead inhabited their house, influencing her daughters to view their world as inhabited by an array of spirits. As a result, their different anomalous experiences reinforced their belief that the farmhouse was haunted. Waking dreams seem to have run in the family. One does not have to be in bed to have one. Clearly Cindy was experiencing them. On the first day of her summer vacation, the eight-year-old was playing with toys on her bedroom floor, alone, when "many hours passed without her recognizing it." Then she saw the figure her mother had told the children about and that Cindy had later seen "*in a dream.*"[46] Suddenly, the bedroom was "awash in a soft glow":

> Directly before her eyes an entity of substance slowly approached, floating above the surface of a bedroom floor. Horrified, the eight-year-old could not move, could not breathe the putrid air. . . . Appearing as some form of a solid mist, Cindy identified the apparition as a woman by her garb. She had no features, only a grayish oval mass. . . . She drifted across the room, arms outstretched, extended toward the terrified child. . . . It positioned itself directly in front of her then began leaning in toward her; closer and closer she came. The air pressure was stifling, pushing on her from every direction.[47]

Cindy suddenly regained her ability to move and bolted from the room. As the girls discussed these and other "encounters" with one another, it is easy to see how they came to believe that the house was haunted by a variety of entities.

Cindy also experienced similar dreams. Early one morning at 3:00 a.m., she became aware of a "dark presence" in the room, hovering just inches above her sister Andrea. The "black, vaporous apparition" reminded her of a storm cloud. It appeared to be fusing with Andrea's body. As she propped herself up for a better look, the entity suddenly shifted and began moving toward her. It enveloped her, knocking her to the floor. Curiously, her screams could not be heard by anyone. She found it difficult to move and difficult to breathe. The force eventually left the room, leaving Cindy so traumatized that she wet herself and ended up sleeping the rest of the night on a sofa. Cindy said that she kept this encounter secret for over two decades.[48]

Cindy also exhibited many of the traits associated with a fantasy-prone personality, and once she whispered to her mother, "Mom, there's a whole bunch of people eating in our dining room."[49] On another occasion, Cindy saw several "little ghosts"—"native children"—playing in a nearby pine grove.[50] The family's isolation certainly would have encouraged their visions of strange entities, as such environments force children who spend much time alone to develop their imaginations. Did the supernaturally inclined Cindy *really* have her hair "knotted" by a spirit?

Was she "dragged to the floor" by a mysterious force, as she claimed? On another occasion—a humid August day—while playing hide-and-seek with her sisters, she crawled inside a wooden box with no latches or locks, later claiming to have been trapped inside, unable to budge the lid. Christine and Nancy opened the lid with ease, while Cindy protested adamantly that she had indeed been trapped and was suffocating when her sisters rescued her. It is more plausible that Cindy was play-acting or immersed in her imagination.[51] Cindy said that when she was under attack by the spirits, it was like being inside a bubble. She told Andrea that during these encounters, "you cannot be heard" and "no one can hear you." A more likely explanation is that Cindy was immersed in her own inner fantasy world.[52]

Poltergeists

Poltergeist phenomena were common at the farmhouse, such as the time when Andrea set up after-school classes with herself as teacher, using an old, oak-framed, slate blackboard. She tells us that "some scoundrel spirits from the Netherworld did not appreciate having to attend school and would play nasty tricks." The chalkboard was repeatedly smeared, often erased, and eventually smashed. Though Andrea believed it was the girls' "favorite pastime," it is likely that one of them secretly resented the extra "school" time their big sister was subjecting them to. Andrea writes the following:

> As one of the most active rooms in the house, the kitchen attracted someone, maybe more than one spirit. The telephone was frequently tampered with, as were several appliances. Antique bottles were routinely arranged and rearranged, moved from open shelves to windowsills then back again; someone had a flair for interior design! A pile of dirt left on the floor, the broom propped beside it, leaning against a chair; a message received then ignored. Household provisions spilled and splashed about the premises, chairs pulled out from beneath children; hair pulling was always a less-than-gentle reminder of their omnipresence. And the flies![53]

Investigators will need more convincing evidence than the recollections of schoolgirls, thirty to forty years late, in order to conclude that there were real poltergeists.

Poltergeist activity was also common in the horse barn, where curry combs and other horse paraphernalia would go missing, only to turn up in another part of the barn. Often an object would suddenly vanish, only to be found in its original spot minutes later. Andrea writes that the bridle that always "hung on the same peg on the nearest wall to the stall, would suddenly vanish, only to be found later on the opposite side of the barn." She dismisses the possibility of practical joking by her sisters and concludes that the mysterious happenings were the result of "supernatural shenanigans."[54] On one occasion, Nancy went to the barn to check on the horses, and she said she was overcome by an "unnatural cold" and fell to the ground. At about the same time, the horse, Pineridge, reared up in fright. It was assumed that a supernatural force had frightened the horse. Nancy said later, "Something grabbed me from behind and dragged me to the floor!"[55]

As with most classic poltergeist outbreaks, strange incidents centered on one person more than any other: in this case, Cindy. On numerous occasions she reported being tormented after entering the kitchen. Several times she claimed that the refrigerator door would suddenly begin to open and shut, flapping wildly back and forth as food "would fly out all over the place." Andrea wrote, "[F]or some reason, Cindy was the one most frequently subjected to the cruel and unusual behavior, a particular stunt occurring in her presence on a fairly regular basis. It seemed to be a deliberate act, initiated with some forethought and malice."[56] Curiously, it was observed that Cindy's strange encounters with the so-called haunted fridge "almost always occurred just prior to Roger's return home."[57] Such tactics may have been the ploy of a young girl seeking the attention of an absentee father, trying to get him to remain at home more and to stop taking long business trips.

Not only did Cindy have a strange influence on the family fridge, but on her bed as well. Over several years, she claimed that her bed would levitate and vibrate. The saga began one evening while she was alone, sitting on the mattress and doing homework. Suddenly, she said, it lifted into the air, shaking with such intensity that she feared she would be thrown to the floor. Clinging to the bedpost, she pleaded for the force to stop, repeating aloud the prayer that Lorraine Warren had advised her to say in an emergency: "In the name of Jesus Christ, go back to where you came from!" It had no effect, and the "attack" continued:

> The bed came alive. It vibrated furiously, tipping side to side. Then it began banging down onto the floor with such a force, it shook the entire structure; one strike after another. Steam escaped from Cynthia's mouth with each panicked shriek; the room became unbearably frigid. Books were bouncing off the walls as papers

and pens flew imprecise patterns, trapped within a spiraling shaft of stench; a whirlwind as circling projectiles crashed into this child, over and over again; punishment time!

Oddly, despite her screams and the ruckus, no one downstairs heard the clamor from above. Is it possible that Cindy had made up the story for attention? There is another possibility: she had entered a trance-like state that psychiatrists refer to as dissociation, and the episode was a figment of her imagination. Andrea wrote that Cindy later told her that "time itself seemed virtually suspended whenever they occurred." The aftermath of this episode is equally confusing: "a sudden drop ending with a bang finally silenced her screaming and stilled the bed." The perception of time seeming to stand still is a classic feature of altered states of consciousness. The sudden "bang," ending with the bed supposedly dropping to the floor, may have been her snapping out of it.[58] There is something distinctly odd about the claims of the levitating and vibrating bed: no one ever witnessed it. Had Cindy trashed her room in order to get attention by walking downstairs and venting at her mother and sisters for not coming to her aid? The story gets stranger and more improbable: when it came time to sleep, she refused an offer to sleep with her mother and instead steeled herself and retired for the night in her own bed! These actions stretch credulity. Her explanation? "Nothing and no one is going to scare me away from my room. I waited a long time to have it and I won't give it up for anything . . . or to anyone . . . not even for one night."[59] So let's get this straight: a young girl had a terrifying experience during which her bed levitated, she was left bruised and bloodied with scrapes and cuts, and her room is in a shambles, as a mysterious force has scattered her belongings. Her reaction? She scolds her mother and sisters for not hearing her screams, and then she proceeds to sleep in the same bed—declining an offer to sleep elsewhere. During the ordeal she was described as "traumatized," "frantic," and "crying hysterically"—a young girl who was "out of her mind with terror."[60] Her actions are incongruent with her claims.

The incident with the vibrating bed was not a one-off; it occurred over and over, according to Cindy. To prove her story, all she would have had to do was to keep a camera under her pillow and take snapshots when the bed levitated. Given that this was supposedly a routine occurrence, how come no one else was able to see it and snap photos? To accept that this happened on a regular basis, traumatizing Cindy on each occasion—yet she continued to sleep in the bed—is beyond belief. Andrea writes, "The same scenario played out again and again over the course of the next four years but Cynthia held her ground then held onto her bed knobs for dear life. Every time the bed levitated it would shake violently. She would cling to the headboard or grab onto its spindles; something sturdy enough to keep her from being flung off the mattress." How could anyone remain in the house when such dramatic encounters were happening, let alone sleep in the same bed?[61]

On another occasion, Cindy claimed that as she entered the kitchen, she saw a broom sweeping the floor—by itself. "With flair and rhythm, the broom swished and sashayed around the room, as if dancing in the arms of another, then abruptly fell onto the floor," Andrea recounted the story as later told to her by Cindy. Cindy was just nine at the time of the first incident.[62] Again, if there were so many supernatural encounters, as claimed by the Perrons, and they were occurring on a daily basis, then why didn't anyone manage to take a single photo of a levitating bed, a self-sweeping broom, or a fridge that flapped its doors and expelled food? The most likely answer is that it is because these events never happened. Either they were figments of the imaginations of frightened, impressionable people in an isolated farmhouse, or they were a series of pranks. Based on the accounts written by Andrea Perron, the answer is most likely a combination of both, with Cindy responsible for much of the poltergeist activity. An equally appropriate title for this chapter would have been "The Family That Scared Itself—With a Little Help From Cindy."

Over time, the cellar became another focus of strange events, and when family members entered it, there was an expectation of paranormal happenings. One evening while the family was watching a movie on TV, loud noises similar to a trumpet being sounded during a fox hunt rang out from below. Andrea described the scene when Roger went down to investigate: "Huddled beside each other in the middle of a parlor, frantic females shivered and shuddered with anxious anticipation, awaiting father's return." The woodshed door was found ripped off its hinges, twenty feet away. Carolyn immediately took the incident to be "an act of war" and a blatant "intimidation tactic" by an unholy entity in the house.[63]

Witches and Demons

Even when the best evidence warrants a mundane explanation, Andrea still invokes the supernatural. For instance, her father was once angry about something and "touched a handle on the pot of meatballs" cooking in the kitchen, whereupon "it flew off the stove and hit the floor," splattering him with sauce. Andrea insists she "saw that pot of meatballs go *flying* off the surface of the stove *without* the assistance of her furious father." She wondered if the "Kitchen Witch"—a historic local figure named Bathsheba Sherman with whom the Perrons were obsessed—was actually responsible.[64]

According to Andrea, Bathsheba was the most frightful spirit in the house. She had supposedly been charged with the murder of a child, but her case was dismissed. Carolyn claims that she researched the local history and found that there were rumors of Bathsheba having been a witch who sacrificed an infant to the Devil.[65] Born Bathsheba Thayer in 1812, she married Judson Sherman in 1844. Mrs. Warren told the Perrons that Bathsheba was "the lone demonic presence in their house."[66] In reading Andrea's book, one could get the impression that Lorraine Warren had used her psychic powers to divine this. Yet Carolyn previously had told the Warrens about Bathsheba. Andrea says that her mother let the Warrens have her notebook—which was filled with "meticulous notes" about the strange goings-on at the farmstead, including details on Bathsheba and sketches of frightening entities—but it was never returned.[67]

After the Warrens became involved in the case, something curious happened. The farmstead was besieged with curiosity seekers, from ghost hunters to Devil worshippers. It turned out that the Warrens had been giving public lectures on the "haunting" and divulging the names of both the town and the farmhouse. Carolyn was horrified when she learned the news and felt a deep sense of betrayal because of the hassles her family was forced to endure with this invasion of privacy.[68] Andrea wrote that vehicles "slowed to a crawl" in the vicinity of Round Top Road as thrill-seekers sought to identify the house from the landscape. Excited by the prospect of seeing a "haunted house," the Warrens' seminars inspired people to make the pilgrimage. "Individuals would simply show up at the door, sometimes in small groups, wanting to meet the family, to ask questions and see the house."[69] The situation angered Carolyn, who confronted Lorraine over the breach of confidence. At first, Lorraine "claimed to be unaware she'd mentioned the town or the names involved," but she later confessed to speaking about the family and the house during a speaking trip.[70]

Ed and Lorraine Warren entered the picture in October 1973. Their involvement only intensified the belief of Mrs. Perron and her daughters that the house was haunted. For instance, Andrea quoted her mother as saying she believed that the appearance of a swarm of flies in winter was a supernatural occurrence. "Those flies were all sent here on a mission, to observe the new occupants . . . to size us up." She drew this conclusion in part because no one ever found them breeding! "No one has thousands of flies in the dead of winter. No one. Certainly not in Rhode Island! . . . [T]hey'd attack us and buzz our heads. . . . They'd stare at us! They did not even look like normal flies. Those fat, black little bastards," Carolyn quipped.[71] Her explanation for holding such an absurd belief was Lorraine, who had told her that botflies gravitated to corpses and that their appearance was a warning that spirits were around.[72] In reality, fly swarms are a common winter occurrence in Rhode Island homes. The most likely candidate is the pesky cluster fly. According to Environmental Health Services (EHS), a pest control company serving parts of the Rhode Island, "If there was ever a pest that made you feel like you are living in the Amityville Horror it is cluster flies. They invade your home by the hundreds or thousands causing even the most battle tested person to freak out. They are also mistaken for Bottle flies as people think something must have died if I have this many flies."[73] Mrs. Perron remarked that the flies were impossible to get rid of, despite her best efforts. "How many times did we treat this house? How many different ways did we try to kill them? We couldn't do it!"[74] The Perrons tried fly swatters and then mothballs before caving and reluctantly summoning pest controllers to spray the house, but the flies kept swarming. EHS pest experts note that while treatments can provide some relief, eradication is difficult because cluster flies hibernate in cracks, gaps in siding, and unscreened vents. They are attracted to places like windowsills that are in the sun, where they typically swarm. Cluster flies have such a notorious reputation for resisting pest controllers that EHS recommends waving a white flag and simply grabbing a vacuum cleaner and sucking them up whenever they appear.[75]

The Warrens' presence legitimated the girls' belief that spirits were everywhere in the house—both good and evil. For instance, Lorraine suggested that vague knocking sounds and shaking and rattling in the house were not due to the wind but were "demonic in nature."[76] Another time, when it was revealed that the girls had dabbled with a Ouija board, it prompted a sudden outburst by Lorraine: "Under *no* circumstances should a Ouija Board be allowed in this house. No Tarot cards. No Ouija Board. *Nothing* connected with the Dark Arts." She called it a "very dangerous game" that was "literally inviting disaster."[77] Once, Lorraine abruptly stopped near the parents' bedroom. She closed her eyes and began to shake. "No one should sleep in this bedroom," she blurted out. Soon after, as Lorraine stepped inside the laundry room, a disturbed look came over her, and she quickly backed out, complaining of negative energy. "Something awful happened in there. Violent. The poor thing. So young. A girl. Blood. Definitely a female." Lorraine then lectured Mrs. Perron on the danger posed to her children, whom she said were "highly susceptible to supernatural energy." After hearing that her children were in grave danger, Carolyn was so upset that she began to tremble uncontrollably.[78] There was only one solution: a séance.

The Séance

The Warrens arrived for the séance at dusk with the intention of exorcising the house. They brought with them an entourage including a female medium, a parapsychologist from Duke University, a priest, and a camera crew to record the anticipated events. Carolyn told Roger nothing of the planned demonic intervention until less than an hour before the Warrens showed up at their doorstep. Roger was livid, but he let them in. As the "cleansing" ritual began, Carolyn looked "unresponsive," with "vacant hollow eyes." Lorraine said, "Someone invited a demon into your house. It might have happened many years ago before you arrived here. Or it might have come in because of mischievous children playing with fire, disguised as a game. . . . [B]ut make no mistake, *someone* invited this demon."[79] Carolyn began to weep; anguish and fear came over her face. As the séance continued, and seeing his wife in obvious distress, Roger grew more and more angry, unimpressed with what he viewed to be a pagan ritual filled with superstitious mumbo jumbo. Roger found the spectacle difficult to bear as his wife began to shiver, her teeth chattering. Soon Carolyn was letting out piercing screams, with an angry, evil tenor.

With the group holding hands (except for Roger, who had refused), Carolyn let out a "howling, growling" sound, as if she were experiencing "horrific pain." Suddenly, her chair appeared to lift and move backward, spilling Carolyn hard to the floor. "She hit the floor with such force everyone present could hear the air rushing from her lungs."[80] Andrea suggests that Carolyn's chair was propelled supernaturally and perhaps even levitated. Given all of the video equipment that was there, why wasn't this fantastic event captured on film? The chair could have been pushed by Carolyn and—far from levitating—acted in accordance with the laws of physics, until it stopped abruptly and tipped over. This explanation seems more likely than the presence of demonic forces. If Carolyn's chair *had* levitated as Andrea claimed, such a dramatic event surely would have converted Roger on the spot. But that did not happen. Roger Perron did not respond like a man who had just witnessed a defiance of natural law. He rushed to his wife's aid, and as Ed Warren attempted to pull him back, he "whipped around and punched Ed directly in the face, dropping him to the floor." Seeing Ed's nose bleeding, Lorraine wiped his face. Roger wanted the demon busters gone and ordered the Warrens and their entourage out of his home. When the ghost "techs," who had set up ghost detecting equipment throughout the house, went to fetch their equipment from the "haunted" cellar, they discovered that one or two "poltergeists" had managed to smash every one of their devices during the hubbub. Two of the girls, Andrea and Cynthia, had secretly watched the dining-room séance "through a crack in the door," putting them near the cellar door; Chrissy had, unbelievably, slept through it all; and April was in and out of her room. None of the girls would confess to destroying the devices.[81] Conveniently, the photos and film all turned out to be blank and unusable, so there was no verification of the dramatic séance as claimed by the Warrens.[82]

After slamming the front door behind the group, Roger blasted his wife. Andrea writes, "He bitterly resented the intrusion, the theatrical farce of a pseudo-intellectual endeavor: ritualistic nonsense." Roger viewed the spectacle that he had just witnessed as "an artificial make-it-up-as-you-go-affair" resembling a circus sideshow.[83] In a promotion for her books at the release of the movie *The Conjuring*, Andrea Perron lauds the film as highly accurate. However, anyone familiar with the film will realize that the producers took great liberty with what was claimed in the book. In the film, there is no mention of Ed Warren being punched in the nose and Roger ordering the ghost hunters, "Get the hell out of my house!"[84] Roger's assessment of the Warrens may not have been far off the mark. In August 2014, poltergeist investigator Guy Playfair said he had "only met the Warrens briefly and all I remember was him telling me what a lot of money I could make out of the Enfield [England] case, which seemed to be his main interest. I never took either of them seriously for a minute."[85]

Haunted Houses and Faded Memories

Much of what we know about the Perron "haunting" is based on the recollections of family members, decades after the events were reported. Psychologists Leonard Zusne and Warren Jones observe that when subjects recall events in haunted houses—events that occurred years earlier—the mixing of memory with imagination is the rule, not the exception, as memories are easily distorted. They write, "Dreams are remembered as actual physical events, a dream that comes after a significant event is remembered as having come before it and, therefore, as being prophetic of it, and the story itself gets better and better, in the retelling, with significant but inconvenient details being omitted and other details added."[86] A classic example is the case of Sir Edmund Hornby, the former chief justice of the Supreme Consular Court of China and Japan. He recounted an incident from 1875 in which a newspaper editor entered his bedroom at 1:20 a.m. and sat on his bed, ignoring his request to leave. The editor insisted on knowing the judgment of a case from the previous day. Fearing an argument might break out and awaken his wife, he relented. He said that the man stated, "This is the last time I shall ever see you anywhere."[87] The following day he learned that the visitor had died of a heart attack the previous day at 1:00 a.m.—twenty minutes *before* he showed up in Hornby's bedroom. An inquest uncovered the following note: "The Chief Judge gave judgment this morning in this case to the following effect," followed by illegible writing. In recalling the story nine years later, Judge Hornby asserted that his memory of the incident was clear and that he was wide awake at the time. A friend of the editor and the judge, after making inquiries, found "that the editor had died at 9 in the morning of the day in question, that no inquest was held on his death, that there was no record of the judgment that figures so prominently in the story, and that Judge Hornby was not married at the time. Thus, what had probably been a vivid dream had turned, in the Judge's mind, into reality wrought with ghostly implications."[88]

There is no concrete evidence that there were ever ghosts, poltergeists, or demons in the Perron home, only a one-time Catholic family given to occultish beliefs—beliefs that shaped their perception of everyday events and conditions well known by psychologists: lucid and waking dreams, sleep paralysis, fantasy-proneness, and imaginary companions. In addition, there was another powerful force at work, a force long studied by social psychologists: the power of the group and the spread of emotional contagion from person to person by suggestion. Within this context, it was not long before Mrs. Perron and her daughters were viewing their world within a supernatural framework. The appearance of the Warrens reinforced their beliefs about the haunting. They were well-known outsiders and experts who were seemingly finding spirits behind every door. Within this atmosphere of fear, common events became reinterpreted as paranormal, including something as simple as answering the telephone. For instance, on occasion, the phone would ring and only static could be heard. "More frequently there would be an unnerving noise, a crackling rather convoluted sound, as if someone was calling from far beyond the realm of possibility; from long ago and far away." Andrea suggests that instead of technical issues with the line or the phone, it was likely some type of otherworldly force trying to communicate.[89]

Another factor adding to the cauldron of excitement and fear was the likelihood of pranking by one or more of the girls. Certainly, the reaction by Carolyn Perron was not typical of a Rhode Island housewife during the 1970s. When most people see fly swarms in winter, they do not assume that the flies are a portent of evil forces that are going to haunt your house. When most people learn that their child is playing with an imaginary companion, they do not believe that the "companion" is actually a spirit. Many people who experience paralysis in bed while seeing terrifying visions would consult a psychiatrist; Mrs. Perron did not. In fact, if a psychiatrist or psychologist had been consulted, he or she might have been able to explain the occurrences as natural events, events that are fairly common within the general population.

It remained for the Warrens to plant the idea of potential possession. Although *The Conjuring* exaggerates the case and suggests that a possessed Carolyn Perron was freed of her "demon" after a wild exorcism, it is apparent that Mrs. Perron was simply caught up in suggestion and role-playing. Moreover, the Perrons would continue to be plagued by nine spirits, or rather their belief in such entities, for several years to come.[90] The series of extraordinary events at the Perron farmhouse begs the question of why a family tormented by spirits for a decade would remain for so long. Several times, family members felt that their lives were being threatened by an array of supernatural forces that terrified them. In the trailer for the movie, an announcer says chillingly, "What happened to the family was so disturbing that they refused to speak of it—until now."[91] If these events *were* so frightening, *why remain in the house for even one night? The Perrons stayed for ten years!* Andrea said that she was petrified during the séance because she thought her mother had died. She was traumatized. Her books detail hundreds of incidents with apparent supernatural forces in what was an emotional roller coaster for Mrs. Perron and her daughters. They remained in the house for six more years following the séance. In a recent interview, Andrea said that even though her family realized that the property was haunted, they would have lost a significant sum of money by selling, as the early seventies were marked by an economic downturn.[92] It is difficult to believe, given the sheer volume of terrifying encounters reported by the family, that they would have risked their lives and mental well-being by remaining in a house that posed so many constant threats. The obvious answer is that these events have been exaggerated over time. One cannot understate the constant, unrelenting stress and fear that the girls faced on a daily—even hourly—basis. For instance, Andrea Perron told a TV interviewer, "We packed like wolves . . . we became a pack.

We travelled in numbers. We used the bathroom in multiples of three or more because there was an evil male presence in that house . . . [and] you couldn't use that bathroom without feeling that you were being watched."[93] Christine even complained of feeling like someone or some *thing* was watching her "all of the time." "When I look there's no one there but I know someone is in the room with me. It creeps me out," she said.[94] Yet the feeling of being watched is very common. While paranoia is a key symptom of a variety of mental disorders, it also occurs in everyday life. Professor Colin Clifford of Sydney University believes that everyone is "hard-wired to believe others are staring at us." He notes, "A direct gaze can signal dominance or a threat, and if you perceive something as a threat, you would not want to miss it. So simply assuming another person is looking at you may be the safest strategy."[95]

A Never-Ending Story

The drama of the Perron family versus the spirit world continues even today. During filming of *The Conjuring* in 2012, the Perron sisters visited the set. Andrea says that while they were giving an interview to promote the movie, "a bizarre wind" suddenly kicked up and knocked over much of the set and the cameras. It was obvious to Andrea what had just happened: it was Bathsheba's curse. This event is telling, for it shows just how easily the Perrons were prone to redefining mundane events in a supernatural light. At about the same time the interview was taking place, Mrs. Perron (who did not make the trip) fell and broke her hip. She too concluded that the fall was a result of Bathsheba's spirit.[96]

When we ponder what really happened at the "haunted" Perron farmhouse for over a decade, one cannot help recalling the words of Shakespeare: "Or in the night, imagining some fear, How easy is a bush supposed a bear!" To Mrs. Perron and her daughters, hidden meanings were everywhere. A vague noise became a restless spirit; a gust of wind was a supernatural force; a swarm of flies was a sure sign that spirits were about. When most people have terrifying visions of their house burning down or of a strange entity hovering above them, they seek the opinion of a professional such as a psychologist or psychiatrist. Not Carolyn Perron. She assumed these events were caused by spirits, yet they could not have been as terrifying as described in the book, because the family remained in the house for over a decade. Most claims by the girls were accepted as gospel by Mrs. Perron, despite a lack of witnesses or corroborating evidence. It is also evident that some pranking was going on, with the suspicion falling on Cindy. One can hardly blame the daughters for thinking that the house was inhabited by spirits, given their isolation, the influence of their mother, and their propensity to experience a variety of psychological phenomena within a supernatural framework: small-group dynamics, waking dreams, sleep paralysis, fantasy-proneness, and imaginary companions.

Carolyn Perron and her daughters grew up in an enchanted world inhabited by an array of paranormal entities. Ultimately, these "encounters" were appealing because they offered them a glimpse of immortality: proof of an afterlife. Each encounter was an affirmation of this reality, a reality that was both terrifying and reassuring. The books that purport to document their many interactions with the supernatural, *House of Darkness House of Light*, read like gospels. At the end of volume 2, Andrea writes that "the Perron family intermingled with immortality and each was transformed by the experience. They would emerge from the engagement profoundly changed and spiritually stirred, shaken and awakened by personal encounters they will never forget. . . . When they emerged it was with a realization. There is no death. There is only transformation."[97] Viewing the world through a spiritual prism may explain why they looked at the mundane and ordinary and saw the extraordinary and fantastic. Time and again family members had the opportunity to consider natural explanations for an array of predominantly mundane events, and instead they chose the supernatural hypothesis. Belief is a powerful force—and the intense desire to believe is an even stronger one.

The events as described in Andrea Perron's books *must have been exaggerated*. How could anyone stay in a house with a supposedly "haunted" fridge routinely scattering its contents on the kitchen floor; levitating beds that left Cindy terrified, bruised and battered; an animated broomstick that swept the floor by itself; and so many other strange visions and creepy happenings? Andrea even claims that one of the two phones in the house would routinely lift off the cradle and float in midair.[98] Why was none of this activity caught on film? How could any responsible parents allow their daughters to stay in such a dangerous house, and how could the girls—repeatedly frightened—remain for over ten years?

New Revelations

After *The Conjuring* was released in 2013, the owner of the farmhouse for the past 26 years, Norma Sutcliffe (along with her husband, Jerry), said that her life became a nightmare. "We will never feel safe and secure again; we have forever lost our sense of peace and privacy," she laments. She has had to endure ongoing harassment and the invasion of her privacy by trespassers at all hours of the day and night, who have turned her life into "a circus." Mrs. Sutcliffe is a skeptic when it comes to ghostly spirits and haunted houses, and she places the blame on Hollywood for the intrusions by curiosity seekers. "Those responsible who created this movie caused this to happen to us and they do not care."[99]

Sutcliffe decided to research the suicides, murders, and drownings that Andrea Perron said had taken place on the property. After a check of local historical records, she says that there is not a single shred of evidence to support these assertions, including the claims that Bathsheba Sherman had murdered a child as part of a satanic sacrifice. While Andrea says that she confirmed this with a local historian, Sutcliffe reports tracking down the historian mentioned in the book and says that Andrea fabricated the story. Sutcliffe has teamed up with retired journalist Kent Spottswood to investigate the claims made about the house, claims they say are false. Spottswood's research shows that Bathsheba Sherman died of "paralysis" in 1885 (a code word of the time for what was most likely a stroke).[100] In January 2014, Andrea Perron told a journalist for the *Providence Journal*, "I'm not in dispute with Mrs. Sutcliffe about Bathsheba. . . . That was the story line of a made-up movie . . . it was a movie designed to highlight the career of Ed and Lorraine Warren. It was their version of events turned into a Hollywood feature film."[101] Perron then suggested that the spirit haunting the farmhouse was that of a Mrs. John Arnold who was supposedly found hanging in what had been the Perron barn during the eighteenth century. Spottswood says that is impossible, because records show that Arnold had hanged herself in 1866, and not in what was once the Perron barn but in a house a mile away.[102]

Sutcliffe also says that during some stretches, she and her husband are unable to sleep well for days at a time due to outsiders disturbing the peace, observing that "we wake up at 2 in the morning . . . there are people with flashlights in our yard." Other times they are pestered by those who have somehow obtained their unlisted phone number, who ask, "Is this 'The Conjuring' house?" The local Burrillville Police had to be called to the property to shoo away thrill-seekers.[103] A very similar outcome would happen several years later in the wake of another reported haunting investigated by the Warrens. The location of the house was a village named Amityville. It would soon become a household name.

CHAPTER 5

The Amityville Horror:
Haunting or Hoax?

'Tis strange—but true; for truth is always strange;
Stranger than fiction.

—Lord Byron[1]

It is arguably the most famous haunting in American history. Images of the eerie six-bedroom Dutch colonial house on the south shore of western Long Island are instantly recognizable to millions around the world. For many, the house at 112 Ocean Avenue in Amityville, New York, epitomizes evil, and the terrifying events that were reported to have occurred there defy explanation. After all, the mysterious occurrences of December 1975 and January 1976 were not only affirmed by the family who lived there, but also by a priest, a police officer, and numerous visitors, including a television news crew. They all claimed they were attacked by demonic forces. It is difficult to believe that so many people could have been involved in an elaborate hoax or were victims of their imaginations. The two principal witnesses, George and Kathy Lutz, even passed lie detector tests.[2] There would seem to be compelling evidence that something extraordinary and unexplainable happened at the Lutzes' former home. Enough evidence has now come to light to be able to piece together an accurate picture of what transpired in this small seaside village thirty miles east of New York City. The episode has made such an indelible impression on popular culture that the word "Amityville" is synonymous with demonic forces and the paranormal. What Roswell is to UFOs, and Loch Ness is to lake monsters, Amityville is to hauntings. Adding to its mystique are claims that the book and the movie by the same name, *The Amityville Horror*, are based on a true story. Some may accept the reality of the Lutzes' accounts based on this assertion alone, reasoning that publishers and filmmakers would not be allowed to make such statements unless they were true. Were the events in Amityville a genuine case of paranormal activity or something more mundane?

It was April 1977 when the story of a terrifying haunting in Amityville was thrust into the national media spotlight.[3] During that month the popular women's magazine *Good Housekeeping* published a summary of the ordeal, under the title "Our Dream House Was Haunted," by Paul Hoffman.[4] By September, Jay Anson's *The Amityville Horror: A True Story* arrived in bookstores and quickly became an international bestseller. It would give rise to a major movie by the same name, earning $86 million at U.S. box offices since then: a huge success for a project that cost a mere $4.7 million to make.[5] In the book, Anson chronicles the distressing ordeal reported by George and Kathy Lutz and their three children: Daniel, age nine, Christopher, age seven, and Melissa ("Missy"), age five. The family, along with their dog, Harry, moved into their new home shortly before Christmas on December 18, 1975. They had snapped up the house for the bargain price of $80,000. It even had a heated swimming pool, a large boathouse on the Amityville River, and an enclosed porch. It sounded too good to be true, but there was a catch: thirteen months earlier, it had been the scene of a gruesome mass murder involving six members of the same family, and it had stood unoccupied since. In the early hours of Wednesday, November 13, 1975, Ronald "Butch" DeFeo Jr. methodically shot his parents, two brothers, and two sisters as they lay in their beds. That night, Suffolk County medical examiner Dr. Howard Adelman arrived on the scene amid a swarm of police. He assumed that the victims had been drugged, as he observed that "all of the bodies were found face down with their arms extended."[6] Media outlets soon reported that the family had been slipped a sedative.[7] However, extensive toxicology tests on their blood, urine, and major organs were negative, leading Adelman to describe their state at the time of the killings as "stone cold sober." This led to public speculation that an "evil force" may have held them down while DeFeo went from room to room.[8] The 23-year-old car mechanic would later claim that dark voices in the house told him to shoot. At his trial, his plea of innocent by reason of insanity was rejected. He was sentenced to six consecutive life terms.

Extraordinary Claims

The story told by the Lutzes is chilling. They say that a supernatural force left them so badly shaken that they abandoned the house after just 28 days, leaving behind all of their possessions except some clothing. The strange happenings were said to have begun with mysterious knocking, glimpses of shadowy figures, and George's incessant feeling of being cold. Family members began to undergo personality changes, growing uncharacteristically ill-tempered. The Lutzes said that on their fourth night, they exploded in anger when the children accidentally cracked a windowpane. As punishment, they grabbed a strap and a wooden spoon and beat their children. This was followed by foul stenches and a massive fly swarm in the middle of winter.[9]

On December 22, a powerful, unseen force reportedly ripped open a 250-pound door, leaving it hanging from a single hinge. Before long, the reports of strange happenings grew wilder and more bizarre. During the family's stay, this force was said to have thrown open windows, bending their locks; caused green slime to seep from a ceiling and keyhole; flip a crucifix upside down; and cause beds and dresser drawers to slide rapidly back and forth. Kathy claims to have been levitated two feet into the air one time. On another occasion she peered into a mirror, only to see herself as a wrinkled, toothless, ninety-year-old woman. They say a strange creature left cloven-hooved tracks in the snow, peered into the house at night with penetrating red eyes, and appeared to the Lutzes' five-year-old daughter, Missy, as an invisible friend whom she called Jodie: a sinister pig-like creature. George says he was once attacked in bed by an invisible entity with hooves: "heavy feet struck his legs and body."[10] The Lutzes also claim that a Catholic priest who was blessing their house heard a masculine voice order him to get out. Shortly after, he felt a slap on his face by an invisible force, and later he developed mysterious blisters on his hands.

The events in Amityville contain classic elements of a poltergeist: strange knocking, moving objects, cold spots, levitating people, mysterious lacerations and bruises from an unseen force, oozing liquid, and malfunctioning equipment, such as their telephone. These events are mostly confined to a specific site: 112 Ocean Avenue. But instead of a central figure around whom the events occur, we have three: George, Kathy, and Missy. The shadowy figures and demonic features are also uncharacteristic of poltergeists. Their story is a strange mixture of traditional haunting, poltergeist disturbance, and demonic possession, with elements suspiciously similar to those from *The Exorcist*, which had been released only two years earlier in December 1973.

Unraveling a Mystery

Nearly three weeks after fleeing their "dream home," on February 14, 1976, the Lutzes appeared on the local TV news: Channel 5 Metro Media, where reporter Steve Bauman recounted the tragic history of the house, which he said seemed to be haunted. He claimed that in researching the site's history, he found that tragedy had befallen almost everyone who had lived in the house—and in an earlier house on the site, which had since been torn down. Bauman told his viewers, "They talked of feeling the presence of some energy inside, some unnatural evil that grew stronger each day they remained."[11] Then came the surprising announcement: Ronald DeFeo's lawyer, William Weber, said that he was investigating the possibility that a mysterious force inside the house may have influenced his client to murder his family. Weber's strategy was clear: while it was a long shot at winning a new trial, it was true that DeFeo had claimed that voices in the house had instructed him to do the killing. DeFeo would later contend that while high on drugs, he became paranoid after overhearing family members plotting to kill him. A hooded figure then appeared, a female demon with black hands, who handed him the rifle that he used to shoot his family.[12] Weber said he was commissioning studies to determine whether the influence was natural (such as "electrical currents" created by the unique structure of the house) or paranormal (resulting from "psychic" forces).[13]

On February 16, the Lutzes held a press conference with William Weber, reaffirming their account of the events at 112 Ocean Avenue but refusing to discuss the case further, claiming that journalists were distorting the story.[14] A second factor appears to have been involved: as would later be disclosed, the Lutzes and Weber were intending to get rich off of a book deal about the "haunted house" and were reluctant to release too much information that could undermine sales. Not long after, two well-known psychic investigators entered the picture: Ed and Lorraine Warren. After being asked by representatives of a local TV station to visit the house and give her impressions as a clairvoyant, Lorraine entered the house on February 24, accompanied by her well-known, demon-hunting husband, Ed. Before long, Lorraine said she could feel an evil presence. Ed reported having been attacked by a sinister force while he was inspecting the cellar. "Suddenly I felt as though I were under a heavy waterfall, and the pressure was driving me down to the floor." Ed said that he fought off the force by reciting prayers. [15]

On the night of March 6, 1976, and early into the next morning, a series of séances were held in the house at the behest of Channel 5 News, which had been given exclusive permission to visit the house with a team of reporters, accompanied by an entourage of psychics and parapsychologists.[16] During the first séance, which began at 10:30, one of the mediums, Mrs. Albert Riley, went into a trance and gasped, "It's upstairs in the bedroom!" She complained that the force was making her heart race. During the same séance, another medium, Mary Pascarella, suddenly fell ill and described seeing a large, threatening black shadow.[17] Psychic researcher George Kekoris then became "violently ill" and left the table. Soon an observer from radio station WNEW-FM, Mike Linder, reported feeling cold and numb, while TV cameraman Steve Petropolis suffered heart palpitations, chest pains, and shortness of breath.[18] Ed Warren also reported severe heart palpitations, which lasted for three weeks after the "attack" that night.[19] The Warrens were convinced that the strange happenings were the work of Satan. Yet despite the excitement experienced by the psychics and some outside observers who became convinced there was a demonic presence, two TV journalists who were present were unimpressed. News anchor Marvin Scott and intern Laura DiDio reported nothing out of the ordinary except for several overly excited people.[20] Scott later quipped, "The only voices I heard that night were of my crew wanting to know when we were going to eat the sandwiches we brought along."[21]

Before Anson's book appeared on store shelves, paranormal investigators Rick Moran and Peter Jordan obtained an advance copy and traveled to Amityville to check out the Lutzes' claims. In searching early press reports, they noticed something odd. There was no mention of any damage to the house, such as a 250-pound wooden door being ripped off or locks bent. Moreover, the pair was intrigued by the incidents involving a Catholic priest. In the book, George Lutz summons a "Father Mancuso" to bless the house, and as the priest is doing so, a voice orders him to get out, followed by an invisible force that slaps his face. The priest soon feels unwell, and while he is driving home, the force appears to take possession of his car. Suddenly the hood flies up, smashing into the windshield, and the passenger-side door bursts open. Father Mancuso slams on the brakes and narrowly averts a disastrous accident. Moran and Jordan tracked down the real-life priest, Father Ralph Pecoraro, who denied that any of these events happened.[22] Supporters of the Lutzes point out that this is blatantly untrue, for a 1979 episode of the popular TV show *In Search Of* presented an interview with a silhouetted man claiming to be the priest. He said that the book accurately portrays his experiences in the house. "I also started sprinkling Holy Water, and I heard a rather deep voice behind me saying, 'Get out.' It seemed so directed toward me, that I was really quite startled. I felt a slap at one

point on the face. I felt somebody slap me, and there was nobody there."
Soon after, he says, mysterious blisters appeared on his hand.[23]

There is something odd about this story. Imagine you are a priest
blessing a house. You are alone in a room, and suddenly a strange masculine voice forcefully orders you to leave, followed by an unseen force
slapping your face. So what does he do? He leaves without telling a
soul. It is not until 5:00 PM on Christmas Eve that he rings the Lutzes
and tries to warn them about the evil force that he believes inhabits
the house, but midway through the conversation, "an irritating static"
drowns out their voices. Over the next three weeks, numerous attempts
are made by both parties to phone each other, but each time, mysterious crackling and static prevents the priest from warning the Lutzes. It
was not until several months after the Lutzes fled their home that the
priest would finally tell them of the strange voice and slap in the face,[24]
yet Rockville Center is a mere 25-minute drive from the Lutzes' house.
He easily could have driven there or sent them a letter warning of the
evil force that he had supposedly encountered. It is difficult to believe
that he would withhold this information for so long. What happened
while he was blessing the house forms the centerpiece of the book. It
gives the story integrity ("If a priest said it happened, it must be true")
and introduces a religious component. Yet in the *Good Housekeeping*
article, which appeared *before* the Anson book was released, there is no
mention of this dramatic claim or that the priest even blessed the house.
Instead, Paul Hoffman writes that George Lutz, in an effort to exorcise
the evil spirits, went through every room while reciting the Lord's Prayer
and shouting, "Get out!"[25] This is a remarkable coincidence as it is strikingly similar to the priest's account—yet the priest is never mentioned
in the article. In November 1977, reporters from *Newsday*, a respected
newspaper serving western Long Island and New York City, contacted
the Catholic Diocese of Rockville Center and were told that the event
never happened.[26] So, how do we account for this discrepancy? Is the
Catholic Diocese trying to cover up the case? In 2004, Moran clarified
what had happened: "Father Pecoraro, whom Peter Jordan interviewed
several times and I once, never said he saw anything in the house . . .
he *felt* it was a very dark, possibly evil place, feelings that seemed to be
telling him to 'get out' immediately." Moran said Pecoraro later recanted
his claims and said "that he never went in the house at all . . . adding
that when Kathy Lutz told him they were moving into the DeFeo house,
he said they would say a mass for their happiness in their new home."[27]

Jay Anson admits that he had taken "artistic license" in writing the
story, and he told Moran that the injection of Father Pecoraro into the

story "served only to stretch a short story into a full-length book."[28] In the late 1970s, the same priest was called upon to testify under oath in a U.S. district court in Brooklyn, New York, as to the authenticity of his story, as part of a lawsuit. The record of his testimony was sealed until May 2001, when Ron DeFeo's wife, Geraldine, managed to get a judge to release it. Crime researcher Ric Osuna describes the outcome: "What was unsealed was the simple affirmation of the Catholic priest, who testified under oath that the events described in Jay Anson's book never transpired."[29]

On July 27, 1979, *The Amityville Horror* opened to packed movie theaters. At about the same time, DeFeo's attorney, William Weber, unleashed a bombshell revelation to the Associated Press: the Lutzes' story was a hoax. "We created this horror story over many bottles of wine that George Lutz was drinking," he said. The goal was to create a story that "the public wanted to hear."[30] Weber was unhappy with the Lutzes because he claimed they had reneged on a deal to collaborate on a book about the strange events at the house. Weber said that he supplied details about the DeFeo murders to the Lutzes to help them craft a more believable story using what he called "creative imagination." For instance, he says he told Kathy Lutz that DeFeo had shot his victims around 3:00 AM. "So Kathy said, 'Well, that's good. I can say I'm awakened by noises at that hour of the day and I could say I had dreams at that hour of the day about the DeFeo family.'"[31]

Weber says he showed the couple numerous crime-scene photographs, some of which revealed "black gook" in the toilet bowls, which he attributed to police fingerprint powder.[32] But why would the Lutzes make up a story of a haunted house? Weber says that the Lutzes were desperate to get out from under a crushing mortgage that they could not afford.[33] While his admission was not likely to enhance his personal and professional standing, Weber stood to gain financially if he could convince the judge that he helped to create the story that would eventually be published as *The Amityville Horror*. While Weber sued Anson and Lutz for $60 million for "stealing ideas," he settled out of court for the paltry sum of $2,500 and an additional $15,000 for his contribution to the book and film.[34] Many researchers and Web sites continue to have a skeptical view on Weber's hoax claim, noting that it was in his financial interest to make such a claim in hopes of striking it rich in his lawsuit against the Lutzes. How much weight should we place on this argument and on claims that the Amityville haunting really happened, as the Lutzes claim? Let's look at the case in greater detail.

A Closer Look

In the book, Anson writes that the police conducted an on-site inspection of 112 Ocean Avenue during the Lutzes' 28-day ordeal.[35] Amityville police deny this. Could the police have been covering up their involvement in order to distance themselves from a controversial case? Such conspiracy theories belong to the realm of fiction. Even before the book reached stores, Rick Moran and Peter Jordan went to Amityville and checked the police records. They state that "no police officer was in that house and no report was ever made of physical damage, prowlers, or intruders in the house or on the grounds during the time the Lutzes were in residence." It was only *after* they had abandoned the house that they bothered to contact police.[36] *Newsday* journalist Ed Lowe confirms these claims, observing that during their 28-day "siege," they never once contacted police—and he should know: his father was the Amityville police chief at the time. Think about it. Mysterious and terrifying events occur in your new home and continue unabated for four weeks: strange noises, shadowy figures, and mysterious levitations. Yet, despite their claims to the contrary, the Lutzes never once contacted the police, and they supposedly stayed in the house, battling these evil forces, for no less than 28 days!

The inconsistencies between the events reported in the book and real life do not stop with the inaccurate claims about the police and priest. If one scrutinizes the *Good Housekeeping* article further, George Lutz never claims that his wife levitated two feet off the bed—arguably the most dramatic part of the story in Anson's book. Instead he says that she "slid" across the bed "as if by levitation."[37] In September 1979, George Lutz gave testimony in a U.S. federal court in his $1 million lawsuit against Paul Hoffman, claiming that Hoffman invaded his privacy by writing the *Good Housekeeping* article and a spinoff piece for the *New York Daily News*. During his testimony under oath, Lutz gave a third version of the event, admitting that she had indeed levitated but that it had been exaggerated in the book. How much so? He said that his wife had floated just *two inches in the air*. In dismissing the suit against Hoffman and two others, presiding judge Jack Weinstein ruled that the Lutzes had "deliberately made themselves public figures."[38] Weinstein observed, "Based on what I have heard, it appears to me that to a large extent the book is a work of fiction, relying in a large part upon the suggestions of Mr. Weber."[39]

But if the Lutzes conspired to create a hoax, how do we explain that they both passed polygraph tests? In their study of the over-hyped claims of neuroscience, psychiatrist Sally Satel and psychologist Scott Lilienfeld document why lie detector tests are inadmissible in courts of law and inherently flawed. They observe that polygraphs monitor subjective responses to control questions, which are then used to set a baseline against lies. It is an inexact science because it measures arousal, not truth. They note that habitual liars and psychopaths often have nervous systems that do not respond to threats as many people do. On the other hand, truth-tellers may become anxious under high-stakes questioning. The results, if allowed into the courts, would be disastrous, because innocent people may appear guilty and the guilty may appear innocent. They write, "Under interrogation, they become frightened or agitated, their hearts pound, their breath labors, and their palms sweat. They may even *feel* guilty." Polygraph examiners even have a name for these people: "guilt grabbers," as "the mere thought of being accused of wrongdoing gooses their autonomic nervous systems." The bottom line is that research on polygraphs consistently demonstrates that they are unreliable. The National Academy of Sciences estimate is that polygraph exams correctly identify between 75 and 80 percent of those who tell lies, but they mislabel people as liars about 65 percent of the time.[40] Even the CIA, which is known for using polygraphs, has made serious blunders. In 1998, a scientist working for the Department of Energy, Wen Ho Lee, was accused of spying for the Chinese government but was later found to be innocent. Conversely, the notorious Soviet secret agent Aldrich Ames passed polygraph exams in 1986 and 1991.[41] He was not arrested until 1994, after electronic surveillance. Ames described the polygraphs he was given as "witch-doctory" that required "no special magic." He said that the key was to remain confident and exhibit "a friendly relationship with the examiner . . . rapport, where you smile and you make him think that you like him."[42]

Meteorology 101

One of the strengths of Anson's writing is the detail that he includes from the 35 hours of tape recordings with George and Kathy Lutz. Meteorological expert Tim Vasquez examined records from the National Climatic Data Center and the National Oceanic and Atmospheric Administration (NOAA) in order to verify the Lutzes' claims. His findings are revealing. For instance, Anson writes that at 3:15 on Christmas morning, "winter moonlight" was "flooding the bedroom." In reality, the sky was overcast.[43] We are told that on December 27, conditions were "bright and clear," with "temperatures hovering in the low teens." At no time was the daytime temperature below freezing. It was overcast with a predawn high of 46°F, falling slowly to 39°F.[44] Anson states that on January 10, George Lutz heard a loud thunderclap, and upon looking out a window, "he saw the first raindrops strike the panes. Then somewhere in the distance, a flash of lightning hit the darkness and again, a few minutes later, came another boom of thunder." George said he could then distinguish "the silhouettes of trees swaying in the rising gusts. . . . The rain was coming down much harder now, beating heavily against the windows and outside walls." When he went outside, George described "sheets of icy rain that lashed at him" and "hurricane-force winds" that "whipped the front door of the house back against the building."[45] Local weather records reveal a very different scene: at 8:00 PM, nearby John F. Kennedy Airport recorded clear skies and 24°F. The following morning, clouds moved in, and light snow fell. Vasquez writes of the night in question, "The air mass was far too cold and stable to support thunderstorm activity."[46] Even the claim that George Lutz found eerie cloven hoof prints in the freshly fallen snow near the house does not correspond with weather records. There had been no snow at the time.[47] In fact, after analyzing the verifiable weather-related claims in the book, Vasquez was able to find just one accurate description! At about 1:00 on the morning of January 1, 1976, a violent wind gust was reported, coinciding with the time when the Lutzes said it had awakened them. That actually *did* happen.[48] The book also has astronomical inconsistences. For example, George Lutz says that at 3:15 on Christmas morning, he looked at his daughter's window and saw a pig's face staring back. At the time, he said, "the orb of the full moon was like a huge flashlight, lighting his way."[49] Impossible. The moon was in its third quarter, and it had set several hours earlier, well before midnight.[50]

The near-total failure of weather data to coincide with the Lutzes' claims shows just how poorly thought out their plan was. All they had to do was to look at back issues of local newspapers to know what the weather had been on any given day, or they could have consulted the weather bureau. Did they think that no one was going to check these dates against weather records, simply taking their word for it, given the extraordinary claims? While their hoax may have been elaborate and their acting good enough to obtain a book deal and a film, much of their success can be attributed to good fortune, given the amateurish way it was constructed. The deception was always going to fall apart; it was only a question of time. The book is filled with so many discrepancies and inconsistencies that it was soon being poked full of more holes than a block of Swiss cheese. For instance, an early hardcover edition of the book says that when George supposedly found mysterious pig-like footprints in the snow, they were investigated by the Amityville police—who later described the claim as "absolutely false."[51] In the book, Amityville police sergeant Al Gionfriddo supposedly checked on the Lutzes, yet there was no such officer on the force, and there is no record of his ever existing. We were also told that Gionfriddo had been on duty the night of the DeFeo murders and that he radioed an Officer Cammaroto from outside the house. Sergeant Pat Cammaroto was indeed a police officer on the Amityville force at the time of the supposed haunting, and he did go to the crime scene immediately after the shootings. He says that the radio incident never happened.[52]

Physical evidence for the haunting, as described in the book, also crumbles under closer scrutiny. Anson writes of serious damage to doors and windows, including a doorknob, locks, and hinges. Shortly before the book appeared, Rick Moran and Peter Jordan conducted a check of area repair shops and locksmiths; several recalled doing work for the DeFeo family, but none said they had been to the house since the Lutzes moved in. In spite of claims of extensive damage to the house over their 28-day stay, the Lutzes neither filed an insurance claim nor rang police about possible vandalism.[53] Joe Nickell talked with the couple that purchased the house after the Lutzes fled: the Cromartys. They said that these items of hardware had not been newly replaced or repaired. In some cases, they never existed. For example, in the book we are told that a green slime oozed from the playroom door; the "only source seemed to be an empty lock hole in the door." When journalist Dennis Hevesi interviewed the Cromartys, it was evident that the door in question has no lock hole or lock. "There is only an antique keyhole plate fastened over the spot where a keyhole might be drilled."[54]

Shortly after the "haunting" made headlines in November 1977, just after publication of the book, more anomalies surfaced. For instance, the man who bought the Lutzes' previous home in nearby Deer Park, James Mullally, observed that two weeks after the Lutzes had moved into 112 Ocean Avenue—when the demons were supposedly in full riot—he and his wife had visited the Lutzes and were given a tour of the house. Far from being exhausted from fighting off an evil force and desperate to stay warm, they seemed very happy, Mullally says. "I remember my wife saying as we left if she were living in that house"—considering the murders—"she wouldn't be in as good a mood as Mrs. Lutz."[55]

Several accounts in the book have a distinct ring of implausibility, even if we were to assume that what was claimed actually occurred. For instance, Anson writes that on one early January morning at 2:00, George was horrified to see that Kathy's face had aged sixty years and she resembled an old woman. Later, in an exclusive interview, Kathy Lutz would describe the terrifying ordeal after seeing her reflection in a mirror, in her own words. "Ugly creases and crow's-feet scarred my face. I drooled all over my shriveled up, dried skin." She continued, "I ran my fingers down my craggy face and touched my dry lips. I shivered and broke out in a cold sweat. I burst into sobs." Kathy described the feel as "like looking through a Halloween mask." Now place yourself in Kathy's position. You awaken to find that your face is so badly wrinkled that your husband barely recognizes you. It is not a stretch of imagination to speculate that most people would seek immediate medical help. But not the Lutzes. Kathy said that for the next *six hours*, the pair lay awake in bed, watching the snow fall, until 8:00 AM, and her face gradually returned to normal.[56] The story and their reaction are just too far-fetched and implausible. Why did no one think to grab a camera and snap a picture of her face? They had several hours to do so. The photo could have been used to convince others that demonic forces were afoot. And what of the green ooze? The staring red eyes? Kathy's levitation? The fly swarm? The priest's blistered hand? The demonic image in the soot at the back of the fireplace? The book is filled with dozens of strange occurrences, yet there is not a single photo. It is simply beyond belief.

Other reactions appear inappropriate. When George discovered that a 250-pound wooden door had been ripped from its hinges, he returned to bed. Shadowy figures were seen lurking outside the house in the night. Eerie red eyes were spotted peering through windows. With the pluck of General Patton and the patience of Gandhi, both he and Kathy refused to do what most people would have done at this stage: flee the house and phone the police. Perhaps the most incongruent reaction of all is when his wife is supposedly found levitating two feet off the bed. This is an event that would likely send even the most battle-hardened person scurrying from the home. Not George Lutz. The former marine pulled her back to earth, didn't tell a soul, and remained in the house. On another occasion, George raced upstairs to find green slime oozing from the ceiling. He then checked it, like a drug detective in the movies might check for the presence of cocaine: "He looked at the substance, smelled it, and then put a little against the tip of his tongue. 'It sure looks like Jello,' he said, smacking his lips, 'but it doesn't have any taste at all.'" How many people do you know who would spot a strange green goo dripping from the ceiling of a strange house that they have just moved into and actually place some of it in their mouths? In Paul Hoffman's original article, there is no mention of green ooze, which also appeared on walls and the keyhole of the playroom door, at times in such quantity that it had to be removed from the house by the bucketful and disposed of in the Amityville River. Hoffman does mention a red, blood-like substance that trickled from the keyholes of some doors. Like the absence of photographic evidence of the many wild and weird happenings, the Lutzes failed to save any of the supernatural slime for analysis.[57]

Coincidence or Concoction?

At first glance, some of the claims in the book appear to be eerie coincidences. For instance, Anson writes that George Lutz kept waking up at 3:15 AM—around the time that Ronnie DeFeo was widely reported to have killed his family, according to initial reports. But later, police revised the time of the shootings as having occurred anytime between 1:00 and 4:00 AM. Also, preliminary reports on the murders suggested that the victims had been shot in the head. This proved to be incorrect.[58] One couple that does not believe their story is Barbara and James Cromarty, who purchased the house from the Lutzes and reported nothing out of the ordinary. Barbara told Joe Nickell that she possessed evidence that the whole affair was a hoax. At the time, Nickell was a consultant to the then forthcoming TV show *That's Incredible,* which sought his advice about filming inside the house. He recommended to a producer that they have Mrs. Cromarty tour the house and point out various discrepancies close up. On the show, Mrs. Cromarty recalled the extensive damage to doors and windows detailed by the Lutzes, and she noted that the old hardware—hinges, locks, doorknobs, etc.—was still in place. What's more, upon close inspection, one could see that there were no disturbances to the paint or varnish.[59] When the show was reportedly inundated with complaints for challenging the Lutzes' claims, Nickell says, he never heard from the producers again.[60] By the time of the film's release in 1979, 32-year-old Frank Burch had taken ownership of the house and was living a paranormally uneventful existence. "I have never heard sounds of ghosts, ghouls, or the supernatural," he said.[61] A transcript of the September 1979 trial of George and Kathy Lutz versus Paul Hoffman (who published the first article on the "haunting") is revealing. In court, the Lutzes were forced to admit that virtually everything in *The Amityville Horror* was pure fiction.[62] As *Newsday* columnist Ed Lowe observes, "It had to have been a setup since Day 1. The day after the Lutzes fled, supposedly in terror, they returned to hold a garage sale—just lots of junk. It was obvious they hadn't moved in there [the $80,000 house] with anything worth anything."[63]

An Enduring Myth

There is no question that *The Amityville Horror* is a hoax, so why is this very relevant information nowhere to be found in later editions of

Anson's book, which continue to be filed under nonfiction? A responsible publisher would add a preface or even a brief note, updating the story. But this has not happened, almost certainly out of fear of losing future sales, as the interest in profits trumps truth. If librarians are going to continue to shelve copies under nonfiction, the section on fraud and hoaxes would seem to be more appropriate.

Several decades after the events at 112 Ocean Avenue, the story of the Amityville Horror is alive and well in countless books, movies, documentaries, and Web sites. What is so remarkable is that many writers and much of the general public remain either unaware or unconvinced that the events are fictional. How do we explain the ongoing public fascination with the Amityville affair, in the face of overwhelming evidence of a hoax? Perhaps it is best summed up in the old adage, "Why let the facts get in the way of a good story?" But even the "facts" have changed over time. As journalist Dennis Hevesi observes, "Complete reversals of fact have been edited into the book since its early hardcover printings." In an early edition, Father Mancuso is driving an "old blue Vega" when the hood suddenly flies open and smashes back into the windshield. We are told that this happened after a welded hinge had "torn loose." In the paperback edition, he is driving an "old tan Ford." Why the change? Perhaps someone realized that the incident, as described, was physically impossible, as the hoods of all Chevy Vegas "are hinged by the headlights and open away from the windshield."[64]

While Anson's book is no literary masterpiece, he does spin a captivating story that begins slowly and builds to a crescendo. It is an enthralling tale filled with mystery and suspense, a tale of good versus evil and one family's struggle to survive against demonic forces. But perhaps the story's greatest appeal is the religious element, for if true, many of the events would appear to confirm the validity of Christianity: the upsidedown cross, the cloven footprints in the snow, the priest being ordered to get out, and the refusal of Kathy's aunt Theresa, a former nun, to enter certain rooms, as they had an evil vibe.[65] On another occasion a group of priests discussed the likelihood that there was a demonic presence in the house.[66] It is a story that many people would like to believe because it reinforces their Judeo-Christian world view. There is only one problem: *The Amityville Horror* is a work of fiction.

Follow the Money

To gain insight into the underlying motivations in the Amityville saga, one need only follow the money trail. At his murder trial, the prosecution suggested that Ron DeFeo Jr.'s motive for murdering his family was his desire to collect his parents' life insurance policies, after he initially claimed that he knew nothing about the killings.[67] DeFeo later changed his story, saying that his sister Dawn and an unidentified third party were the real killers. "She was plotting to profit from the family inheritance," DeFeo claimed.[68] His appeal was denied, perhaps because of his former attorney, William Weber, who testified that DeFeo was unreliable and had previously given at least fifteen different versions of what happened.[69] Weber was no saint and was motivated by visions of dollars from a book deal with the Lutzes; in 1979, he confessed to creating the hoax with them.

Then there are the Lutzes, who may have perpetrated their hoax in order to gain relief from a mountain of financial woes. Stephen Kaplan, who investigated the case from its early stages, believes it is extremely likely that the Lutzes orchestrated the haunting in order to get out of paying a costly mortgage. "This is a couple who had great financial dilemmas" after looking at buying a house in the $30,000 to $50,000 range, only to suddenly find themselves "in debt for an $80,000 house," he said.[70] Other investigators concur. In 2004, after examining the case for decades, Rick Moran concluded that when he bought the house, George Lutz "didn't have sufficient income to meet the mortgage payments. In fact, I was amazed any bank would give him a mortgage at all, given the tax assessments in Amityville at the time. The house was a liability."[71] Even though the Cromartys bought the house for a mere $55,000, they complained that it was hard to sell, due to the high property taxes.[72] There is no question that after buying the house in 1975, the Lutzes found themselves in an unsustainable situation, with the average cost of a home on their street being over $100,000. Money from George Lutz's surveying company was drying up, and George was planning to save money by turning the basement into an office in order to stop paying rent at his business site. He was also in trouble with the Internal Revenue Service over his business expenses.[73] George also planned to save money on marina fees by putting his speedboat and cabin cruiser in the boathouse that came with the home.[74] The Lutzes' plight was evident as soon as investigators began looking into their story. In 1978, Jordan and Moran observed,

> The purchase of this home was less than logical when one considers not only the cost of taxes, but also the cost of fuel to heat a three-story Dutch colonial that sits on the windward side of a river not half a mile from the Great South Bay of Long Island. All in all,

the logic of such a move would escape anyone who thought about it for more than five minutes, unless other considerations were to enter into the argument, a profit motive perhaps, that would not be readily obvious to the casual observer.[75]

By their own admission, the Lutzes were in a financial bind. As Jay Anson observed, soon after buying the house, they had "a very serious payroll deficit" at the survey business and faced "mounting bills."[76] The Lutzes' scheme to create a haunted house—and profit from the story—worked, and by September 1979, George Lutz testified under oath to a federal judge that he had received $100,000 for the book and another $100,000 from the first movie that opened that summer.[77] He revealed that by 2000, they had made over a quarter of a million dollars from the original book and $160,000 from the movie. Ironically, he said that about one third of this went to lawyers to either initiate or fend off lawsuits over various claims about the case.[78]

Some of the Lutz children have also tried to profit from the Amityville cash cow. One of those is Christopher Quarantino, who was seven years old when he lived in the house with his mother, Kathy, and stepdad, George. In 2011, he gave an interview to *Fate* magazine's Rosemary Guiley. He said he was trying to raise money by organizing an online pay-per-view webcast "fireside chat" where he would talk about his Amityville experiences and the haunting at his home in Phoenix, Arizona, where he was living at the time. He claimed that the haunting had followed him there. In discussing her interview with Chris, one gets the distinct impression that the Amityville "haunting" was genuine, as there is no mention of it being a hoax. To its credit, *Fate* did publish the original exposé on the case, by Peter Jordan and Rick Moran, in 1977. But of course, negative articles are not good for business for a magazine whose core audience is made up of believers in the paranormal. Guiley ends her piece by noting, "FATE has not contacted others originally involved in the case, pending further disclosures from Quarantino."[79] Reminding readers that the Amityville case is a hoax would seem to be pertinent information, but it is conveniently left out!

Then there is writer Jay Anson. In the years after the publication of the book and until his death in 1980, Rick Morgan made numerous TV and radio appearances during which he would debate Anson. Despite his skeptical perspective, Moran says that the pair became friends off the air. As it turns out, privately Anson was a skeptic. Moran writes, "Did he believe it? No! He didn't believe in the 'paranormal,' but that didn't stop him from writing the book." So why write the book? "Anson was open about his need for money: he was not a young man and he earnestly wanted to pen a best-seller."[80] On October 9, 1977, the *New York Times* published an interview with Anson. He said he "approached the story . . . as a reporter, so that by the end of the book, you believe or you don't believe. These are the facts. This is what happened to the family . . . to the priest. You make up your own mind as a reader."[81] Perhaps, but a good reporter verifies facts—or at least attempts to. Anson never bothered to verify that his book was indeed "a true story." In the book's afterword, Anson writes that many of the Lutzes' "impressions and reports were later substantiated by the testimony of independent witnesses such as Father Mancuso and local police officials."[82] Nothing could be further from the truth. One hour of basic research at a public library, a few phone calls to people listed in the book, or a call to neighbors would have set alarm bells ringing. In March 1979, Anson was interviewed by *Writer's Digest*, and he noted that in attempting to verify parts of the Lutzes' story, he had conducted "several hours" of interviews with Amityville police officers, the priest, and members of the Amityville Historical Society.[83] Anson's credibility here is dubious. The police are adamant that they were never called to the house until *after* George Lutz left, and even then they observed nothing supernatural.[84] As early as 1977, the priest told investigators that the claims attributed to him in the book were false.[85] As for the historical society, they say that neither Lutz nor Anson was told that the Shinnecock Indians believed that the land where the house stood was haunted by demons, because the story is false. But that did not stop Anson from claiming otherwise in the book. The Shinnecock *never* lived in Amityville, prompting the society's librarian to observe, "I've lived in this area all my life, and I've never heard these stories before."[86] Peter Jordan says that Anson told him that writing the book was strictly a business proposition. "You're one of those naysayers—one of those skeptics who likes to write non-ghost stories. I like to make money . . . and one day I predict that you are going to be sitting there broke, writing your little non-ghost stories, and I am going to be on an island out in the Bahamas or somewhere, with a truckload of cashmere sweaters."[87] While Anson made millions on the book, he never got to enjoy his cashmere sweaters. He died of a heart attack on March 12, 1980.

The publisher also bears some responsibility for failing to ensure that a book claiming to be "a true story" is actually true. When *Newsday* journalists Alex Drehsler and Jim Scovel made queries about the book being riddled with errors and inconsistencies, the director of corporate affairs for Random House refused to discuss the book but did offer an insightful observation. They were told that "authors are responsible for the content and accuracy of the writing, but that 'many books are published in good faith which include errors.'" Drehsler and Scovel pointed out at the time that despite the cloud over the accuracy of the Lutzes' claims, it was still being marketed as "A True Story" in the subtitle.[88] In December 1977, Curt Suplee of the *Washington Post* contacted Prentice-Hall editor Tam Mossman, who had hooked the Lutzes up with Jay Anson to write the book. After observing that there were obvious factual errors in the manuscript, Mossman did not seem overly concerned. "It's impossible for an editor to go through everything with a fine-tooth comb," he said.[89] Even today, the book contains Jay Anson's affirmation, "To the extent that I can verify them, all the events in this book are true."[90] If there is one indisputable aspect to this case besides the obvious tragedy of the loss of six lives, it is that the Amityville Horror is a story of American greed, for how else can one explain how a book of fiction continues to be marketed as fact? The publishers fail to mention anywhere in the book that the story has been discredited. The reason for this omission is obvious: money. Some recent editions have even dropped the subtitle "A True Story," such as the one by Pocket Star. However, this is little consolation, because on the back cover blurb of the same edition, it states, "This is the spellbinding, bestselling true story that gripped the nation."[91] This is clearly deceptive. It is no wonder so many people still believe that the Lutzes' story is true.

The claim that *The Amityville Horror* is based on a true story has become a profitable Hollywood formula, as a virtual cottage industry has popped up among filmmakers. Despite clear evidence of a hoax and scores of inaccuracies in the book, when the film *The Amityville Horror* was released in July 1979, like the book, it too was billed as "based on a true story." The advertising campaign even featured the phrase "For God's Sake, GET OUT!"—a reference to the priest who recanted his story under oath. This was soon followed by *Amityville II: The Possession* in 1982 and *Amityville 3-D* the following year. But the sequels did not end there. In 1989, *Amityville 4: The Evil Escapes* was released, quickly followed by *The Amityville Curse* (1990), *Amityville: It's About Time* (1992), and *Amityville: New Generation* (1993). In Hollywood, if there is public interest and money to be made, there is no such thing as too much of a good thing. Hence, 1996 saw the release of *Amityville Dollhouse*, followed by *The Amityville Haunting* in 2011 and, most recently, *The Amityville Asylum* (2013). Dozens of books have been written on the subject. Many of them continue to assert that the haunting was genuine. A good example is the popular "Complete Idiot's

Guide" book series, published by Penguin, who commissioned Nathan Brown to write *The Complete Idiot's Guide to the Paranormal.* In it Brown states that it is difficult to tell whether a hoax was perpetrated or not. He also says that parapsychologist Stephen Kaplan made claims that the affair was a hoax. He continues, "It is generally believed that this began a personal vendetta for Kaplan against both the Warrens and the Lutzes. He later recanted his accusations and publicly apologized."[92] What is his source for this extraordinary claim? There is none. In fact, the 286-page *Idiot's Guide* is devoid of references.

The news media also bears some of the blame for keeping the Amityville myth alive. At their core, news organizations are in the business of generating viewer interest and peddling a product—information—and the more sensational the product, the more likely viewers are to tune in and stay tuned in. A good example of this state of affairs took place on Halloween night in 2002, when the American Broadcasting Corporation's *Primetime Thursday* aired a TV segment on Amityville. The show contacted Joe Nickell, who gave an extensive pre-air interview on the Lutzes' hoax. Yet the show deliberately slanted interview clips to marginalize Nickell and give greater credence to the Lutzes' story than the facts warranted. Those viewers tuning in who were unfamiliar with the hoax were led to believe that the case was still in dispute, because the show created a mystery where none exists. Reporter Elizabeth Vargas then presented a photo taken in the Lutz house during an overnight ghost hunt, which purports to show the face of a young boy, mysteriously caught on camera. Vargas closes by saying, "But no one has an explanation for this picture. Is it really an eerie looking little boy, and, if not, what is it?"[93] Nickell, a photographic expert, told Vargas during a pre-air interview that he was convinced the photo was a fake—and that it would have been the simplest matter to produce such an image. Yet his attack on the authenticity of the image as a paranormal artifact was left out.[94] The producers of *Primetime Thursday* were intent on presenting a spooky segment for Halloween. They succeeded, but only because they omitted key facts, the most important one being that the entire affair was a hoax. Clearly, billing the segment as "The Amityville Hoax" would not have been as exciting as an eerie image of "the Amityville Boy Ghost." The moral of the story is that sensationalism sells, but it comes at a cost: credibility.

While on the subject of money, let's not forget the many lawsuits and countersuits that have been filed over the years. In one instance, the Lutzes filed suit for $5.4 million against several parties for invasion of privacy, mental distress, and inappropriately using names for trade purposes. It was later dismissed. Several of the accused banded together and countersued for $2 million, claiming breach of contract and fraud. The Cromartys, who took over the house after the Lutzes, sued Jay Anson and publisher Prentice-Hall for just over a million dollars, claiming that their fictional story was ruining their lives. Even the priest whom the Lutzes had discussed in the book, Father Pecoraro ("Father Mancuso" in the book), sued the Lutzes and the publisher for distorting his involvement in the saga and for invasion of privacy.[95] In 2005, shortly before his death from heart disease in the following year, Lutz told *People* that he had been involved in no less than fourteen different lawsuits related to the case.[96] Many of these suits were settled out of court for far less than was asked.

The Story Refuses to Die

In March 2013, the Amityville haunting resurfaced again with the release of a documentary, *My Amityville Horror*, on the life of Daniel "Danny" Lutz, who was just nine years old at the time of the original uproar.[97] The documentary is a case study of a troubled man who claims to have been physically abused by his stepfather, George Lutz, and of faded, garbled memories. While Danny seems sincere about what he can recall from the 28 days that he spent at 112 Ocean Avenue as a boy, the events, as he describes them, are clearly embellished, if not created entirely from his imagination, either intentionally or through memory distortion. He says that George possessed supernatural powers similar to those of Samantha on the TV show *Bewitched*. For instance, he claims that even before they moved to Amityville, he saw George lift a wrench into the air using only his mind. Among his other claims are that an invisible force threw him *up* a flight of stairs; that an evil spirit took possession of his body, and he had to be exorcised by priests, who beat him in the process; that he killed over a hundred flies in a room, only for the flies to suddenly disappear; and that his bed levitated so high that the bedposts stuck into the sheetrock. Danny's claims stretch credulity. On one occasion, he tells how a window smashed down on his hands, causing them to "swell up to the size of a child's baseball glove, five times their normal size." He says that they suddenly returned to normal "in one second," with the exception of a pinky. Clearly, Danny has a propensity to embellish! The only question is whether he has come to actually believe that these events happened the way he remembers them or he is making them up. It may be that he created these memories after listening to his parents and reading about what had supposedly happened, after the fact.

In the film, it becomes clear that Danny hated George Lutz and tried to undermine his authority. Using typical overstatement, he asserts that he tried to kill George "at least 50 times." Danny said that George would make them march around the house like obedient little soldiers—a house that he did not want to move to in the first place. Danny lashed out. "I . . . started destroying this guy's world every opportunity that I walked into" and would "just do anything" so "that we could go back home," he said. Is it possible that some of the low-level poltergeist effects were actually orchestrated by Danny to scare the Lutzes into moving out? Historically, poltergeist cases typically center on a disgruntled child or adolescent in a home, one who is seeking attention or trying to exact revenge. It may be that Danny is telling the truth—recalling what he believes happened, based on false and embellished memories, combined with a traumatic upbringing in which the reality of ghosts was a taken-for-granted fact of life.[98] Either way, it becomes clear by the end of the film that Danny has had to battle his own personal demons after moving out of 112 Ocean Avenue. He became temporarily homeless at age 15, and he still harbors a seething hatred for George. *My Amityville Horror* is more of a biography of a child from a dysfunctional family than a film about supernatural forces; it documents the emotional scars that remain decades later, which take the form of embellished, distorted memories—ghosts from the past that continue to haunt a little boy who is now all grown up.

A Human Creation

What happened at 112 Ocean Avenue between December 1975 and January 1976 is both a horror story and a haunting, but it is devoid of poltergeists and demons. It is a tale of imaginary events that continue to be widely accepted in the popular imagination as a genuine haunting, in the face of overwhelming evidence and logic. The Internet is replete with Web sites that take positions both for and against the reality of "the Amityville Horror," as do many books. The Amityville affair is an interesting lesson in human psychology in the Internet Age. Nowadays believers in the paranormal can surf the 'net and find Web sites that reinforce their own narrow viewpoints.

For decades, the residents of Amityville have been haunted intermittently by visitors trying to glimpse the house. In April 1977, Barbara and Jim Cromarty moved in for the astonishingly low price of $55,000: a full $25,000 less than the Lutzes had paid. While the house's tragic and haunted past repulsed most would-be buyers, they were happy to take the risk. One week later, the *Good Housekeeping* article appeared, followed soon after by the book. Then the real hauntings began and would drive them from their new home. They were not forced to flee by disembodied voices and disgruntled spirits, but instead by something just as frightening: an invasion of relentless curiosity-seekers. "They usually came late at night. They like to run around the house. Scream and holler," said Jim Cromarty. It got so bad that police had to assign officers to guard the house on Friday and Saturday nights. At Thanksgiving 1977, three hundred people were outside—all uninvited.[99] Souvenir hunters created their own nightmare by grabbing their own piece of history—everything from shingles to wallpaper. On one occasion someone even pulled up a chuck of lawn and ran off.[100]

Amityville resident Ed Lowe recalls that on one Sunday afternoon alone, he was interrupted a dozen times while walking in the neighborhood, by people wanting to know how to get to the "ghost" or "spook house." A journalist, he noted that this included "a van load from Michigan, a Cadillac filled with elderly people from New Jersey; two motorcycles with Texas plates, a Canadian Ford; a fancy sportcar with students from Glencoe, Illin.; two couples . . . from Gastonia, N.C.," as well as cars from Pennsylvania, New England, and upstate New York.[101] One time a group dressed in black robes with macabre hoods marched up to the house and surrounded it. They began chanting while holding candles and crosses. They soon reached a startling epiphany: they had encircled the wrong house! On another occasion, someone placed a ladder on the side of the house, climbed up to the gutters, and scooped out rainwater before dashing off.[102] No one is quite sure why. At the height of the chaos, Frank Burch agreed to house-sit while the Cromartys took a vacation from their fishbowl existence. He recalls one night when he became fed up with the incessant harassment and decided to turn the tables. "These people would be peering in the windows with cameras, and I would go outside and walk down the driveway, snapping pictures of them, and they would back off." The intruders then got angry *with him*. "Can you imagine that? They're peering into the windows of my home, taking pictures, and they get angry when I look out and take pictures of them." Burch said that getting aggressive or scaring them only made things worse. "They would run back to their friends and scream: '*Look! There's somebody moving in there!*'"[103]

Locals became so frustrated by intrusive visitors that there was even a community-wide effort to fight back. As Lowe observed in 1980, "almost everyone in Amityville has lied to scores of intruders. I have told people that the house was moved, burned out, that it sank into the ground, and that it was eaten by pigs." Misleading outsiders turned into a pastime among locals. Hairdresser Yvonne Miller once told how a middle-aged woman entered her saloon in tears. "She had asked a dozen people in town where the horror house was, and every one of them had lied to her. It took me fifteen minutes to calm her down. . . . Then I gave her directions to Ocean Avenue in Massapequa, five miles away."[104]

The circus atmosphere and parade of strangers peering into windows at all hours of the day and night eventually took its toll. In late 1978, the Cromartys put the house up for sale; it sold the next year.[105] The Amityville Horror may have been fictional, but when people believe in imaginary poltergeists and demonic forces, their actions can become real in their consequences. Just ask the Cromartys, Frank Burch, neighborhood residents, and the Amityville police force, historical society, and village council. As American social commentator Walter Lippmann once wrote about the news media's affinity for creating reality, "[I]t is clear enough that under certain conditions men respond as powerfully to fictions as they do to realities, and that in many cases they help to create the very fictions to which they respond."[106] The myth of the Amityville Horror will continue to endure because, ultimately, it is a story that many people want to believe in order to validate their belief in the existence of demonic forces, which in turn supports their belief in God. The facts, however, tell a different story. The real Amityville Horror story is every bit as interesting as any haunting, and it is valuable for the insights it affords us into the human psyche and its penchant for greed, deception, and myth. That is the real story of what happened at Amityville. It is a story that continues to be exploited by Hollywood.

CHAPTER 6

Don Decker: The Man Who Could Make It Rain

What makes this case very unique is that all of the witnesses are so credible. We're dealing with very good, well-seasoned police officers that were obviously rather frightened and shaken by this, but also had the powers of observation.

—Chip Decker, paranormal researcher[1]

It is one of the most compelling claims of paranormal activity on record. It is supported by the testimony of no fewer than four police officers, a jail supervisor, two respected couples, a restaurant owner, and a reverend. For decades, this case has been touted as defying scientific explanation. In 1983, a young Pennsylvania man named Don Decker was reported to have performed remarkable feats, including making it rain inside buildings and levitating his body in front of astonished onlookers. The case has been promoted as a genuine episode of paranormal activity on such TV programs as *Unsolved Mysteries* and *Paranormal Witness*.[2] Even skeptics have had difficulty coming up with a plausible alternative explanation for what happened. A decade after he first investigated the case, parapsychologist Peter Jordan, who was one of the first researchers to unmask the Amityville hoax, remarked, "The Donald Decker case is by far the singularly most fascinating and important case I have ever personally been involved in."[3]

On February 24, 1983, twenty-year-old Don Decker of Stroudsburg was on a furlough from the local Monroe County jail to attend the funeral of his grandfather, 63-year-old James Kishaugh, who had passed away four days earlier.[4] Decker was serving time for receiving stolen property. During the service he grew distraught upon seeing the outpouring of sympathy for his grandfather, whom he despised because he said he had been abusive. Two days later, witnesses claim that Decker entered a trance and was responsible for a mysterious indoor rain, that he floated and exhibited telekinesis (moving objects with his mind), and that he made a cross heat up. Does the Decker case offer proof of paranormal powers, or is there a scientific explanation?

The Episode

The public first learned of the story in 1983, when a report appeared in the *Pocono Record* that rumors about "Strange Happenings" were sweeping Monroe County.[5] The case rose to prominence when the popular NBC TV show *Unsolved Mysteries* aired a segment on the claims,[6] and it was featured on the nationally televised *Maury Povich Show* the following year.[7] According to the story, while on compassionate leave from the jail, located in the Pocono Mountains of extreme east central Pennsylvania, on the evening of Saturday, February 26, Don Decker was staying at the home of family friends Bob and Jeannie Keiffer at 528 Ann Street when a series of strange events took place. Decker said that he was in the upstairs bathroom, washing before supper, when he felt strange and confused, fell to the floor, and had a vision of a sinister-looking old man wearing a crown, staring at him through a mirror. He then noticed three deep scratches running down his right wrist. Struggling to his feet, he washed away the blood and went downstairs to eat with the family. When Bob Keiffer saw the blood, Decker told the devoutly religious couple of his vision of the evil face in the mirror, and he attributed the wound to Satan. Before long, water began dripping from the walls and ceiling of the living room, which coincided with a loud noise from above. Mr. Keiffer phoned his landlord, Ron Van Why, who soon arrived to fix what he assumed to be a leak. To their surprise, when they went upstairs to investigate the only plausible explanation they could think of—leaky pipes—nothing appeared to be out of the ordinary. Keiffer later observed, "We thought there had to be some kind of leak but there's no water in that end of the house [where it was "raining"] . . . there's no water lines in any place but the kitchen and the bathroom which were in the back of the house." The two men were mystified.

After going downstairs, Decker appeared to be in a daze. They immediately drew a connection between the "rain" inside the house and Decker's strange mental state. Believing that the house was possessed by an evil force, Mr. Keiffer phoned local police. Officer John Baujan and patrolman Richard Wolbert soon arrived and were baffled by what they saw. Baujan said that not only was there "rain" falling but that "droplets would come from the floor ... defying gravity." After the two officers left, the Keiffers and Van Whys—both devout Christian families—confronted Decker, accusing him of causing the "rain." Decker stood in silence with a blank stare. Pots and pans hanging in the kitchen began clanging. Suddenly, Decker levitated off the ground and was flung against a wall. He then drew attention to deep, bloody scratch marks running the length of his forearm and forming the shape of a cross near the joint of his inner elbow. By now the Van Whys and Keiffers were convinced that Decker was possessed by the Devil. When Officer Baujan later returned to the house, he walked into a tense, electrifying scene. Mrs. Keiffer was in the living room, reading the Twenty-Third Psalm of the bible in an effort to "exorcise" Decker. "The Lord is my shepherd; I shall not want. . . . He restoreth my soul; he leadeth me in the paths of righteousness." After surveying the scene, Baujan said that he too now believed that Decker was possessed by the Devil. Adding to the eerie atmosphere, the mysterious "rain" was confined only to the living room.

Puzzled by what they had seen, Baujan and Wolbert contacted Stroudsburg police chief Gary Roberts and brought him to the house. Roberts walked in, surveyed the scene, and was unimpressed. He ordered his officers to leave the house and not file a report, as indoor rain was not a criminal act. The next day Stroudsburg police officers William Davies and John Rundle visited the Keiffer home, against their chief's wishes, and claimed to observe Decker's body being flung through the air. Davies said that when he handed him a gold cross, Decker dropped it, claiming that it burned his skin. "All of a sudden, he lifted up off the ground and he flew across the room with a force as though a bus had hit him. There were three claw marks on the side of his neck, which drew blood," Rundle said.

Decker was soon back in the Monroe Correctional Facility, but when he entered his cell, the rain reportedly returned, and water began to drip from the ceiling. His cellmate began to panic at the sight of the water and was moved to a separate block. Decker was now in the cell by himself. Two guards then began to joke with him about his supposed ability to make it rain. They issued a challenge: to use his "powers" to make it rain on their shift supervisor, Dave Keenhold. A short time later, Keenhold, who was in his office in a distant part of the jail, says that he was struck in the chest by a drop of water that seemed to materialize out of nowhere. The incident convinced Keenhold that Decker was possessed by an evil force, and he summoned the jail's chaplain, William Blackburn, to perform an exorcism. The two men were placed in a room, where Blackburn performed a brief exorcism, during which they both said it began to "rain." Afterward, Decker said he felt a great relief and lost his paranormal powers.

In the Eye of the Beholder

At the time of the events, Don Decker was under extreme stress, serving jail time and experiencing a range of emotions after the death of a relative whom he loathed. Trance states can be triggered by stress and do not necessarily denote mental illness or disorder; they are also easily feigned. It is remarkable that Decker did not receive medical attention and that outside experts from the government or a university were not called in to investigate. Instead, attempts were made to exorcise him. If those around him—the Keiffers, the Van Whys, the police, and the prison supervisor—were all so quick to assume a demonic explanation, their perceptions may have been affected by their willingness to interpret other natural events within a supernatural framework.

The witnesses' actions are also inconsistent with the nature of the claims. Imagine you are in a house where supernatural events are supposedly occurring: an indoor "rain" is moving upward from the floor, and a man supposedly levitates and can move objects with his mind. If documented, it is a monumental event in the history of science, for it would defy the laws of physics as we know them and prove the existence of paranormal activity. It was an event spanning several days and supported by numerous eyewitnesses. So why didn't anyone bother to record these happenings with a video camera or take photos? On Officer Baujan's first visit to the Keiffer house, he reported seeing a drop of water suddenly materialize from nowhere and fly horizontally through the room. So what did he do soon after witnessing this amazing happening? He and his partner left! Surely they had access to video equipment or a camera that could have documented this remarkable occurrence. Why not phone the local TV station to record the happenings? Decker's forearm supposedly had deep scratches that formed the bloody image of a cross. Why didn't anyone have the presence of mind to photograph the scratches and the image? It is the equivalent of a flying saucer landing on someone's front lawn and no one thinking to record the event. Such lack of foresight is inconceivable. It is important to remember that these events were not said to have happened over a few seconds or minutes but over the course of several days—during which time any one of those involved could have snapped photos or gotten access to a video camera. Yet not a single photo or video of the event was taken for later analysis. The failure by so many people, many of whom were trained professionals, to take such a fundamental action leads to an inevitable conclusion: there was likely nothing out of the ordinary to photograph. However, their actions *are* consistent with events that were almost certainly exaggerated over time. In the end, we are left with eyewitness accounts from excited observers with a worldview that includes the reality of the Devil.

Police are often touted as trained observers whose testimony is beyond reproach, yet they are not trained to detect trickery, and they too can be easily fooled, despite their status. Officer Baujan observed, "Droplets would come from the floor, absolutely defying gravity. It was truly amazing. . . . When all of a sudden this drop materializes . . . [i]t flies through the living room, through the dining room and into the darkness of the kitchen and out of sight." If it was so amazing, why not record it or contact the media? The local newspapers and radio stations would have had cameras. He did return later with Chief Roberts, who did not interpret the "rain" as paranormal. If the activity was so remarkable, why didn't Baujan return with a camera? Human perception is notoriously unreliable, even under ideal conditions. Stress can alter our perception of the world, and it is difficult to imagine many events more stressful than believing that you are in the presence of a man who is possessed by demonic forces. Shortly after the "rain" began, Bob Keiffer and his landlord examined the upstairs pipes for leaks, but in their excitement, they failed to check the most likely cause: the roof, because as Mr. Van Why observed, "it hadn't been raining outside for days." Officer Baujan, Bob and Jeanette Keiffer, and Ron and Romayne Van Why all concluded that an evil force was responsible for the "rain." Ron said, "There was no shadow of doubt in my mind. I was in the presence of evil." Mr. Keiffer concurred: "I thought there was some kind of spirit controlling him. Some kind of demon in him." Officer Baujan even concluded at the time that the strange events were the work of "the Devil." It is notable that Baujan says that the police chief observed the same phenomenon that they witnessed. "When the chief got to the house, he was pelted with rain just as Rich (Wolbert) and I were," he said. Yet Chief Roberts considered the water to be a natural event.[8] Roberts was called to the house on two separate occasions and saw nothing unusual. "Sometimes what people believe happens and what actually happens are two different things," he said defiantly.[9] A skeptic on such matters, he was also an outsider and had moved to Stroudsburg three years earlier to take up the position of chief.[10]

A person's education level does not necessarily make him or her immune from deception. One of the most brilliant minds of the late eighteenth and early nineteenth centuries was Sir Arthur Conan Doyle (1859–1930), who was duped by two schoolgirls into believing that they had photographed fairies in their yard. Of course, one's preexisting belief system has a powerful influence on how one interprets the world. In this instance, it just so happens that all of the principal observers had deeply held religious convictions that affected their interpretation of what they were seeing.

In watching two nationally broadcast TV programs on this case, *Paranormal Witness* and *Unsolved Mysteries*, one cannot help but be impressed by the use of firsthand interviews with people who were there. In fact, almost all of the dialogue in *Paranormal Witness* is from the witnesses in their own words. While these interviews were conducted two decades after the events, they are valuable pieces of primary evidence. But in reality, the TV reenactments were far from accurate, because of two processes: one intentional, through selective editing, and the other unintentional, through distorted memories. An example of selective editing occurred in 2012, when Mr. Van Why told a local reporter that when he first arrived at the house, he noticed nothing out of the ordinary, and that it was not until he sat in the living room that he first noticed very light rain coming from the ceiling.[11] Yet on both the *Paranormal Witness* and *Unsolved Mysteries* segments, Mr. Van Why arrives to see heavy "rain" pouring down inside the house.

At one point, the Keiffers took Decker out of the house to a pizzeria across the street. When owner Pam Scrofano saw Decker's trance-like state, she too assumed that it was likely triggered by demonic influences. "You looked at Donnie and he was . . . in a trance. He would look at you, but not knowing you were there. I said to Jeannie, 'He's got to be possessed.'" Then she suddenly noticed that there was "water all over the pizzeria." Instead of calling a roof specialist or plumber to locate where the water was seeping from, she immediately assumed it was demonic possession and went straight to the cash till to grab a crucifix. When it touched Decker's skin, he said it made his skin burn.[12]

Later that night, Officer Baujan returned to the house out of concern for the Keiffers. He said that when he entered, "there was panic in the room." Jeannie Keiffer stood there, reading from the Twenty-Third Psalm and holding a bible in an effort to rid Decker of his possession, which eventually seemed to work. According to *Paranormal Witness*, which presented the events using the witnesses' own words, the "rain" stopped by the next morning when Decker returned to the county jail.

Inexplicably, *Unsolved Mysteries* reports that Decker's ordeal at the house endured for three days.

Decker's Return to Jail

When Decker reported back to jail, the rain supposedly followed. Yet before he arrived, word had spread of his rainmaking powers, and many guards and inmates were expecting some type of rain event. "All the inmates heard what was going on at the house. They were all scared. The guards—they were scared too," Decker recalled. Keenhold said that after looking at Decker's demeanor, he became convinced that "there was an evil presence around him . . . [that] was so abnormal that we felt that the supernatural was present." Later, when his cell was found to have water dripping from the walls and ceiling, his cellmate screamed to the guards, who transferred Decker to another cell. Keenhold told *Paranormal Witness* matter-of-factly, "Water was all over his cell. Water was going horizontal, vertical, climbing up the walls, defying the laws of gravity." Yet Keenhold told reporter Christina Tatu in 2012 that *he never visited Decker in his cell.*[13] How can he appear so certain of this event if he is relying on second-hand accounts? At the very least, *Paranormal Witness* is guilty of *giving the impression* that Keenhold was there. What other selective use of evidence were viewers not told about? The documentary gives only one side of the story; there are no interviews with skeptics, and conspicuously absent is the testimony of then police chief Gary Roberts. Is the purpose of the show to uncover the truth, or is it to create the impression of a mystery when one does not exist, in order to attain high ratings? Where are the other witnesses? Surely, if one were to see water moving up a wall, one would summon others to observe this remarkable event. Why not contact university experts in physics to investigate? The news media? The FBI? The water in his cell could have been thrown there from the sink or a leaky roof at a time when ice dams would have been common. Instead of assuming one of these natural explanations or an optical illusion is responsible, Keenhold believes it is coming from Decker, who is possessed by the Devil.

In 2011, *Paranormal Witness* depicts Keenhold sitting in his office, several locked doors away from Decker, when he is struck in the chest by a massive water droplet that hit "in about the center of my sternum about 4 inches long, two inches wide. I was just saturated with water," Keenhold said. But in 1993, Keenhold told *Unsolved Mysteries* that he was unaware of having been struck by the water until a guard entered the room and pointed out that he had a wet patch on his chest and told him that Decker had said he would make it rain on him. It was only then that he attributed the moisture to Decker and became convinced that he was possessed by an evil force. Of course, it is not uncommon for people to sweat near their sternum. While Keenhold said he was "saturated," the dampness could not have been too significant, as he said he was not even aware of it until the guard noted it! Keenhold said that his first thought was that he had spilled something on his shirt, but he had not recently been around water.[14] Yet on *Paranormal Witness*, Keenhold said that prior to the incident, he "had just finished with the evening meal," a scenario that would have placed him amongst a variety of liquids.

Between Decker's strange mental state and the mysterious water that had appeared in his cell, word quickly spread about his feats, and the entire jail was on edge. Convinced that Decker was possessed by the Devil, Keenhold felt that he had only one alternative: to contact a priest to conduct an exorcism. So he phoned the Reverend William Blackburn, who soon arrived and was placed in a room with Decker. Keenhold and the guards waited outside. The Reverend Blackburn said he grabbed Decker's hand and began reciting passages from the bible in order to cast out the evil spirit. Eventually, Decker said that he felt a calm feeling come over him and that he was free from the Devil. The two men claimed that during the exorcism, it began to rain inside the room. *Paranormal Witness* shows rain pouring down and Decker observing, "I never saw the liquid as intense as it was in that room." Decker reported that the rain fell only on the priest, drenching him and pooling on the floor. Yet in his 1993 interview with *Unsolved Mysteries*, Reverend Blackburn recounted a far less dramatic scene, describing the "rain" as "a mist." If this much embellishment has occurred between the 1993 and 2011 interviews, one wonders if there was ever a "rain" to begin with. Would a priest lie about such an event? Perhaps not, but given the supernatural mindset of the two participants and their heightened emotional state, sweat is a distinct possibility. While ice damming may explain the "rain" in the Keiffer home, how do we account for the rain inside the local pizzeria and the jail cell? Leaky roofs and ceilings are common after such unusual weather conditions, and little drips and drabs often go relatively unnoticed. Years later they are described as rain.

An Extraordinary Coincidence

Building expert Sandra Ho rates Pennsylvania as being at "moderate to high risk for winter moisture problems," with one of the most severe events being ice damming. This is caused by warm air entering an attic and melting snow on the outer surface of a roof, resulting in an accumulation of ice, under which pools of water form and eventually leak. Ice dams are common after major snowstorms in areas where temperatures rise above freezing during the day and drop below 32°F at night.[15] Such conditions were applicable in Stroudsburg, Pennsylvania. According to weather archives for the nearby city of Scranton for February 11 to 28, 1983, 13 days before the strange indoor "rain," there was a record snowfall across central and eastern Pennsylvania. Philadelphia measured its heaviest accumulation for any February storm, with 21.3 inches.[16] East Stroudsburg University measured one inch of snow on February 10 and sixteen inches the following day.[17] Scranton is the nearest weather station with temperature readings, 37 miles from Stroudsburg. After the storm on February 11, clear, cold weather settled in. Then between February 14 and 25, the daytime temperatures were above freezing by up to 20 degrees, and with three exceptions they were below freezing at night—ideal conditions for ice damming, as the snow would have melted by day and refrozen overnight. On the fateful evening of February 26, there was a mild cold snap, with a daytime high of 26° and an overnight low of 20°.[18]

One of the features that perplexed the house occupants and Officer Baujan was that the "rain" was confined to one room. Patrick Huelman of the University of Minnesota is an expert on environmental design and ice damming. He says that it is common for ice damming events to be limited to a small portion of a house, such as a room. But how does one explain Bob Keiffer's remark that the "rain" dripping down the walls had a strange consistency? "It wasn't water as you know water ... it was a sticky, tacky feeling," he said. Huelman says that such observations are common: water running down ceilings and walls often mixes with resins in the wood or residue from plaster, giving the water a tacky feel.[19] The first sign that anything was amiss with the house, water was seen dripping down the walls and was soon falling from the ceiling.[20] Huelman observes that ice dam events commonly involve "symptoms beginning at the outer edge and working in toward the ceiling." Just as the "rain" first appeared in the Keiffer home, the occupants reported hearing a loud crash from above. Such sounds are consistent with ice damming. Why would the ice crack on February 26? As water expands when freezing, it commonly results in popping and crackling noises, accompanied by what was likely a section of ice cracking or falling off the roof, releasing the dammed water.

The occupants noted a damp chill in the house, particularly in the living room, where the "rain" was falling. "Within seconds of entering that room I had this cold feeling," said Baujan. This observation is consistent with ice damming. As water began seeping into the insulation, the house turned cooler because it was a poor insulator of heat. Combined with the cold water dripping from the walls and ceiling, this could easily make the indoor temperature feel several degrees cooler—and damp. In folklore, the presence of ghosts, spirits, and demons is traditionally associated with a chill; this only served to enhance the belief in a demonic presence at the house. The sensation of a cold chill is also a common reaction to stress.

Enter the Poltergeist

In many instances, "poltergeist" outbreaks soon evolve into "demonic possession." Just such a transformation happened in the case of the "true story" behind the 1973 horror movie *The Exorcist,* as discussed in Chapter 2. The teenage boy was always around when objects went flying, and in time, scratches began to appear on his body as he showed additional signs of "possession," including "trance." An analysis of the case, based on information in a priest's diary, showed that all of the phenomena could have been accomplished by the teenager, who was indeed observed on one occasion inflicting scratches on himself.[21] Such cases illuminate the Rain Boy poltergeist manifestations.

How do we explain Lt. Davies's observation that when he and two colleagues visited the Keiffer home, Decker levitated, and that when he gave Decker a gold cross to hold, he dropped it on the floor, complaining that it burned his hands? In reality, Davies never said the cross was so hot as to burn him. "Not hot hot, but it's hot," he told *Unsolved Mysteries.* Sensations of hot and cold are notoriously subjective. As for the levitation claim, it is worth recalling the context of the visit by Davies and his colleagues. Decker reportedly exhibited a variety of supernatural powers, and the next day police visited the house to verify it; that was their explicit purpose for being there. Surely they would have taken a camera or video recorder, and that they did not do so immediately raises red flags. Perhaps the events were so unremarkable that the officers did not deem them worthwhile. It is more likely that Decker flung himself into a wall and this event became exaggerated with time. It stretches credulity that the officers did not think to record these remarkable events— if they were as remarkable at the time as we have been led to believe.

In 2012, reporter Christina Tatu asked both Keenhold and Mr. Van Why why they did not take photos. "He [Keenhold] said most people used Polaroids back then which would have been too slow to capture the events. Van Why said people just didn't carry around cameras back then."[22] This is untrue on both counts. Pocket cameras were inexpensive and plentiful at the time. The *1983 Montgomery Ward Catalogue* lists pocket cameras for as little as $17.95.[23] Also, there is no reason why a Polaroid would have been too slow to capture the alleged events! Such a claim is absurd. The difference between a Polaroid and a conventional camera of the period is that the former produced no negatives, and the image developed within a few minutes instead of waiting to undergo chemical processing. If these key witnesses failed to recall that cameras were plentiful at the time—and clearly they did—what else did they get wrong? Another example of how events likely became exaggerated over time is claims about the mysterious "rain" pouring down inside the Keiffer home during police visits. It could not have been too perceptible, as at one point police placed a bag over Decker's head to eliminate the possibility of his causing the "rain" by spitting![24] Yet in both the *Paranormal Witness* and *Unsolved Mystery* versions of events, those inside the house are drenched by a heavy rain. Both programs also show rain pouring down in the jail cell. In 2013, Keenhold was asked why, if there was so much water as was reported, no one thought to take a sample for scientists or investigators to analyze. "It evaporated within a minute or so," Keenhold asserted.[25]

Natural or Supernatural?

The most plausible explanation for the events in Stroudsburg, Pennsylvania during February 1983 is that Decker cut and scratched religious symbols into his skin to gain attention and sympathy from the Keiffers, knowing they were religious. Whether this was deliberate or subconscious is open to debate. Coincidentally, an ice dam broke on the Keiffers' roof, which served to reinforce the belief in a demonic force that was also responsible for the "rain." It just so happened that most of the key people who were called on to explain the mysterious "rain" were themselves devoutly religious and interpreted a series of natural events (Decker's self-harm and the ice dam) within a Christian frame of reference. Where most residents would phone a building expert at the first sign of a leaky ceiling, the Keiffers rang the police. Where most people would have sought medical or psychiatric aid for someone who was unresponsive and in an apparent trance, neither the police nor the Keiffers did so. Where most corrections supervisors who saw a prisoner with a "strange look" would have thought little of it, Keenhold assumed that Decker was possessed by a demonic presence. When most police go to a house and cannot explain something such as dripping water, they do not automatically assume that one of the occupants is possessed by the Devil. The events that took place in Monroe County in February 1983 can best be summed up using an old medical adage cautioning against drawing exotic conclusions when more mundane explanations are likely: "When you hear the sounds of hoofbeats in the night, first think horses, not zebras."

The most likely explanation for the "rain" is snowmelt seeping through the ceiling from the attic as a result of ice damming, in conjunction with psychological stress and human imagination. Deception is also a distinct possibility. Decker could have augmented an existing phenomenon with tricks. As for his purported levitation, it is a recurrent pattern in poltergeist cases that the central figure is caught throwing objects or engaging in other trickery to convince those present of his or her powers. In this instance, the one person who supposedly could make objects move and who levitated had a criminal record. Three years after the episode, Decker was back in jail after pleading guilty to burglary.[26] In October 2012, Decker was again arrested and charged with arson and mail fraud.[27] He claims that during the 1983 saga, he was twice flung through the air. In the one instance where detail is provided, we are told that he traveled just five or six feet, landing against a wall. Did he hurl himself through the air when no one was looking directly at him? That is the simplest explanation.

The Rain Boy case is seductive, because if accepted at face value, it offers modern-day proof of the existence of the Devil (and hence God) and, ultimately, evidence of life after death. Keenhold would later observe, "One of the officers actually told me, 'We were looking into the eyes of the devil. We didn't realize who we were messing with.'"[28] This is a major reason why the story appeals and endures.

Despite the overwhelming evidence against Decker's supposed ability to make it rain and levitate, the events continue to be touted widely as a genuine mystery. For instance, in October 2012, shortly after Decker turned himself in to authorities for arson, Pennsylvania TV station WNEP reported that Decker was "the rain man"—a case that "remains a mystery to this day." The news presenter observed that the events continued to baffle Stroudsburg police, who considered it unsolved. There is no mention of former police chief Gary Roberts, who visited the house and labeled what he saw as unremarkable.[29]

When believers in the paranormal attempt to support their claims that a certain event happened, they often cite the number and credibility of the witnesses. There is no doubt that the officers involved in this case were credible, respected members of their community who have since risen to positions of high responsibility. Officer Baujan was eventually promoted to police chief, while patrolman Wolbert became a detective. Then there is the numbers game. Not counting Decker and his cellmate as credible, due to their criminal records, we are still left with no fewer than eleven respected witnesses: officers Rundle, Davies, Wolbert, and Baujan; warden Keenhold; Mr. and Mrs. Keiffer and Mr. and Mrs. Van Why; Pam Scrofano; and the Reverend Blackburn. Despite so many experienced and responsible people claiming to have witnessed these strange events that lasted over several days, how is it possible that not a single person documented these happenings with so much as a photograph? Why did they fail to seek outside help? The answer is clear: they were blinded by their religious worldview and became carried away in the excitement of the moment.

The story of the Rain Boy grew from an extraordinary series of events: a record snowstorm followed by just the right temperature sequence; and eleven people, all of whom appear to have been devout Christians, interpreting mundane happenings as evidence of the demonic. It was a perfect storm. If any one of the series of events had failed to occur, it is likely that no one ever would have heard of the Rain Boy. Without the record snowstorm followed by warm days and cold nights, there never would have been an ice dam on the roof. If the Keiffers and investigating police had not been devout Christians, they almost certainly would not have concluded that Decker was possessed by the Devil. If any of the visitors to the house had been experienced builders, they almost certainly would have checked the roof for an ice dam; or if they were familiar with psychiatric conditions such as dissociation, they may have taken Decker to a hospital for a psychiatric evaluation. In the end, there was no physical evidence to examine:—no photos and no water samples—and no outside experts were called in to examine the house. When one first hears the story, it sounds remarkable, given the number of credible witnesses who render their accounts of what happened in their own words. Yet the more one delves into the accounts, the more it becomes clear that the events could not have happened the way they were described—through selective editing and distorted memories.

Psychiatry 101

A review of the psychiatric literature on people who engage in self-mutilation, such as cutting their bodies, reveals an interesting pattern. There is a clear association between those who engage in self-harm and those who have suffered abuse as children: they are much more likely to exhibit dissociation, and they readily enter trance states. Self-mutilation is a common response to distressing events—the very situation that Decker found himself in. Decker almost certainly cut himself while in the upstairs bathroom prior to supper. Throughout the ordeal, several observers commented on his mental state, noting that he often appeared to be in a trance. On several occasions while at the Keiffer home, Decker was said to have been unresponsive to questions and stared straight ahead with a blank look on his face.

While feigning trance is a possibility, at times Decker genuinely may have been in a dissociative state, given his history of abuse and propensity for self-harm, as he gave himself deep scratches or cuts on his arms at least twice while at the Keiffers'. After the death of his abusive grandfather, the positive attention his grandfather received at the funeral was clearly causing Decker great frustration. A leading expert on self-mutilation and trauma, psychiatrist Sandra Bloom observes that acts of self-mutilation are a traumatized person's way of managing negative feelings "while simultaneously expressing, nonverbally, the extreme rage, despair and agony of the tormented child."[30] The most common form of self-mutilation is cutting, although one variant is giving oneself deep scratches, to the point of drawing blood.[31] Self-mutilation often produces temporary relief from acute distress, possibly due to the release of endorphins, which can explain why cutters typically report feeling "little or no pain." Bloom observes that "many patients self-mutilate while they are in a dissociative state. Under stress they enter a trance state, another part of themselves or an alter personality inflicts the wounds, and they come to their senses without recall for what transpired."[32]

In *Bleeding to Ease the Pain*, clinical psychologist Lori Plante writes that being abused in childhood often results in lifelong emotional damage that triggers dissociation: "Often the abuse is so traumatic that the child can only cope with the overwhelming horror of the act through dissociation, a form of psychological distancing that helps the child disconnect physically and emotionally from the experience as if in a dreamlike trance." Plante also says that the abuse often results in "self-destructive patterns," which would fit with Decker's propensity for getting into trouble with the law.[33]

Whether Decker was consciously aware of what he was doing to his body, later he clearly relished the attention and likely played along with the belief of those around him, who thought he could make it rain. For instance, be began consciously rubbing his fingers together while in jail when he claimed he would try to strike Dave Keenhold with a drop of water. Once he had undergone an exorcism and was supposedly freed from the Devil, Decker received a great deal of attention. He became part of local folklore; he was the focus of paranormal research by the likes of prominent investigator Peter Jordan; he became the subject of public talks; and later he appeared on two popular, globally syndicated TV shows. The key question is whether Decker intentionally master-minded a hoax once the ice dam broke or whether he was truly slipping in and out of a trance. The truth may be a combination of both. Like every other case in this book, a closer examination of the facts reveals more about the eyewitnesses and their states of mind than about the presence of any supernatural force.

CHAPTER 7

The Haunting in Connecticut: A Disturbing Truth

Three things cannot be long hidden: the sun, the moon, and the truth.
—Buddha[1]

In 2009, Gold Circle Films released *The Haunting in Connecticut,* a movie about the fictional Campbell family who reported a series of chilling supernatural attacks after moving into their new home—a former funeral parlor. The movie is said to portray the real-life experiences of Al and Carmen Snedeker and is based on their coauthored book, *In a Dark Place: The Story of a True Haunting.*[2] The film earned $77 million at the box office.[3] Carmen says that just three hours after moving in, her teenage son said to her, "Mom, this house is evil. We need to leave here right away."[4] She said that strange things began to happen on the very first night and would soon escalate. "My son started seeing this young man with long black hair down all the way to his hips. . . . He would talk to my son every day. Sometimes he would threaten him, other times he would stand there and just say his name, which was enough to scare him."[5] As with *The Amityville Horror* and *The Conjuring* before it, the case was investigated by Ed and Lorraine Warren, and a book was written about it that became a major motion picture.

Background to a Haunting

In 1986, Alan and Carmen Snedeker moved into the old Hallahan House on Meriden Avenue in the town of Southington, in central

Connecticut, twenty miles southwest of Hartford. Soon strange things began to happen—or so the story goes. Alan was a foreman at a local stone quarry; Carmen was a former bowling alley cocktail waitress. The family had three sons, ages thirteen, eleven, and three, and a six-year-old daughter. Two nieces would later move in.[6] The Snedekers say that they moved into the house after thirteen-year-old Philip was diagnosed with blood cancer and needed to commute five times a week from where they were living in upstate New York to the John Dempsey Hospital in Farmington, Connecticut, a wealthy suburb of Hartford.[7] This would seem to be an odd claim, given that there are world-class hospitals in New York State capable of treating the boy's Hodgkin's lymphoma. However, they say that as his condition was very serious, they opted for an experimental treatment that was being offered by the hospital, so they soon moved into a nearby townhouse.[8]

According to the story, the family soon discovered a number of creepy items in the basement: a box of coffin handles, a chain-and-pulley casket lift, and a blood drainage pit—unmistakable relics of the previous business, the Hallahan Funeral Home. The eerie setting may have had a powerful suggestive effect. Spooky phenomena began with the oldest son, Philip, whose basement bedroom was adjacent to the gruesome area. He soon reported seeing ghosts, although his parents say they first attributed this to the cobalt treatments he was receiving for his cancer. Philip's personality is said to have undergone a worrisome metamorphosis, and it included an interest in demonology. He is reported to have broken into a neighbor's home and to have told his mother he wanted a gun so he could kill his stepfather.[9] The strange events allegedly continued for two years. A seventeen-year-old niece named Tammy claimed that an unseen hand fondled her on several occasions as she lay in bed. Many other oddities were reported: apparitions, noises, and physical attacks, especially alleged demonic sexual attacks on Carmen.[10] She later told a CNN reporter that mattresses in the house would breathe and vibrate; and whenever she mopped the floor, the water would turn red and give off a putrid smell.[11]

Enter, Stage Right: Ed and Lorraine Warren

The Snedekers soon brought in Ed and Lorraine Warren, who continued their pattern of arriving at a "haunted" house and transforming the case into a "demonic infestation," in keeping with their own medieval-style Catholic beliefs. Like the Lutzes at Amityville, the Snedekers were devout Catholics. Bringing with them two "psychic researchers"—their grandson and nephew—the Warrens eventually moved into the house for nine and a half weeks. While they denied that there was a book deal in progress, there is evidence that the researchers had made just such an arrangement. Mrs. Snedeker had already told her upstairs neighbor about the deal, saying that she and her husband were to receive one third of the profits.[12] Soon Al and Carmen Snedeker were publicly claiming to have been raped and sodomized by demons: the same claim made in a previous case involving the Warrens.[13] They would repeat these claims on national television shows, notably *Sally Jessy Raphael*, to promote their 1992 book with the Warrens, *In a Dark Place*.[14] It was written with professional horror-tale writer Ray Garton and timed—like the *Sally* show—for release near Halloween.

The Investigation: Red Flags Galore

When Joe Nickell examined the case more closely, it quickly unraveled. For instance, the Snedekers maintained that when they moved in on June 30, they had no idea that the house had been a funeral parlor, as the sign had been covered by plywood. But many neighbors insist otherwise, and the previous owners emphatically say that the Snedekers *were* informed of the house's former use prior to moving in.[15] Sandy, a woman who worked for the real estate agent that rented the property, coincidentally lived on the second floor during the supposed haunting. She said that Carmen "was totally made aware that . . . this was a funeral home."[16]

Although Nickell appeared with Carmen Snedeker on *The Maury Povich Show* in March 1992, his investigation intensified when *Sally Jessy Raphael* producers sent him an advance copy of the Snedekers' book with the Warrens and invited him on the show.[17] Nickell later visited Southington as a guest of one of the Snedekers' neighbors. On the *Sally* show, he appeared with the Warrens and Snedekers, along with several skeptical neighbors.[18] During the taping, the Snedekers sat on a brass bed while telling their story of demonic sexual attacks.[19] Mrs. Kathy Altemus lived across the street from the Snedekers during the entire time they resided in the Hallahan House. Beginning in mid-July 1988, Mrs. Altemus kept a journal of events relating to 208 Meriden Avenue. She told Sally, "I discovered that there were usually things going on in the neighborhood that explained the things they put in the newspaper." It corresponds with her written records, with news clippings arranged chronologically. The outcome is revealing. For instance, the television program *A Current Affair* mentions the sound of clanking chains in the house, presumably from the coffin lift in the basement. But Mrs.

Altemus's journal shows that at the same time, a truck passed by, making a sound like it was "dragging a chain." Other events also had plausible explanations, such as pranksters hiding in the shadows and racing past the well-known "haunted house" in the early morning.[20]

The journal sheds light on another incident. The *New Britain Herald* reported on either a "bizarre coincidence or ghost," as indicated by a mysterious power outage that occurred just after *A Current Affair* aired a broadcast segment on the Snedeker family haunting. A utility spokesman "was at a loss to explain just why the limb chose that particular time to knock out the power." A closer examination of the claim reveals that the incident did not occur at the time of the television program but nearly two hours later. Similar outages have occurred several times on tree-lined Meriden Avenue, when limbs have fallen on the uninsulated line. When Joe Nickell was visiting Southington at the Altemus home in June 1993, he also experienced a power outage. It seems unlikely that demonic forces were heralding his arrival or had no better means of attempting to scare him away.

Long before the *Sally* show, in response to the Warrens' media exploitation of the case, the Snedekers' landlady, who had served them with an eviction notice for failing to pay rent, said that she and her husband had owned the property for two and a half years and experienced no inkling of any supernatural presence. "I find it ironic that after more than two years as tenants, suddenly we are told about these alleged ghosts and then read in the paper that the Warrens will be conducting a seminar and will be charging the public for it. . . . If the ghosts really are there, then why did the Snedekers stay there over two years and why are they staying there now? Are they looking for publicity or profit, or what?"[21] The Snedekers' upstairs neighbor held similar views. Referring to the Warrens as "con artists," she said, "I haven't experienced anything." She told reporters that the Warrens, who she was convinced were exploiting the situation for personal gain, "have caused a lot of problems here and they are not ghost problems."[22]

The events in the house clearly center on Philip and reflect classic poltergeist claims, beginning innocuously and building in severity. The ordeal began when shortly after moving in, Philip said he could hear a voice calling his name. This became a nightly occurrence, followed by visions. After six months, one night Philip claimed that he could see spirits in the room, which appears to have frightened his brother Brad—who was with him at the time and thought he might have glimpsed them as well. They also began to notice that the crosses above the doorways had been taken down. The family suspected Philip, who was described as angry and distraught from his ordeal with cancer.[23]

They soon found Philip's notebook, with dark, eerie sketches and writings. Then one evening at the dinner table, Carmen said she noticed something unusual about Philip's arm, which she grabbed and pulled up the sleeve. Philip had deep, bloody scratches on both arms and claimed that an unseen force was causing him to make the lacerations. This aspect of the case is strikingly similar to the 1983 incident involving Don Decker in Stroudsburg, Pennsylvania. Self-mutilation is a cry for help and attention. It is common among adolescents. The key difference here is that it was happening in a suspected haunted house.[24]

Philip became aggressive and began harassing his brother; he even threw punches at him. He also trashed his sister Tammy's room, and when she tried to stop him, she said he "threw me across the room as if I was nothing."[25] After this incident, she said that he would peek around corners and stare at her. That's when something odd began happening at night. Tammy reported that during the night, she would awaken after someone or something had pulled off the bedcovers. Other times she awoke with a startle after feeling her shirt lifting up. Once she woke sensing what felt like a hand pulling at her bra strap.[26] Other revealing information came to light in the book, including Philip's drug use, vandalism, and other misbehavior. There was even an explanation for the sexual touching that Carmen's niece had felt "from an unseen hand." The boy was caught fondling his cousins while they slept. Philip "was taken away by the police that afternoon. He was questioned, at which time he confessed that he'd been fondling the girls while they slept at night, and that he'd attempted unsuccessfully to have sex with his twelve-year-old cousin." He was later taken to the juvenile detention center, where a psychiatrist diagnosed him as schizophrenic.[27] These are not baseless allegations from a disputed third party: they appear in the Snedekers' own book.

Admissions of a Horror Writer

Many people have branded the Warren-Snedeker-Garton book a work of fiction. The husband of the Snedekers' landlady observed, "It's a fraud. It's a joke. It's a hoax," adding, "It's a scheme to make money."[28] One of the coauthors of the Warrens' books has since admitted that Ed Warren (who died in 2006) told them to make up incidents and details to create scary stories.[29] Ray Garton, the award-winning horror writer who authored the book about the Southington case on which the movie *The Haunting in Connecticut* is based, now repudiates the book. He is glad that it went out of print, and he notes that writing the manuscript was challenging because the various players involved gave different versions of events. In a 2009 interview, Garton made several extraordinary admissions. He said that he took the job to write the book about the supposed haunting because he grew up reading about various exploits of the Warrens in the tabloids like the *National Enquirer*, but that his view of the Warrens was quickly deflated after meeting them in Connecticut. What Garton says happened at that meeting is extraordinary and disillusioning, and it is best told in his own words. "I went to Connecticut and spent time with the Warrens and the Snedekers. When I found that the Snedekers couldn't keep their individual stories straight, I went to Ed Warren and explained the problem. 'They're crazy,' he said. 'All the people who come to us are crazy, that's why they come to us. Just use what you can and make the rest up. You write scary books, right? Well, make it up and make it scary. That's why we hired you.'"[30]

This is a remarkable claim. It is important to remember that Garton was not just *any writer* hoping to attain fortune and fame: he already had both. Why would he risk his reputation by making such remarks? His revelations cast doubt on *all* of the Warrens' investigations. So why did he become associated with such a suspect project? He said he took the job assuming that he would be telling the story of a family that genuinely believed they had been involved in a haunting (hence the "true story" billing); later he realized that the story was a fraud "concocted by people looking for a book deal and a possible movie deal," but by then he was locked into the project. When he approached the publisher about his reservations, he said they "had no interest in anything I had to say. I was contracted to write this book, and the book was always meant to be 'non-fiction.'"[31] Garton says that he has since been in contact with other writers who have worked with the Warrens, leaving him in no doubt that the Warrens and the Snedekers are frauds, as "their experiences with the Warrens have been almost identical to my own." As for what he thinks of the film *The Haunting in Connecticut*, he reports never having seen it, stating bluntly, "I've had my fill of this con."[32]

While some have accused him of holding a grudge against the Warrens because he did not receive money from the film, Garton says that he has been denouncing claims that the book is nonfiction ever since it first appeared in 1992. He says he did this because he was disturbed that it was being promoted on the nonfiction shelves and not as a work of fiction. "I wanted to make sure I had a clear conscience, so I've given my account at every opportunity."[33] Carmen Snedeker (now Carmen Reed) has denounced Garton's comments, claiming that the book was inaccurate and that her family had little or no involvement with it. Garton fired back, "That's a lie. They were very involved. They signed off on the whole thing. I spent a lot of time with them in their home. But they've reinvented this story for the movie and the new book that's being written about it, so it's important for their presentation that they dismiss the book I wrote." Garton chided Carmen by noting, "If my book was inaccurate, it's because I was told to make up whatever I needed to. I have been telling my story since *In A Dark Place* was published because my name is on that book."[34]

The Film versus the Original Story

The Haunting in Connecticut is a fictitious story that fails to follow key parts of the story that it is supposedly based on. In the film, "Sara Campbell" fears that the long road trips that her son "Matt" (Philip in real life) must endure to receive cancer treatments are proving to be too much of a strain on him. The solution is to rent a house near the clinic. Beyond this point, little else is based on the original claims, as the film quickly plunges into a melodramatic supernatural thriller. Troubled by the many visions reported at the house, when Matt looks into the history of the property, he learns that during the 1920s, mortician Ramsey Aickman mutilated corpses at the funeral home and then held séances in an effort to contact the spirits of the deceased. Not surprisingly, this was a bad idea, as Aickman and several others were killed by the angry spirits. A terminally ill priest (Reverend Popescu) tries to rid the house of the many spirits inhabiting it, but in the process, he angers them and makes matters worse. We also learn that Mr. Aickman had not only desecrated their memories through mutilating their bodies, but that he also placed many of their remains in the walls. Matt is able to save the day when he becomes possessed, locates the various remains, and has them cremated. The haunting ends, and he is cured of cancer.[35]

One of the most important weapons in the arsenal of a detective is the technique of examining interviews by the same persons, over time. When we engage in this most basic of practices, cracks in the Snedekers' stories begin to appear. In a 1992 TV interview, Carmen states emphatically that when her family first moved in, she "didn't realize it was a funeral home." In 2012, the producers of *Paranormal Witness*, which tells paranormal accounts in the words of the witnesses, reenacted a scene in which the Snedekers first entered the house. They immediately realized that the home had been a funeral parlor.[36] To get out of this apparent discrepancy, Carmen later claimed that her first realization that the house had been a funeral home appeared to her in a dream.[37]

Another red flag is the odd behavior of the parents. While the "haunting" included an array of minor events such as flickering lights or ghostly images in windows at night, far more sinister violations occurred, such as the claim that Carmen and her husband were raped by an unseen entity! If we are to believe the Snedekers, they were harassed and terrified by these events. Carmen said there was no pleasure: "[I]t was horrible pain . . . it was so penetrating and so much pain." She said that after intercourse, a voice could be heard laughing. She described the experience as "the most crippling thing I've ever been through in my life."[38] Meanwhile, Alan claimed that he was raped by a demon one night while he lay next to his wife in bed. *Why would anyone remain in a house where they are the victims of ongoing sexual attacks by demons?* It is not as if they claimed that these were rare events. In one interview, Carmen said, "It physically engulfed me [raped her], and every night since I've been under some sort of attack. The next night I was sodomized. The following night I was raped. My husband's been sodomized. My husband's been taken into a deep trance and showed horrible things." They also claimed that the bed would vibrate and that a tiny invisible entity would occasionally walk around it.[39] During one interview, Carmen said, "It told me it would kill my daughter . . . it told my husband it would kill our son."[40] It is difficult to imagine anyone being subjected to such experiences yet remaining in the house for two years! Certainly, most people would have fled at the first signs of trouble, in the interests of their safety and that of their children. While these strange events were supposedly happening, the woman living above them said that she neither heard nor experienced anything unusual.[41]

While many of the claims appear to have been fabricated, others can be explained by mass suggestion after the family members realized they were living in a former funeral parlor. We also have classic poltergeist elements, with a central figure—an angry, frustrated adolescent—suspiciously at the center of many of the claims, one who later confesses to molesting his cousin. It is possible, perhaps even likely, that Carmen and her niece Tammy perceived one key event to have happened. When Tammy reported feeling that she had been inappropriately groped in the night, Carmen came to the conclusion that Philip was the culprit. "She was very frightened because she didn't see what was pulling at her . . . but at the end of the day there is no way I believed that it was ghosts. The only conclusion I could come up with was that it was my son."[42] Carmen said that the realization that Philip was the perpetrator left her numb and emotionally distraught. "I didn't know what to feel or what to think. I was like a robot running on battery power." She called his psychologist, who had him committed to a mental hospital. She said, "My emotions were just completely void." Carmen said that as she drove home from the hospital, Philip's last words to her—"Now that I'm gone, they're going to come after you"—played in her mind. "I felt very conflicted . . . I was in such a rage that I was ready to believe anything other than that my son was going to be a schizophrenic the rest of his life."[43] She went into the house, sat at the bottom of the stairs, and said, "Alright you . . . want to play, you come play with me." She sat there for several hours, but nothing happened. As she and Tammy claimed, that night they saw the outline of a hand move under Tammy's clothing and up to her chest on two occasions.[44] However, given their emotional state and the intense desire to believe that Philip was innocent, Carmen and Tammy may have allowed their imaginations to deceive them. This was the year 1987. Given all of the events that allegedly occurred in the house—and the invisible hand that supposedly moved up Tammy's nightshirt—why didn't anyone think to grab a camera and take a picture in order to convince others? The circumstances of this supposed encounter are suspicious. Tammy had come to Carmen and said she felt that an unseen force was coming for her; Carmen says she grabbed her bible, went to Tammy's room, and began reading from Psalms 24. It was within this emotionally charged environment, where she was expecting something supernatural to happen, that she thought she saw the hand move under Tammy's shirt.[45]

It is now clear that the events as claimed by the Snedekers did not happen, and for Hollywood to promote the film as "based on true events" is a stretch of the imagination. It is an interesting story that was made into a chilling movie, but the film bears little resemblance to the alleged story, which lacks tangible evidence that any paranormal events took place. But as with *The Amityville Horror* and *The Conjuring*, while the new homeowners failed to experience any paranormal happenings, they were forced to endure the aftermath. Susan Trotta-Smith lived in the house for over a decade after the alleged events and says that she and her neighbors have been in contact with police about the house—not out of a fear of ghosts, but because of inconsiderate sightseers.[46] Even before the film officially appeared in theaters, the publicity about the house had unleashed a torrent of curiosity seekers who shattered the peace and tranquility of the neighborhood. Trotta-Smith observed, "It's been a total change from a very quiet house in a very quiet neighborhood to looking out the window and seeing cars stopping all the time. It's been very, very stressful, and sometimes worrisome."[47]

CHAPTER 8

Weighing the Evidence: Separating Fact from Fiction

I believe in observation, measurement, and reasoning, confirmed by independent observers. I'll believe anything . . . if there is evidence for it. The wilder and more ridiculous something is, however, the firmer and more solid the evidence will have to be.

—Isaac Asimov[1]

There is nothing with greater emotional appeal than to think that when our physical bodies die, our consciousness lives on as a spirit or soul. It is also appealing to think that the human mind is capable of extraordinary feats that could someday be harnessed. For these reasons, we must approach the subject of poltergeists and hauntings with caution and stick to the facts as we know them, not as we wish them to be. Keeping our emotions from influencing our conclusions is a cardinal rule of scientific investigation. When we carefully examined the best cases that were chosen by film and documentary makers for their compelling nature, we found no tangible evidence to support the existence of haunted houses and poltergeists. When we surveyed the literature, a curious pattern emerged: a pattern that dates back centuries, is clustered around adolescents, and is best described as "poltergeist faking syndrome." We also found complicity within the film and television industries, which were quick to promote "true" aspects of these storylines, despite clear evidence to the contrary. The "based on a true story" genre and the paranormal continue to be characterized by a disregard for facts and a desire to place profit over truth. When there is a vested interest in something as alluring as the evidence for life after death, people are susceptible to self-deception. Hollywood producers know this feature of human nature all too well. But as the saying goes, "Never let the facts get in the way of a good story."

The Social History of Poltergeists

To the novice and the uninitiated, the evidence for poltergeists appears formidable if not indisputable; for how could so many people in so many parts of the world report similar experiences over the centuries? Surely there must be some truth to these reports. Yet the uniformity of poltergeist reports appears mythical. Pagan folklore tells of malicious ghosts with many poltergeist qualities, who lived in the countryside on the outskirts of human settlements. These spirits could enter villages when someone cut down a tree they inhabited and incorporated it into a house, transforming the spirit into a benign, domesticated one. Paranormal historian James Houran observes that until the early sixteenth century, there are many accounts of friendly ghosts coexisting in domestic harmony with humans. He writes, "They have been described as supporting and caring, giving advice and telling the future, taking the blankets away when children have been sleeping too long, and so on. They lived in friendship with humans."[2] This state of affairs changed abruptly when Christianity began to view paganism as a threat, and poltergeists were transformed into more demonic entities. Houran continues, "From Martin Luther onward, we have documents about threatening ghosts being perceived now around and inside of houses instead of far away in the countryside ... [and they] became the noisy and stone-throwing ghosts later known as poltergeists."[3] This shifting nature of poltergeist activity suggests that they are a human creation. But even if we accept Houran's historical evolution of the poltergeist, it is undeniable that for the past five hundred years, the descriptions of cases have been relatively uniform and consistent. There are essentially two explanations for poltergeists: they are either real or imaginary. Of course, "real" refers to manifestations of psychic powers, such as telekinesis, or to supernatural entities. The term "imaginary" not only includes hoaxes but also incidents of self-deception. In either case, the scientific community remains overwhelmingly skeptical of their reality, and it must do so, in accordance with the tenets of science, until more concrete evidence is produced.

The many hundreds of documented cases of poltergeists present us with a conundrum. On the one hand, scores of people from different parts of the world have reported remarkably similar experiences for centuries. It seems inconceivable that they could all be the product of tall tales, fraudsters, hallucinations, and misperception. Time and again the same key features crop up: strange knocking sounds with no apparent cause; stones, pebbles, and other small objects flying through the air; or larger objects, such as furniture, found mysteriously smashed to pieces. Occasionally, people and objects are said to levitate. On the other hand, with the proliferation of mobile phones capable of capturing images, and with the widespread use of video surveillance cameras, why are there so few claims by everyday citizens recording poltergeist images? Why are there so many photos from paranormal investigators that were taken under dubious circumstances or are indistinguishable blurs? Why can't scientists replicate these results in laboratory or in field studies? This is why, despite the persistence of reports and many credible witnesses, most scientists remain steadfastly unwilling to accept that poltergeists exist. Are they being so conservative and inflexible in their thinking as to deny a significant body of evidence amassed over the years? The trouble is that the evidence compiled to date is "soft" and is mostly based on unsubstantiated claims and eyewitness testimony.

It is possible that we live in a mysterious world filled with strange creatures, otherworldly spirits, and nefarious entities—an exciting, enchanted universe where, like in the TV show *The Twilight Zone*, the known laws of physics do not apply. While at times scary, this world is also seductive, because the creatures and forces that inhabit it defy what science says is possible. Strange phenomena such as poltergeists serve as cautionary tales about the inadequacy of science. In this sense, mysterious entities may be viewed as anti-scientific symbols undermining conventional paradigms of reality. The underlying message in poltergeist cases is clear: the mainstream scientific community has yet to accept their existence, but each year, ordinary people continue to report instances of these "noisy ghosts." The stubborn persistence of these encounters, like sightings of Bigfoot and the Loch Ness monster, challenges the authority of science for those people who are unfamiliar with rules of evidence and the unreliability of eyewitness testimony. This helps to explain the gulf between the skepticism that typifies most scientists and popular beliefs as reflected in opinion polls. Some people conclude that scientists are either close-minded or are afraid to publicly support the existence of the supernatural, for fear of hurting their careers. The truth is that for scientists to conclude that the paranormal is real will not inhibit their career advancement, if they can produce the evidence to support their conclusions—and if they are able to replicate their findings. If they could do this, the scientific community would be forced to accept their findings. But this has not happened, because to date, they have been unable to produce the evidence.

Fraud: A Universal Human Tradition

Poltergeist believers often argue that it stretches credulity to think that so many people would be creating hoaxes and deceptions in such a similar fashion, across vastly different cultures and time periods. Yet throughout *all* cultures and *every* period of recorded history, humans have been known to engage in guile and trickery. It is part of the human condition. This raises the question of whether there are precedents in nature involving similar phenomena. One only need pick up a basic anthropology textbook. A classic example that has been thoroughly studied is "the sucking cure." All over the world, anthropologists have observed a curious act practiced by native healers, shamans, witch doctors, and medicine men. These tribal priests claim to rid people of diseases and evil spirits by literally sucking the illness from their patients and spitting it out as a tangible object such as pebble, a piece of wood, or a chunk of bone. Observers often note that shamans appear to believe they possess special powers to heal, but that they use this technique—what is essentially a magic trick—to bolster the patients' belief in their cure. While it can be interpreted as a tradition, ritual, or secret practice, it is still deception. A typical example can be found among in various tribal groups that reside throughout the Andes mountains of Chile. When people get sick, it is widely believed that it is from an imbalance caused by a foreign spirit or object that has invaded the body. The shaman supposedly enters a deep trance, and amid the sounds of pounding drums, bells, and rattles, he sucks the entity into his mouth, restoring the patient's natural balance. He then typically spits out the entity.[4] Ruth Underhill observes that the "sucking cure" is found in every Northern American Indian group. She writes, "The medicine men whom I knew believed in their powers, although they were quite aware that sucking out the disease object was a matter of sleight of hand." As one shaman admitted, "[P]eople need something to see."[5] At best, one could rationalize their actions and view it as a form of primitive placebo.

A regional example of a tradition of deception occurred when Robert Bartholomew investigated the so-called mental disorder of *latah* in Malaysia and Indonesia. He concluded that it is not a disorder at all but instead a local idiom of distress that has developed throughout parts of Southeast Asia and *always* involves deception and fraud. *Latah* is a bizarre behavior whereupon being startled, ordinarily shy, timid women may react with obscenities and outrageous sexual gestures. Severe cases almost always involve elderly women, who may engage in "automatic obedience," doing whatever they are told. Yet there is a pattern to these cases: "severes" are almost always elderly Malay women who are socially isolated and depressed, often after losing a husband. Until recently, psychiatrists have assumed that stress from their social situation triggered this culture-specific form of mental disorder. Instead they should have been looking at the conditions under which people are likely to feign behavior for attention.[6] Michael Kenny concludes that "severe" subjects do not enter trance states but are instead engaging in a *latah* "performance" or "theater." Never are the words "fraud" or "fakery" used, yet anthropologists may be guilty of using double standards here. For instance, when studied, Western faith healers are typically viewed as fraudulent, but place an exotic label on essentially the same behavior involving a shaman in an exotic tribe, and anthropologists are quick to point to their "symbolic" qualities. A fraud explanation explains the appearance of *latah* in a waxing and waning fashion in Malaysia and Indonesia since the latter 1800s. Today the condition has nearly died out. In a similar manner, Bigfoot and kindred monster traditions exist around the world, and people often create hoaxes involving footprints and sightings. Feigning poltergeist outbreaks is just one more example.

In a variety of fields that are on the margins of scientific acceptance, from cryptozoology to UFOs to the Loch Ness monster, there will always be a small group of rogue scientists who believe in their existence. It does not matter whether 99.9 percent of mainstream scientists are skeptical on these topics; journalists will gravitate to maverick scientists, as it makes for an exciting, interesting story. Unfortunately, this situation can often give the distorted impression that more scientists believe in poltergeists and haunted houses than actually do. While a handful of qualified scientists claim to have observed evidence for poltergeists, their results have never been consistently replicated under strictly controlled conditions. Furthermore, when most respected researchers conduct rigorous investigations by setting up tight controls and cameras, either they uncover clear evidence of deception and fraud, or the phenomenon fails to materialize. Like UFOs, Bigfoot, and the chupacabra, given the absence of definitive proof of something extraordinary, do all poltergeist cases have mundane explanations? We have not seen any convincing evidence to indicate otherwise.

Each of the cases that we have explored contains a clear religious element. This may explain why so many of the participants were fooled. Don Decker was thought to be possessed by the Devil. In Amityville, a cross was turned upside down and a priest attacked. At Seaford, the Herrmann family placed bottles of holy water throughout the house to ward off the poltergeist, and eventually a priest came to bless the house, and the possibility of an exorcism was discussed. Religious symbolism was also prominent in the outbreaks involving the Perron family in Rhode Island and the Snedekers in Connecticut. For many people, these cases go far beyond being the temporary infestation of a "noisy spirit"; they are proof of the reality of God and the bible. To believe in their existence offers us a glimpse of a black-and-white world of good versus evil, where God is watching over us.

The Warrens

No discussion of our "based on a true story" cases would be complete without mention of the role of Ed and Lorraine Warren. Their involvement in the investigations of cases that were turned into *The Conjuring, The Amityville Horror,* and *The Haunting in Connecticut* is revealing. A number of years ago, Connecticut neuroscientist Dr. Steven Novella made a sincere attempt to investigate the Warrens' claims. While skeptical and an atheist, Novella said that he made a conscious effort not to confront their belief system. His goal was to objectively evaluate the evidence that they had accumulated after forty years of investigating hauntings. "He showed us a lot of ghost photos where if you've ever just gone on the web and look up ghost photos, you've seen them. It's all the same thing. Basically, the three, four most common photographic artifacts. You get some flashbacks and camera cord reflect, occasional double exposure, all very unimpressive, just blobs of light on film," he said.[7]

Novella estimates that 90 percent of their evidence consisted of vague photos of "ghosts." They made little or no attempt to critically evaluate what they were photographing. "They claim that the ghostly images get on the film psychically . . . but they were surprised to find that that happened more often when you used a flash and the brighter the flash, the better. Yet, it didn't occur to them that the flash was producing the effect that was producing the light on the film. They still thought it was psychic effects from the ghost or at least that's what they professed to believe." According to Novella, when he pointed this out to them, "they just quietly took that off their web site without ever acknowledging our correction."[8] So much for integrity. At best, the Warrens appear to be gullible, uncritical, and influenced by their medieval Christian beliefs about the existence of demonic forces.

When Novella and his fellow skeptics continued to politely challenge the Warrens, things began to turn ugly. During one local TV appearance, Novella said that Ed turned confrontational, produced evidence they had never heard of before, and exclaimed, "Explain that, skeptics!" Novella said he was shocked by the tactic as his group had been asking the Warrens to provide them with evidence for years. As for the remarkable evidence that Ed had produced, Novella said it consisted of a video of "a white lady" at a cemetery. Novella said that it "was at that perfect distance and resolution that it was suggestive of a ghostly figure but you couldn't really see it well enough to know if it was Lorraine in a bed sheet. . . . It wasn't close up, it wasn't in focus enough . . . the quality was not there. It was like, if you were trying to fake a ghost video, that's exactly what it would have looked like."[9] Whether they are sincere but gullible and misguided or are conscious hucksters, perhaps the best description of the Warrens was made by Joe Nickell when he confronted them on national TV. He observed that after decades of investigating haunted houses, "I've not met a house that I thought was haunted. I think the Warrens have not met a house that they didn't think *was* haunted!"[10]

A good example of the Warrens' lack of scientific rigor occurred when they "investigated" the Snedeker haunting in Connecticut. When asked why he thought that spirits had chosen that particular house, Ed speculated that it was because it had been a funeral home and necrophilia had taken place there. "You have itinerant embalmers from time to time, who will help out. . . . We think it was one of them. . . . What happened was . . . a body was abused, or maybe more than one, and we know that this can bring about terrible phenomena and hauntings."[11] For such an elaborate theory, Ed could not produce any evidence to support it. It was based on a feeling. Detectives and scientists do not make accusations based on hunches; they deal in facts and weigh evidence. In this instance, there are no supporting facts. There are two basic types of speculation: informed and wild. Police use the former all the time to solve crimes and track criminals. Ed Warren's inklings fall into the latter category.

Adolescents Behaving Badly

There is no credible evidence to conclude that poltergeists result from the hypothetical existence of "psychic energy" or are the noisy spirits of the dead. Instead, they appear to be a reflection of the troubled minds of the living, which have a propensity for deception and mischief. Poltergeists are universal because the belief in ghosts and spirits is universal, and the propensity to hoax and deceive is found in every culture. The global belief in otherworldly entities allows adolescents who are experiencing feelings of rage and revenge a convenient label under which to blame their destructive actions, getting their point across while deflecting the attribution of guilt. *They* didn't do it—it was the ghost. Poltergeist behaviors are temporary and soon pass as the adolescent matures or fears being caught, because ultimately, outbreaks are unsustainable. A young boy who is unhappy in his new home and desperately wishes to move can argue that the spirit is sending them a message, when in reality, it is the boy. In the case of "Robbie," he wanted to go to St. Louis after his aunt died and conveyed his message by carving "LOUIS" on his chest. Not long after, the family was on a train bound for St. Louis. Why are these deceptive acts so common among adolescents? Perhaps it is because they are old enough to pull off these deceptions successfully in the absence of a fully developed set of moral values; they possess a state of mind where "the ends justify the means."

In the early twenty-first century, advances in technology have failed to produce definitive proof of monsters, extraterrestrials, or poltergeists. More often than not, instead of recording mysterious happenings, the "haunted" subject is captured in the act of deceiving investigators by throwing objects, setting fires, or rattling pots and pans. In the rare instances where a seemingly mysterious act is recorded, the circumstances are such that the image is of dubious origin. If the outbreaks we have examined are the best available, then these episodes likely reveal more about the researchers and the claimants themselves than any poltergeists they are supposedly depicting. A classic example occurred at Seaford, Long Island, when William Roll and Gaither Pratt lost their objectivity and failed to recognize numerous signs pointing to Jimmy Herrmann as the poltergeist, while rejecting the offer of help by Milbourne Christopher, who was able to duplicate *every disturbance created by the poltergeist*. Despite this, Christopher's name never once appeared in their final report. Neither did the negative findings of Dr. Osis. Roll and Pratt were simply reinforcing an existing dogma under the guise of science. In the case of Don Decker, the investigating authorities and the families involved were blinded by their religious beliefs. As a result, a leaky roof became a manifestation of evil, an apparent trance state became demonic possession, and sweat on Warden Keenhold's shirt was interpreted as proof of supernatural powers. But more than this, these events became proof of the presence of the Devil and served to reinforce a belief in God. The main participants saw what they wanted to see.

Every psychologist should be made aware of the poltergeist faking syndrome, so that when they encounter a family where a "noisy ghost" is supposedly causing disturbances, they can focus immediately on the subject who is the center of the   ' seek the underlying causes of that person's anger. Poltergeists a   of distress and signals that something is amiss. In this regard, instead of reflecting spirits of the dead, poltergeists reflect problems of the living. They are not signs from the hereafter but from the present. Like UFOs, Bigfoot, and the Loch Ness monster, their existence tells us more about ourselves than it does about them, because they originate in the human imagination and reflect our hopes and fears.

A common factor in all of the cases in this book is that they were supposedly "based on a true story" and immortalized in films and on TV. It may be a good selling point to gain viewership, but did the events really happen as described? The unequivocal answer is no. When we carefully examine the original claims and compare the testimony of the participants over time, each story unravels. In every case in our study, there is clear evidence of human deception. In every instance, there are gullible bystanders and outsiders who come in to "examine" the case and accept the story at face value—either other family members or journalists and paranormal investigators. They share a common element: their lack of expertise in deception. It is worth remembering that these are not just any cases that we have put under a microscope. We chose seven of the best cases we could find: cases that were so compelling that they inspired Hollywood directors to invest large sums of money so as to bring these stories to wider public attention; cases that researchers point to for their meticulous documentation; cases that witnesses have attested to as being genuine and truly inexplicable.

In his book *Science in the New Age*, anthropologist David Hess briefly surveys films on hauntings and observes that Hollywood tends to lend credence to ghosts, hauntings, and possession claims and typically features believers in heroic roles, while skeptics fare poorly.[12] Media studies expert Emily Edwards concurs. In her review of popular film and television portrayals of "ghostly narratives," she writes that the typical horror film featuring the paranormal makes scientists "appear helpless, even silly. The skeptic in the narrative must convert to belief or be defeated." Thus, skeptics in films like *Poltergeist* must embrace the fringe discipline of parapsychology in order to successfully do battle with the spirit world.[13] Yet when one looks at the evidence for poltergeists and kindred phenomena, there is a huge gulf between public perception and the scientific reality. The story of poltergeists is the story of us—of the human condition that faces the possibility of death on a daily basis. The desire to believe in an afterlife is the driving force behind the poltergeist myth. It is the same desire that blinds those who look at the evidence and see what they want to see.

Notes

Introduction

1. Myrna Blyth and C. Winston, *How to Raise an American* (New York: Three Rivers Press, 2008), p. 91.

2. A Harris Poll released in December 2013 found that 42 percent of those surveyed believed in ghosts. See "Americans' Beliefs in God, Miracles and Heaven Declines" (Harris Poll number 97, released December 16, 2013). Unlike other polls, Harris does not use the term "margin of error," as they consider it to be misleading. They write, "All that can be calculated are different possible sampling errors with different probabilities for pure, unweighted, random samples with 100% response rates. These are only theoretical because no published polls come close to this ideal." A 2012 poll of a representative sample of American adults places this figure at 45 percent. Refer to "Omnibus Poll," accessed April 22, 2014, at http://big.assets.huffingtonpost.com/ghosttoplines.pdf. The poll was conducted on December 17 and 18, 2012, and had a margin of error of 3.1 percent. The question was asked as follows: "Do you believe in ghosts, or that the spirits of dead people can come back in certain places and situations?" These polls are in line with earlier surveys such as the CBS poll conducted between October 3 and 5, 2005, with a sampling error of plus or minus 4 percent. The question asked was worded as follows: "Do you believe in ghosts?" See http://www.cbsnews.com/news/poll-majority-believe-in-ghosts/. The reference in the title to a majority believing in ghosts refers to those samples between the ages of 18 and 45, which was placed at 56 percent. Older persons were more skeptical. See also the Online Paranormal Society Directory, accessed March 14, 2015, at http://www.paranormalsocieties.com/, which lists 3,220 active paranormal organizations in the United States alone.

3. This is a rough approximation, as there is no precise translation from German to English. It has been described in various definitions as a boisterous, troublesome, mischievous, playful, knocking, rattling, or rumbling spirit or ghost.

4. Owen Davies, *Witchcraft, Magic and Culture, 1736–1951* (Manchester: Manchester University Press, 1999), p. 29.

5. Pamela Rae Heath, *Mind-Matter Interaction: A Review of Historical Reports, Theory and Research* (Jefferson, NC: McFarland, 2011), p. 65; Leo Ruickbie, *Ghosts, Vampires and the Paranormal* (London: Constable and Robinson, 2012).

6. Prominent paranormal historian Colin Wilson mistakenly gives the date as "858 BC." See Colin Wilson, *Poltergeist: A Classic Study in Destructive Hauntings* (Woodbury, MN: Llewellyn, 2009), p. 83, citing the chronicle *Annales Fuldenses*. However, references to the "Bishop" and "holy water" show the truth of the matter—positively confirmed by other numerous sources. For a brief survey of possible very early cases, see Heath 2011, op. cit., pp. 65–67.

7. Cheryl A. Wicks, *Ghost Tracks* (Bloomington, IN: AuthorHouse, 2004), pp. 41–42.

8. Alan Gauld and A. D. Cornell, *Poltergeists* (Boston, MA: Routledge & Kegan Paul, 1979), p. 227.

9. Also known as telekinesis, some fancy-sounding names have been used by parapsychologists to describe this process, such as "recurrent spontaneous psychokinesis" and "repressed psychokinetic energy."

10. Guy Playfair, *This House Is Haunted: The Amazing Inside Story of the Enfield Poltergeist* (Guildford, UK: Whitecrow Books, 2011), p. 279.

11. James C. Bozzuto, "Cinematic Neurosis Following 'The Exorcist': Report of Four Cases," *The Journal of Nervous and Mental Disease* 161(1) (1975): 43–48.

12. Several books have examined so-called real hauntings in Hollywood. See Tom Ogden, *Haunted Hollywood: Tinseltown Terrors, Filmdom Phantoms and Movieland Mayhem* (Guilford, CT: Globe Pequot Press, 2009); Laurie Jacobson, *Haunted Hollywood: A Ghostly Tour of Filmland* (Santa Monica, CA: Angel City Press, 1999); Tammy Mahan, *Hometown Hauntings: Celebrity Ghosts of Hollywood* (New York, NY: Aurora Borealis, 2013); Frank McSherry, Charles Waugh, and Martin Greenberg, eds., *Hollywood Ghosts: Haunting, Spine-Chilling Stories from America's Film Capital* (Nashville, TN: Rutledge Hill Press, 1991). Several books analyze claims of hauntings and poltergeists in terms of plot, genre, and cinematography. Examples include Lisa Kroger and Melanie Anderson, *The Ghostly and the Ghosted in Literature and Film* (Lanham, MD: University of Delaware Press, 2013); Tom Ruffle, *Ghost Images: Cinema of the Afterlife* (Jefferson, NC: McFarland, 2004); Joseph Natoli, *Hauntings: Popular Film and American Culture 1990–1992* (Albany, NY: State University of New York Press, 1994); Lee Kovacs, *The Haunted Screen: Ghosts in Literature and Film* (Jefferson, NC: McFarland, 1999).

Chapter 1

1. Sir Arthur Conan Doyle, *The Sir Arthur Conan Doyle Reader: From Sherlock Holmes to Spiritualism* (New York: Cooper Square Press, 2002), p. 53.

2. Box Office Mojo, "*An American Haunting*," accessed August 2, 2014, at http://www.boxofficemojo.com/movies/?id=americanhaunting.htm.

3. Trailer for *An American Haunting*, accessed November 20, 2013, at http://www.youtube.com/watch?v=WxcfXDBqpUQ.

4. Nick Schager, "An American Haunting." *Slant Magazine* (2006), accessed November 20, 2013, at http://www.slantmagazine.com/film/review/an-american-haunting.

5. Personal communication between Fred Rolater and Robert Bartholomew dated December 20, 2013. He is a retired professor of history from Middle Tennessee State University.

6. Claudette Stager, *National Register of Historic Places Continuation Sheet, United States Department of Interior, Supplementary Listing Record* (NRIS Reference Number: 08000237, 2007), at p. 3 of section 8. This is the official document granting the Bell Witch Cave its legal historical status. It was submitted by Stager in December 2007 and was approved and enacted on March 21, 2008. Stager was representing the Tennessee Historical Commission, 2941 Lebanon Road, Nashville, Tennessee (forty pages).

7. Workers of the Writer's Program (compilers), *Tennessee: A Guide to the State*. Produced by the Works Progress Administration (during the Great Depression) by the State of Tennessee, Department of Conservation, Division of Information (American Book-Stratford Press, 1939), p. 392.

8. See, for example, Carol Gist, *Is It Really Haunted? A Concise Resource for Ghost Enthusiasts* (Lincoln, Nebraska: iUniverse, 2009), pp. 89–95.

9. Martin Van Buren Ingram, *Authenticated History of the Bell Witch and Other Stories of the World's Greatest Unexplained Phenomenon* (1894, reprinted, Adams, Tennessee: Historic Bell Witch Cave, Inc., 2005). The legend's most vocal proponent, Ingram, claims that it even surpasses the disturbances of the Epworth rectory poltergeist, an early eighteenth-century case involving the Wesley family, among the children of which was the future founder of Methodism, John Wesley. For a description of the Wesley case, refer to Rosemary Ellen Guiley, *The Encyclopedia of Ghosts and Spirits*, second edition (New York: Checkmark Books, 2000), pp. 122–124.

10. "Story of Witchcraft: In the South—Old Kate Batts' Awful Spell." *The Hartford Herald* (Kentucky), July 25, 1984, p. 1.

11. Earl Shaub, "Worry over Scheduled Return of Legendary Witch," *Hamilton Daily News Journal* (Hamilton, Ohio), April 14, 1937, p. 12.

12. Robert Talley, "America's No. 1 Ghost Breaks a Date Made 110 Years Ago," *Arizona Independent Republican*, December 19, 1937, p. 6. This story appeared in many American papers near this date.

13. William T. Brannon, "The Mystery of the Bell Witch," *Family Weekly Magazine*, October 30, 1955, pp. 8–9. See p. 9 for quote.

14. Alan Spraggett, "The Unexplained: Andrew Jackson Heard the Witch's Voice," *The Robesonian* (Lumberton, North Carolina), October 17, 1973, p. 11.

15. Pat Fitzhugh, *The Bell Witch: The Full Account* (Ashland City, TN: Armand Press, 2009), p. 14.

16. Stephen Wagner, "The Bell Witch," accessed November 17, 2013, at http://paranormal.about.com/od/trueghoststories/a/aa041706.htm.

17. Charles A. Stansfield Jr., *Haunted Presidents: Ghosts in the Lives of the Chief Executives* (Mechanicsburg, PA: Stackpole Books, 2010), p. 41.

18. Michael Schmicker, *Best Evidence* (Lincoln, NE: iUniverse, Inc., 2002), p. 229.

19. Ted Olson and Anthony Cavender, *Tennessee Folklore Sampler: Selections from the Tennessee Folklore Society* (Knoxville: University of Tennessee Press, 2009), p. 236. This composition places the witch in North Carolina, not Tennessee.

20. See Olson and Cavender 2009, p. 236, citing Gladys Barr, "Witchcraft in Tennessee," *Tennessee Valley Historical Review* II (Fall 1983): 29. The article took a romantic angle. The writer suggested that the "spirit" was a male ventriloquist who was infatuated with Betsy Bell and wanted to scare off her suitor, Josh Gardner.

21. "Tennessee Witch Now the Star of a Play." United Press International report appearing in the *Pharos-Tribune* (Logansport, Indiana), October 31, 1976, p. 36.

22. See http://www.clarksvilleonline.com/2008/10/29/last-weekend-for-david-alfords-play-spirit/, accessed November 20, 2013; Fiona Soltes, "Bell Witch Tales Possesses Spirit: Performer's Love for Bell Witch Play Never Dwindles Despite Strange Occurrences," *The Tennessean*, October 17, 2013.

23. Film trailer for *The Bell Witch Haunting*. Accessed November 17, 2013, at http://www.thebellwitchhaunting.com/trailerpage.html.

24. S. Shane Marr (director), *Bell Witch: The Movie* (Big River Pictures and Cinemarr Entertainment, 2005); Robert Maughon, *Bell Witch: The Movie Novel* (Sugarlands Publishing, 2005).

25. Press release, "Seven Tennessee Sites Added to National Register of Historic Places," *United States Federal News Service, Including US State News* (Washington, D.C., May 6, 2008).

26. Stager 2007, op. cit., section 8, p. 8.

27. http://www.bellwitchfallfestival.com/index.php/tickets/events-listing/2012-08-09-00-07-03, accessed November 20, 2013.

28. http://www.bellwitchfansite.com/our_bell_witch_story.html, accessed November 20, 2013.

29. Richard Williams Bell, Chapter 8, "'Our Family Trouble': The Story of the Bell Witch as Detailed by Richard Williams Bell" (allegedly 1846). The authenticity of the manuscript, which is supposedly cited verbatim by Richard Bell in Ingram's book, is almost certainly a hoax. Alleged authorship and date given in Ingram 1894, op. cit., pp. 101–186.

30. Ingram 1894 (2009), op. cit., p. 7. The references to Ingram 2009 refer to a different reprinted edition of Ingram's original book. Joe Nickell worked with the 2005 reprint, while Robert Bartholomew used the 2009 edition. The books are identical, except for slightly different titles, but the page numbers do

not sync. Therefore, anywhere "Ingram, 1894 (2009)" appears, it refers to the following edition: Martin Van Buren Ingram, *An Authenticated History of the Famous Bell Witch* (1894, reprinted, Rockville, MD: Wildside Press, 2009).

31. Ingram 1894 (2009), op. cit., p. 2.

32. Both Jesse Glass and Jack Cook have researched the story over the years and searched for historical documents to corroborate it in everything from diaries to letters and church documents. They found nothing predating 1886. Glass observes that it is beyond belief to think that detailed records of the Red River Primitive Baptist Church, which excommunicated Bell in 1818, would have failed to mention something as significant as the Witch, given that these events took place when the Great Revival was sweeping through the region, given the emphasis at the time on repudiating the Devil (Glass, personal communication dated December 31, 2013).

33. Ingram 1894 (2009), op. cit., p. 55.

34. Ingram 1894 (2009), op. cit., p. 55.

35. Ingram 1894 (2009), op. cit., p. 56.

36. Ingram 1894 (2009), op. cit., p. 56.

37. Ingram 1894 (2009), op. cit., p. 56.

38. This is not an unheard-of practice in poltergeist cases. For a prominent example where such acts were uncovered, see the case of the Enfield Poltergeist, in which such deception was effectively discovered. See Joe Nickell, "Enfield Poltergeist," *Skeptical Inquirer* 36: 4 (July/August 2012a), pp. 12–14.

39. "Bell" 1846 (2009), op. cit., p. 58.

40. "Bell" 1846 (2009), op. cit., p. 59–60.

41. "Bell" 1846 (2009), op. cit., p. 87.

42. Arthur Edward Waite, *A New Encyclopedia of Freemasonry* (New York: Weathervane Books, 1970), volume 1, p. 366.

43. Waite 1970, op. cit., Volume 1, p. 367.

44. Waite 1970, op. cit., Volume 1, p. 174.

45. Ralph P. Lester, *Look to the East! A Ritual of the First Three Degrees of Masonry* (Chicago: Ezra A. Cook Publications, 1977), p. 181.

46. Albert G. Mackey, *The Symbolism of Freemasonry* (Chicago: Charles T. Posner Co., 1975), p. 320.

47. Mackey 1975, op. cit., p. 339.

48. Lester 1977, op. cit., p. 91.

49. Ingram 1894 (2009), op. cit., p. 87.

50. Mackey 1975, op. cit., pp. 125–129; Lester 1977, op. cit., pp. 40–41.

51. Capt. William Morgan, *Illustrations of Masonry* (reprinted, Chicago: Ezra A. Cook Publications, 1827), pp. 105–110.

52. These include allusions in the Bell narrative to "signs," knocks at the door, and "mauls," which also have their counterparts in the secret symbols, rituals, and language of Masonry. See Lester 1977, op. cit., pp. 22, 47, 143.

53. Ingram 1894 (2009), op. cit., pp. 116–120.

54. Ingram 1894 (2009), op. cit., pp. 116–117.

55. Ingram 1894 (2009), op. cit., p. 118.

56. Michael Norman and Beth Scott, *Historic Haunted America* (New York: Tom Doherty Associates, 2007), p. 324.

57. Don Wick, "The Strange True Story of the Bell Witch of Tennessee." Parts 1–5 (February–June 2007), *The Mountain Laurel: The Journal of Mountain Life*, accessed November 23, 2013, at http://mtnlaurel.com/ghost-stories/1166-the-strange-true-story-of-the-bell-witch-of-tennessee-part-1.html.

58. See Sue Hamilton, *Ghosts and Goblins* (Edina, MN: ABDO Publishing, 2005), p. 5; Hans Holzer, *Poltergeists: True Encounters with the World Beyond* (New York: Black Dog & Leventhal, 2010).

59. Donald B. Cole, *Vindicating Andrew Jackson: The 1828 Election and the Rise of the Two-Party System* (Lawrence: University of Kansas Press, 2009).

60. Michael Franz, Paul Freedman, Kenneth Goldstein, and Travis Ridout, *Campaign Advertising and American Democracy* (Philadelphia: Temple University Press, 2007), p. 7; Thomas Ayres, *That's Not in My American History Book* (Lanham, MD: Taylor Trade, 2004) p. 106. The allegation of mass murder was for Jackson ordering the execution of deserters in the War of 1812.

61. Charles Albert Snodgrass, *The History of Freemasonry in Tennessee, 1789–1943: Its Founders, Its Pioneer Lodges and Chapters, Grand Lodge and Grand Chapter, the Cryptic Rite, the Templars the Order of High Priesthood, and the Ancient and Accepted Scottish Rite* (Nashville: Ambrose Printing Company, 1944), inside cover page and pp. 390–394. The local lodge for Adams was the Western Star Lodge No. 9, which was first organized in 1812 at Port Royal, about five miles away. It was also known as the Rhea Lodge. Coincidentally, in 1817, the year that the strange happenings were first reported at the Bell home, this lodge was moved to Springfield. "The History of Robertson County," pp. 827–867. See p. 844. Jackson was the head of the Tennessee Masons between 1822 and 1823.

62. Obituary of M. V. Ingram, *Clarksville Leaf-Chronicle*, October 5, 1909; reproduced at http://bellwitch02.tripod.com/martin_van_buren_ingram.htm; accessed October 31, 2014.

63. "Bell" 1846, op. cit., pp. 143–144.

64. Spartacus Educational, "Pinkerton Detective Agency," accessed November 22, 2013, at http://www.spartacus.schoolnet.co.uk/USApinkertonD.htm.

65. See Joe Nickell, *Literary Investigation: Texts, Sources, and "Factual" Substructs of Literature and Interpretation* (doctoral dissertation, University of Kentucky, 1987). For other textual analyses conducted by Nickell, refer to "Did Shakespeare Write Shakespeare? Much Ado About Nothing," *Skeptical Inquirer* 35(6): 38–43.

66. "Bell" 1846, op. cit., p. 132; Ingram 1894, op. cit., p. 34.

67. "Bell" 1846, op. cit., pp. 130–131, 185.

68. Ingram 1894, op. cit., p. 6, 315.

69. "Bell" 1846, op. cit., p. 102.

70. Ingram 1894, op. cit., p. 37.

71. For example, see "Bell" 1846, op. cit., pp. 104–112; Ingram 1894, pp. 38–43.

72. "Bell" 1846, op. cit., pp. 143–144; Ingram 1894, op. cit., p. 206.

73. "Bell" 1846, op. cit., pp. 122, 126, 127.

74. Ingram 1894, op. cit., pp. 4, 10, 35, 189, 213.

75. "Bell" 1846, op. cit., pp. 121–123, 126, 173, 178.

76. Ingram 1894, op. cit., pp. 19, 33–34, 36, 43, 86–87.

77. "Bell" 1846, op. cit., p. 171.

78. Ingram 1894, op. cit., p. 67.

79. "Bell" 1846, op. cit., p. 173.

80. Ingram 1894, op. cit., p. 101.

81. See Courtland L. Bovée and John V. Thill, *Business Communication Today*, second edition (New York: Random House, 1989), p. 126. This formula is based on the average length of independent clauses together with the number of words of three or more syllables.

82. "Bell" 1846, op. cit., p. 149, 150; Ingram 1894, op. cit., p. 14.

83. "Bell" 1846, op. cit., p. 117; Ingram 1894, op. cit., p. 82.

84. "Bell" 1846, op. cit., p. 139, 145; Ingram 1894, op. cit., pp. 193, 196.

85. "Bell" 1846, op. cit., p. 126; Ingram 1894, op. cit., p. 32.

86. "Bell" 1846, op. cit., p. 144, 171; Ingram 1894, op. cit., pp. 37, 187.

87. "Bell" 1846, op. cit., p. 156; Ingram 1894, op. cit., pp. 189–190.

88. Personal communication with Dr. Glass, December 31, 2013, and January 7, 2014, citing various issues of the *Tobacco Leaf*.

89. Joe Nickell, "Uncovered: The Fabulous Silver Mines of Swift and Filson," *Filson Club History Quarterly* 54(4) (1980): 325–345; Joe Nickell, "Discovered: The Secret of Beale's Treasure," *Virginia Magazine of History and Biography* 90(3) (1982): 310–324; Joe Nickell, "The Secrets of Oak Island," *Skeptical Inquirer* 24(2) (2000): 14–19.

90. "The History of Robertson County," pp. 827–867 in *Goodspeed's History of Tennessee*, originally published in 1886 by the Goodspeed Publishing Company (Columbia, Tennessee: Woodward & Stinson Printing Company). See p. 833 for the specific quotation. The original text can be viewed at http://www.tngenweb.org/goodspeed/robertson/robtco.pdf (accessed November 26, 2013).

91. The Library of Congress's "Chronicling America" provides access to 42 digitized Tennessee newspapers published prior to 1893. From 1894 onward, references appear, but none of them includes the names of witnesses or letters from relatives of witnesses. These are *The Columbia Herald* (1850–1873); *Daily Nashville Patriot* (1857–1858, 1860–1862); *The Daily Nashville True Whig* (1851–1855); *Daily Nashville Union* (1862); *Daily Union and American* (1865–1866); *Fayetteville Observer* (1850–1893); *Herald and Tribune* (Jonesborough, 1869–1893); *Knoxville Whig and Chronicle* (1875–1882); *Knoxville Daily Chronicle* (1870–1882); *Knoxville Tri-Weekly Whig and Rebel Ventilator* (1864–1866); *Knoxville Weekly Chronicle* (1870–1875); *Loudon Free Press* (1852–1855); *Maryville Republican* (1867, 1877); *Memphis Daily Appeal* (1847–1886); *The*

Milan Exchange (Gibson County, 1874–1978); *Nashville Daily Patriot* (1855–1857); Nashville Daily Union (1862–1866); *Nashville Patriot* (1858–1860); *Nashville Union and American* (1853–1862, 1868–1875); *Nashville Union and Dispatch* (1866–1868); *Nashville Union* (1851–1853); *Nashville Weekly Union* (1862–1866); *Public Ledger* (Memphis, 1865–1893); *The Pulaski Citizen* (1866–1893); *The Sweetwater Enterprise* (1869); *The Sweetwater Forerunner* (1867–1869); *Tri-Weekly Whig* (1859–1861); *Tri-Weekly Union and American* (1866); *Union and American* (Greenville, 1875–1877); *The Union Flag* (Jonesborough, 1865); *Weekly Clarksville Chronicle* (1857); *Whig and Tribune* (1870–1877); *Winchester Appeal* (1856); *Winchester Army Bulletin* (1863); *Winchester Daily Bulletin* (1863); *The Winchester Home Journal* (1857–1858); *The Winchester Weekly Appeal* (1856); *The Daily Bulletin* (1862–1863); *The Home Journal* (Winchester, 1857–1880); *The News* (Bristol, 1865–1867); *The Union* (Greeneville, 1877); *The Weekly Herald* (1876–1888). See http://chroniclingamerica.loc.gov/ (accessed November 22, 2013).

92.   See, for example, A. W. Putnam, *History of Middle Tennessee, or Life and Times of Gen. James Robertson* (Nashville: Southern Methodist Publishing House, 1859).

93.   Personal communication between Jack Cook and Robert Bartholomew, December 2013.

94.   A search of 130 million newspaper pages from Newspaperarchive.com and an additional 6 million pages from the Library of Congress "Chronicling America" project failed to turn up any mention of the Bell Witch prior to 1893.

95.   Ingram 1894 (2009), op. cit., p. 107.

96.   Harold E. Way, *A White Paper: American County Histories: Their Uses, Usability, Sources and Problems with Access* (Malvern, PA: Accessible Archives, 2010).

97.   Way 2010, op. cit., p. 2.

98.   Way 2010, op. cit., p. 13.

99.   Personal communication between Robert Bartholomew and Jack Cook dated November 22, 2013.

100.   Fred S. Rolater, "Goodspeed Histories," *The Tennessee Encyclopedia of History and Culture, Version 2.0* (Nashville: Tennessee Historical Society, 2012), accessed November 25, 2013, at http://tennesseeencyclopedia.net/entry.php?rec=558.

101.   "The History of Robertson County," op. cit., p. 843.

102.   Personal communication from Fred Rolater to Robert Bartholomew dated December 20, 2013.

103.   Ingram 1894, op. cit., pp. 292–293.

104.   Ingram 1894, op. cit., pp. 251–308.

105.   Glass holds a PhD in American literature.

106.   The papers examined were *Clarksville Gazette*, the *Jeffersonian*, *Clarksville Chronicle*, *Clarksville Weekly Chronicle*, the *Tobacco Leaf*, *Clarksville Semi-Weekly Tobacco Leaf*, and the *Clarksville Daily Leaf Chronicle*.

107. Personal communication between Jesse Glass and Robert Bartholomew, January 31, 2013.

108. Glass to Bartholomew, op. cit., December 31, 2013.

109. Glass to Bartholomew, op. cit., December 31, 2013.

110. "The Spirit of Mud Alley." *Tobacco Leaf*, September 30, 1874.

111. As evidence, Glass cites the following item published in the *Tobacco Leaf* on June 26, 1894, entitled "Honor Well Bestowed: Ross Bourne the Champion Liar of the County": "An unsolicited honor has come to Ross Bourne, Mayor of Port Royal. He has received a certificate of membership in 'The Ancient, Reckless and Independent Order of prevaricators.' This certificate bears the following inscription: 'Liars License. This is to certify that Ross Bourne is entitled to lie from the first day of January to the 31st of December, he being a duly qualified liar, and having satisfied the license committee of the A. R. & I. O. of P. that he is a fit and proper person to hold license.' Mr. Bourne prizes the license very highly and it is an honor well merited. If there is a man in the county who can wear the honor more worthily the Leaf-Chronicle does not know him." See also the *Tobacco Leaf*, August 23, 1894, as an example of a practical joke making front-page news.

112. For an analysis of this event as a social delusion, see Robert E. Bartholomew, "The Airship Hysteria of 1896–97," *Skeptical Inquirer* 14:2 (1990): 171–181; Thomas E. Bullard, *Mysteries in the Eye of the Beholder: UFOs and Their Correlates as a Folkloric Theme Past and Present* (PhD dissertation, Indiana University, 1982); Daniel Cohen, *The Great Airship Mystery: A UFO of the 1890s* (New York: Dodd, Mead & Co., 1981). The calf-napping story first appeared in the *Farmer's Advocate* of Yates Center, Kansas, on Friday, April 23, 1897, and was reprinted in various papers around the state. It stated that Alex Hamilton of Vernon claimed to have seen "an air ship slowly descending over my cow lot about forty rods from the house ... (and) occupied by six of the strangest beings I ever saw. ... When about 300 feet above us it seemed to pause and hover directly over a 3-year-old heifer, which was bawling and jumping, apparently fast in the fence. Going to her we found a cable about half an inch in thickness ... fastened in a slip knot around her neck, one end passing up to the vessel and tangled in the wire. We tried to get it off, but could not, so we cut the wire loose and stood in amazement to see ship, cow and all rise slowly and sail off, disappearing in the northwest. ... We, the undersigned, do hereby make the following affidavit: That we have known Alex Hamilton from fifteen to thirty years, and that for truth and veracity we have never heard his word questioned, and that we do verily believe his statement to be true and correct." It was signed by E. V. Wharton, state oil inspector; M. E. Hunt, sheriff; W. Lauber, deputy sheriff; H. H. Winter, banker; E. K. Kellenberser, MD; H. S. Johnson, pharmacist; J. H. Stitcher, attorney; Alex Stewart, justice of the peace; H. Waymire, druggist; F. W. Butler, druggist; James L. Martin, register of deeds; and H. C. Rollins, postmaster. "Subscribed and sworn to before me this 21st day of April, 1897" (W. C. Wille, notary public).

113. Daniel Cohen, *The Great Airship Mystery: A UFO of the 1890s* (New York: Dodd, Mead & Co., 1981), pp. 98–102.

114. "Three Forms of Thought: M. M. Mangassarian Addresses the Society for Ethical Culture at Carnegie Music Hall," *The New York Times*, November 29, 1897, p. 200.

115. Karen Roggenkamp, *Narrating the News: New Journalism and Literary Genre in Late Nineteenth-Century American Newspapers and Fiction* (Kent, OH: Kent State University Press, 2005), p. xiv.

116. Roggenkamp 2005, op. cit., pp. xv–xvi.

117. "A Mammoth Potato," *Scientific American*, September 18, 1895, cited in http://www.museumofhoaxes.com/hoax/archive/permalink/the_mammoth_ potato_hoax_of_loveland_colorado, accessed November 23, 2013.

118. Personal communication between Robert Bartholomew and Jack Cook dated November 27, 2013.

119. Glass speculates that Ingram's book may have been part of a plan to boost local tourism, in the tradition of the Silver Lake, N.Y., Sea Serpent hoax of 1855. Henry Faxon who worked on the Buffalo *Daily Republic* at the time, claimed to have created the Silver Lake hoax, which generated a tourism surge. In 1869, Henry's older brother Charles, was hired by Ingram to work on *The Clarksville Tobacco Leaf.*

120. See, for example, *The Nashville Banner*, November 3, 1893; the Clarksville *Tobacco Leaf*, June 5, 1894.

121. "Robertson County: An Interesting Trip and Its Incidents," *Semi-Weekly Tobacco Leaf-Chronicle*, July 15, 1892.

122. "Adams Station: Tobacco Season Over—The Old People and Their Hospitality," *Semi-Weekly Tobacco Leaf-Chronicle*, July 22, 1892.

123. Thanks to Jesse Glass for this suggestion.

124. "Cream of News," *Hopkinsville News*, March 12, 1895, volume 16, No. 20, p. 1.

125. Robert Talley, "America's No. 1 Ghost Breaks a Date Made 110 Years Ago," *Arizona Independent Republican*, December 19, 1937, p. 6.

126. Both Jack Cook and Jesse Glass found no record of this alleged trial from searches of local newspapers for 1875.

127. "The Old Bell Witch" (commentary by "an old reporter"), *Rocky Mount Evening Telegram*, December 29, 1955, p. 4A.

128. "Tennessee's Bell Witch Makes Believers of the Skeptics," *The Frederick Post* (Maryland), October 27, 1986, p. E8.

129. "Tennessee's Bell Witch Makes Believers of the Skeptics," op. cit.

130. "Tennessee's Bell Witch Makes Believers of the Skeptics," op. cit.

Chapter 2

1. Arthur Conan Doyle, *The Treasury of Sherlock Holmes* (Radford, VA: Wilder, 2013), p. 117.

2. James C. Bozzuto, "Cinematic Neurosis Following 'The Exorcist': Report of Four Cases," *The Journal of Nervous and Mental Disease* 161(1) (1975): 43–48.

3. "The Exorcist Haunts M.D.'s at Georgetown," *American Medical News* 17(9): 14 (1974); "Behavior: Exorcist Fever." *Time* 103: 53 (1974).

4. M. A. Ingall, "Psychiatric Casualties of *The Exorcist*," *Rhode Island Medical Journal* 57(11) (1974): 472–473, 479–480; James W. Hamilton, "Cinematic Neurosis: A Brief Case Report," *Journal of the Academy of Psychoanalysis* 6(4) (1978): 569–572; Bruce Ballon and Molyn Leszcz, "Horror Films: Tales to Master Terror or Shapers of Trauma," *American Journal of Psychotherapy* 61(2) (2007): 211–230.

5. William Peter Blatty, *The Exorcist* (New York: Harper and Row, 1971).

6. Carl DiOrio, "'Exorcist' Turning Heads Once Again," *Variety* 381(3) (2000): 9, 82.

7. Bill Brinkley, "Priest Frees Mt. Rainier Boy Reported Held in Devil's Grip," *Washington Post*, August 20, 1949, p. 1.

8. Thomas B. Allen, *Possessed: The True Story of an Exorcism* (Lincoln, NE: iUniverse.com, 2013), pp. viii–ix.

9. Alan Brown, *Ghost Hunters of New England* (Lebanon, NH: University of New England Press, 2008), p. 156.

10. "'The Exorcist' Fairly Close to the Mark," *National Catholic Register*, September 1, 2000, p. 7.

11. William Peter Blatty, *William Peter Blatty on The Exorcist* (New York: Bantam, 1974), p. 24; Paul Meehan, Cinema of the Psychic Realm (Jefferson, NC: McFarland, 2009), p. 80.

12. Raymond J. Bishop, typescript diary of an exorcist (1949), 26 single-spaced pages, reprinted in Allen 2013, pp. 245–291.

13. Allen 2013, op. cit., pp. 2–3.

14. British psychologist Chris French observes that Ouija boards are easily explained using mainstream psychology and without recourse to the paranormal. He says that as the participants attempt to answer a question, they put their finger or fingers on the glass or wood, which appears to answer the question by sliding the object to a series of letters that spell out certain words, or over the words "yes," "no," and "maybe." French says the responses are often coherent but result from the idiomotor effect, where those using the board do not realize that they are pushing the glass or board unconsciously. This effect is easily demonstrated and verified: when the participants are blindfolded and attempt to answer the questions without seeing where they are pushing it, inevitably they end up with garbled, incomprehensible messages. See http://www.videojug.com/expertanswer/debunking-the-paranormal-2/how-does-a-ouija-board-work, accessed January 15, 2014.

15. Allen 2013, op. cit., pp. 4–6.

16. Bishop 1949, op. cit., p. 246.

17. Bishop 1949, op. cit., pp. 246–247.

18. Bishop 1949, op. cit., p. 248.

19. Allen 2013, op. cit., pp. 9–10.

20. Allen 2013, op. cit., pp. 14, 17.

21. Allen 2013, op. cit., pp. 19–21.

22. Charles Vanderpool (director), *In the Grip of Evil* (Discovery Channel Pictures and Henninger Media Development, 1997), interview with Thomas Allen.

23. Howard M. Norton, *The Sun* (Baltimore, Maryland), January 9, 1949, p. 1.

24. Vanderpool 1997, op. cit., interview with Elizabeth Bowman.

25. Specifically, between February 27 and March 6.

26. Vanderpool 1997, op. cit., interview with Father Hughes's former colleague Father Frank Bober, who worked under Father Hughes as an associate pastor; Allen 2013, op. cit., pp. 36–37.

27. Vanderpool 1997, op. cit., interview with Thomas B. Allen; Allen 2013, op. cit., p. 223.

28. Allen 2013, op. cit., p. 223.

29. Bishop 1949, op. cit., p. 247.

30. Allen 2000, op. cit., pp. 61–76.

31. Bishop 1949, op. cit., pp. 255–257.

32. Vanderpool 1997, op. cit., interview with Walter Halloran.

33. Bishop 1949, op. cit., p. 258.

34. Bishop 1949, op. cit., pp. 257–262.

35. Bishop 1949, op. cit., pp. 262–269.

36. Allen 2000, op. cit., p. 46.

37. Allen 2013, op. cit., p. 162.

38. Allen 2013, op. cit., p. 161.

39. Bishop 1949, op. cit., p. 282.

40. Bishop 1949, op. cit., p. 291.

41. Allen 2013, op. cit., p. 210.

42. Susan Saulny, "Historian Exorcises Mount Rainier's Past," *The Washington Post*, March 24, 1999, p. M13.

43. Mark Opsasnick, "The Haunted Boy of Cottage City," *Strange Magazine* 20 (2000), serialized in four parts at http://www.strangemag.com/exorcist page1.html, accessed January 14, 2014.

44. Opsasnick 2000, op. cit.

45. Opsasnick 2000, op. cit.

46. Opsasnick 2000, op. cit.

47. Opsasnick 2000, op. cit.

48. Quoted in Edward Brent and J. Scott Lewis, *Learning Sociology* (Burlington, MA: Jones & Bartlett Learning, 2013), p. 20.

49. Nancy R. Stuart, "The Raps Heard Around the World," *American History* 40(3) (2005): 42–80.

50. Joe Nickell, *Entities: Angels, Spirits, Demons, and Other Alien Beings* (Amherst, NY: Prometheus Books, 1995), pp. 79–82, 119–120.

51. Joe Nickell, "The Davenport Brothers," *Skeptical Inquirer* 23(4) (1999): 14–17

Chapter 3

1. Susan Ratcliffe, *Concise Oxford Dictionary of Quotations* (New York: Oxford University Press, 2011), p. 127.

2. "The Numbers, Box Office Data …" accessed August 8, 2014, at http://www.the-numbers.com/movies/series/Poltergeist.php.

3. John D'Auria (director), *Real Fear: The Truth Behind the Movies* (AEP Media, 2012). According to the documentary, the parallels between the Freelings and the Herrmann family are too numerous to be coincidental, including both sites being supposedly built over Indian burial grounds, flying furniture, and university parapsychologists being called in to investigate.

4. *Census of Population: 1960, Volume 1: Characteristics of the Population* (U.S. Department of Commerce, Bureau of Census), pp. 1–87; G. J. Pratt, *Parapsychology: An Insider's View of ESP* (New York: Doubleday, 1964); Robert Wallace, "House of Flying Objects," *Life* 44(11) (March 17, 1958): 49–50, 52, 55–56, 58; "Religion: Long Island's Poltergeist," *Time*, March 17, 1958; Val Adams, "CBS Will Report on L. I. Ghost Home." *New York Times*, September 29, 1958, p. 52; "TV Key," *Arizona Republic*, April 11, 1958, p. 23 (Edward R. Murrow program guide).

5. David Moye, "'Real Fear:' The Spooks That Inspired 'Poltergeist' and 'The Amityville Horror,'" *The Huffington Post*, March 12, 2012, accessed December, 25, 2012, at http://www.huffingtonpost.com/2012/03/09/poltergeist-amityville-horror-survivor-real-fear_n_1335948.html.

6. "L. I. 'Poltergeist' Stumps Duke Men: Expert's Report on Seaford Incidents …" *New York Times*, August 10, 1958, p. 68.

7. Rosemary Guiley, *The Guinness Encyclopedia of Ghosts and Spirits* (New York: Facts on File, 1994), p. 297.

8. Sam Stall, *Suburban Legends: True Tales of Murder, Mayhem, and Minivans* (Philadelphia, PA: Quirk Books, 2006), p. 15.

9. Michael Norman and Beth Scott, *Haunted America* (New York: Tor, 1995), p. 249.

10. Moye 2012, op. cit.

11. Based on calculations from MapQuest. See http://www.mapquest.com/maps?city=Seaford&state=NY#bc74ba99b3d35bfcfe2e23b2, accessed November 17, 2013.

12. Milton Bracker, "Mystery in L. I. House Deepens: Family, Experts, Police Stumped," *New York Times*, March 4, 1958, p. 31, 34; G. J. Pratt, *Parapsychology: An Insider's View of ESP* (New York: Doubleday, 1964), pp. 80–115.

13. Based on a copy of the original sixty-page police file on the case, citing a report filed by Seaford police detective Joseph Tozzi in 1958; Robert Wallace, "House of Flying Objects," *Life*, March 17, 1958, pp. 49–50, 52, 55–56, 58. Mr. Wallace's article is also valuable because he conducted detailed interviews with the family.

14. Original police file in Wallace 1958, op. cit.

15. Wallace 1958, op. cit., p. 50.

16. William Roll, *The Poltergeist* (Old Chelsea Station, NY: Paraview, 2004), pp. 15–16.

17. Copy of the original police report by Detective Tozzi, in Wallace 1958.

18. Pratt 1964, op. cit., p. 110.

19. Wallace 1958, op. cit., p. 52.

20. Roll 2004, op. cit., pp. 15–16; Wallace 1958, op. cit., p. 52.

21. Milbourne Christopher, *ESP, Seers & Psychics* (New York: Crowell, 1971), pp. 157–158.

22. Roll 2004, op. cit., p. 15.

23. Roll 2004, op. cit., p. 15.

24. Pratt 1964, op. cit., pp. 85, 99, 103–104.

25. Pratt 1964, op. cit., p. 104.

26. William G. Roll, "Poltergeists, Electromagnetism and Consciousness," *Journal of Scientific Exploration* 17(1) (2003): 75–86. See p. 75.

27. Tozzi 1958, op. cit., pp. 11–12.

28. Christopher 1971, op. cit., pp. 157–158.

29. Tozzi 1958, op. cit.

30. "Long Island's Poltergeist," *Time* 71(11) (March 17, 1958).

31. Wallace 1958, op. cit., p. 52.

32. Wallace 1958, op. cit., p. 55.

33. Christopher 1971, op. cit., pp. 151–152.

34. F. Brill, "House of Flying Objects," *Life* 44(14): (letter) 18 (April 7, 1958).

35. Arthur Guy Matthews (1958), "House of Flying Objects," *Life* 44(14): (letter) 18 (April 7, 1958).

36. Paul W. Kniskern (1958). "House of Flying Objects," *Life* 44(14): (letter) 18 (April 7, 1958).

37. Tozzi 1958; Roll 2004, op. cit., p. 21.

38. Bracker 1958, op. cit., p. 34. See also Wallace 1958, op. cit., p. 52.

39. "Family Finally Conceded Defeat, Leaves House to Baffling Bottles," *Niagara Falls Gazette*, February 23, 1958, p. 4-A; Wallace 1958, op. cit., p. 52.

40. Wallace 1958, op. cit., p. 58; "Robert F. Wallace '41," *Princeton Alumni Weekly*, March 21, 1990.

41. Karlis Osis, "An Evaluation of the Seaford 'Poltergeist' Case," *Newsletter of the Parapsychology Foundation* 5(2) (March–April 1958): 5–10. See p. 10.

42. W. G. Roll and M. Persinger, "Investigations of Poltergeists and Haunts: A Review and Interpretation," in J. Houran and R. Lange (editors), *Hauntings*

and Poltergeists: Multidisciplinary Perspectives (Jefferson, NC: McFarland, 2001), pp. 123–163. See pp. 128–129.

43. Roll 2003, op. cit., p. 75.

44. Pratt 1964, op. cit., p. 114.

45. Osis 1958, op. cit., pp. 9–10; "'Haunted House' Believed to Be Boy's Prank," *The Knickerbocker News* (Albany, New York), May 15, 1958, p. A2.

46. "'No Trick' Says Victim: Jumping Bottles Still Stump Scientists," *The New Mexican*, June 16, 1958, p. 8.

47. Barbara Budschu, "That House of Flying Objects Subject of Several New Reports," *Delta-Democrat Times* (Greenville, Mississippi), June 17, 1958, p. 8.

48. "L. I. 'Poltergeist' Stumps Duke Men," *New York Times*, August 10, 1958, p. 68.

49. Pratt 1964, op. cit., p. 114.

50. "'Hexpert's' Odyssey," *Newsletter of the Parapsychology Foundation Incorporated* 5(2) (March–April 1958), p. 11, citing the *New York Times*, the *New York Post*, and United Press.

51. Wallace 1958, op. cit., pp. 49–50.

52. Pratt and Roll 1958, op. cit., p. 114.

53. Christopher 1971, op. cit., p. 156; "Press Comment," *Newsletter of the Parapsychology Foundation* 5(2) (March–April, 1958): 5–10. See p. 3.

54. Hans Holzer, *The Phantoms of Dixie* (New York: Ballantine, 1973), p. 127.

55. Roll 1970, op. cit., p. 20; Pratt 1964, op. cit., p. 105.

56. Pratt 1964, op. cit., p. 105.

57. Christopher 1971, op. cit., p. 157.

58. Tozzi 1958, op. cit., p. 2.

59. Tozzi 1958, op. cit., p. 8.

60. Pratt 1964, op. cit., p. 108.

61. "Mystery House Still Jumping: Son's Favorite Victim of Seaford Ghosts," *Long Island Star-Journal*, February 25, 1958, p. 3.

62. "L. I. 'Poltergeist' Stumps Duke Men," *New York Times*, August 10, 1958, p. 68.

63. Cal Bernstein, "What's Haunting These Houses?" *The American Weekly*, April 20, 1958, p. 4 and 6, published in the Sunday edition of the *San Antonio Light* (Texas) of the same date.

64. "Electrical Gremlin makes Madhouse," United Press International report published in the *Panama City Herald* (Florida), August 2, 1957, p. 1; *Lawton Constitution* (Oklahoma), August 2, 1957, p. 7.

65. Bernstein 1958, op. cit., p. 6.

66. Bernstein 1958, op. cit., p. 6.

67. "Illinois Sheriff Tackles Case of the Ghostly Hurler," *Pacific Stars and Stripes* (Tokyo, Japan), August 18, 1957, p. 3; Bernstein 1958, op. cit., p. 6.

68. Michael Norman, *Haunted Homeland* (New York: Tor, 2006), pp. 60–61.

69. Bernstein 1958, op. cit., p. 6.

70. Wallace 1958, op. cit., p. 56.

71. Pratt 1964, op. cit., p. 113.

72. Tozzi 1958, op. cit., p. 17.

73. Pratt 1964, op. cit., p. 105.

74. Christopher 1971, op. cit., pp. 158–159; Pratt 1964, op. cit., pp. 101–102.

75. Christopher 1971, op. cit., p. 159.

76. Christopher 1971, op. cit., pp. 155–156.

77. Pratt and Roll 1958, op. cit., p. 124.

78. Osis 1958, op. cit., p. 10.

79. Pratt 1964, op. cit., p. 100.

80. Pratt 1964, op. cit., p. 109.

81. Christopher 1971, op. cit., p. 155.

82. J. G. Pratt and William Roll, "The Seaford Disturbances," *The Journal of Parapsychology* 22(2): 79–124 (June 1958).

83. Osis 1958, op. cit., p. 7.

84. Pratt and Roll 1958, op. cit., pp. 82, 120–121.

85. Pratt and Roll 1958, op. cit., p. 83.

86. Pratt and Roll 1958, op. cit., p. 113.

87. Nando Pelusi, "Defying the Laws of Physics," *Psychology Today* 45(4) (2012): 24–26. Quote on p. 26.

88. David Moye, "'Real Fear': The Spooks That Inspired 'Poltergeist' and 'The Amityville Horror,'" *The Huffington Post*, March 9, 2012, accessed May 3, 2014, at http://www.huffingtonpost.com/2012/03/09/poltergeist-amityville-horror-survivor-real-fear_n_1335948.html.

Chapter 4

1. Jon R. Stone, *The Routledge Book of World Proverbs* (New York: Routledge, 2006), p. 421.

2. Box Office Mojo, "The Conjuring," http://www.boxofficemojo.com/movies/?id=conjuring.htm, accessed January 20, 2013.

3. Dave McNary, "A Haunting They Will Go," *Variety* 320(14): 16 (July 2013).

4. Andrea Perron, *House of Darkness House of Light: The True Story*, Volume One (Bloomington, IN: AuthorHouse, 2011); Andrea Perron, *House of Darkness House of Light: The True Story*, Volume Two (Bloomington, IN: AuthorHouse, 2013).

5. Peter Mitchell, "Something Freaky in the Farmhouse," *Sunday Herald* (Melbourne, Australia), July 14, 2013, p. 87.

6. Perron 2011, op. cit., pp. 1–10.

7. Perron 2011, op. cit., p. 45.

8. Perron 2011, op. cit., p. xix.

9. Perron 2011, op. cit., p. 60.

10. Perron 2011, op. cit., p. 61.

11. Interview with Andrea Perron on August 7, 2013, on the Dead Air Paranormal Radio Show, accessed February 20, 2014.

12. Perron 2011, op. cit., pp. 112, 195.

13. Perron 2011, op. cit., pp. 59, 63, 108.

14. Perron 2011, op. cit., pp. 146–147, 153.

15. Perron 2011, op. cit., pp. 156–159, 185; Perron 2013, op. cit., pp. 355–363, 393.

16. Perron 2011, op. cit., pp. 249, 278, 279.

17. Perron 2011, op. cit., p. 290.

18. Perron 2011, op. cit., p. 454.

19. Perron 2011, op. cit., pp. 7–8, 260–261.

20. Perron 2011, op. cit., pp. 192–193.

21. Perron 2011, op. cit., p. 25.

22. Perron 2011, op. cit., p. 213.

23. Perron 2011, op. cit., pp. 484–485.

24. Perron 2011, op. cit., p. 131.

25. Perron 2013, op. cit., p. 293.

26. Perron 2011, op. cit., p. 121.

27. Perron 2011, op. cit., pp. 392–393.

28. Perron 2011, op. cit., pp. 431, 438.

29. Perron 2011, op. cit., pp. 73–74, 223; Perron 2013, op. cit., pp. 69, 164.

30. Perron 2013, op. cit., p. 2.

31. Perron 2011, op. cit., pp. 314–315.

32. Perron 2011, op. cit., p. 434.

33. Perron 2011, op. cit., p. 435.

34. Perron 2011, op. cit., p. 454; Perron 2013, op. cit., pp. 95–97.

35. Perron 2011, op. cit., p. 1.

36. D. Pearson, H. Rouse, S. Doswell, et al., "Prevalence of Imaginary Companions in a Normal Child Population," *Child: Care, Health and Development* 27(1) (2001): 13–22.

37. Karen Majors, "Children's Perceptions of their Imaginary Companions and the Purposes They Serve: An Exploratory Study in the United Kingdom," *Childhood* 20(4) (2013): 550–565.

38. Perron 2013, op. cit., p. 258.

39. Perron 2011, op. cit., p. 156.

40. Perron 2011, op. cit., p. 157.

41. Joe Nickell, *The Science of Ghosts: Searching for Spirits of the Dead* (Amherst, NY: Prometheus Books, 2012), pp. 41–43, 109.

42. Paul Davies, "The Power of Pillow Torque," *The Guardian*, November 16, 1995, p. B9.

43. Perron op. cit., 2011, p. 185.

44. Perron 2011, op. cit., pp. 185–187.

45. David J. Hufford, "Sleep Paralysis as Spiritual Experience," *Transcultural Psychiatry* 42(1) (2005): 11–45. See p. 20.

46. Emphasis in original.

47. Perron 2011, op. cit., pp. 222–223.

48. Perron 2013, op. cit., pp. 70–72.

49. Perron 2013, op. cit., pp. 69–70.

50. Perron 2013, op. cit., pp. 164–165.

51. Perron 2013, op. cit., pp. 52–58.

52. Interview with Andrea Perron by Rita Scott, Westport Radio (Ireland), WRFM, 98.2, published June 8, 2013, at http://www.youtube.com/watch?v=8y8 CKlE7ntY.

53. Perron 2011, op. cit., p. 448.

54. Perron 2013, op. cit., pp. 184–185.

55. Perron 2013, op. cit., pp. 187–188.

56. Perron 2011, op. cit., p. 445.

57. Perron 2011, op. cit., p. 445.

58. Perron 2011, op. cit., p. 436.

59. Perron 2011, op. cit., p. 438.

60. Perron 2011, op. cit., p. 438.

61. Perron 2011, op. cit., pp. 438–439.

62. Perron 2011, op. cit., pp. 440–441.

63. Perron 2013, op. cit., pp. 174–175.

64. Perron 2013, op. cit., p. 236; Perron 2011, op. cit., p. 298.

65. Perron 2013, op. cit., p. 299, 321, 404.

66. Perron 2011, op. cit., p. 328.

67. Perron 2011, op. cit., pp. 404–405; Perron 2013, op. cit., pp. 298–299, 314.

68. Perron 2013, op. cit., pp. 324–329.

69. Perron 2013, op. cit., p. 239.

70. Perron 2013, op. cit., p. 330.

71. Perron 2013, op. cit., pp. 265–266.

72. Perron 2013, op. cit., p. 266.

73. "Cluster Flies (*Pollenia rudis*)," accessed January 22, 2014, at http://ehspest .com/cluster-flies.htm.

74. Perron 2013, op. cit., p. 265.

75. "Cluster Flies," op. cit.

76. Perron 2011, op. cit., pp. 53, 311, 313.

77. Perron 2013, op. cit., p. 293.

78. Perron 2013, op. cit., pp. 260–262.

79. Perron 2013, op. cit., p. 350.

80. Perron 2013, op. cit., p. 358.

81. Perron 2013, op. cit., pp. 358–362.

81. Interview with Andrea Perron, August 7, 2013, on the Dead Air Paranormal Radio Show, accessed February 20, 2014, at http://www.youtube.com/watch?v= ppLrirY2_Wo.

83. Perron 2013, op. cit., p. 362.

84. Perron 2013, op. cit., p. 359.

85. E-mail from Guy Playfair, August 11, 2014.

86. Leonard Zusne and Warren H. Jones, *Anomalistic Psychology: A Study of Magical Thinking* (Hillsdale, NJ: Lawrence Erlbaum, 1989), p. 226.

87.   Zusne and Jones 1989, op. cit., pp. 226–227.

88.   Zusne and Jones 1989, op. cit., p. 227.

89.   Perron 2011, op. cit., p. 382.

90.   Peter C. T. Elsworth, "'The Conjuring' Depicts Family's Reported Haunting," *The Providence Journal*, July 17, 2013.

91.   See http://www.youtube.com/watch?v=onALOHGiSVQ, accessed February 20, 2014.

92.   Interview with Andrea Perron by Rita Scott, Westport Radio (Ireland), op. cit.

93.   "The Conjuring Case with Andrea Perron." *30 Odd Minutes* cable TV show (ABMI Cable 8, 10 Williams Way, Bellingham, Massachusetts), accessed February 20, 2014, at http://www.youtube.com/watch?v=xA5FhzmX1zI.

94.   Perron 2011, op. cit., p. 209.

95.   Nick Collins, "Feeling of Being Watched 'Hardwired in Brain.'" *The Daily Telegraph* (London), April 12, 2013.

96.   Interview with Andrea Perron by Rita Scott, Westport Radio (Ireland), op. cit.

97.   Perron 2013, op. cit., p. 474.

98.   Perron 2011, op. cit., pp. 483–484.

99.   "The Conjuring & Perron Story: The Current Owner Speaks Out," narrated by Norma Sutcliffe. Accessed May 1, 2014, at http://www.youtube.com/watch?v=w2dg2Ufavj8.

100.   Andy Smith, "Owner of R. I. 'Conjuring' House: Movie Has Made Life a Nightmare," *Providence Journal*, January 30, 2014.

101.   Smith 2014, op. cit.

102.   Smith 2004, op. cit.

103.   Jim Baron, "Movie Link Conjures up Nightmare for Local Family," *The Call* (Woonsocket, RI), July 25, 2013.

Chapter 5

1.   Eleanor Ayer, *Parallel Journeys* (New York: Aladdin, 2000), p. vii.

2.   Brad Steiger, *Real Ghosts, Restless Spirits, and Haunted Places* (Canton, MI: Visible Ink Press, 2003), p. 34.

3.   According to the 1980 Census, the population of Amityville was 9,076.

4.   Paul Hoffman, "Our Dream House Was Haunted," *Good Housekeeping* (April 1977): 119, 238, 240, 242. On July 18, 1976, Hoffman published a very similar version of this article in the *New York Sunday News*, under the title "Life in a Haunted House."

5.   Samuel Arkoff and Richard Turbo, *Flying Through Hollywood By the Seat of My Pants* (Secaucus, NJ: Birch Lane Press, 1992), p 228; "The Amityville Horror," accessed January 16, 2013, at http://www.boxofficemojo.com/movies/?id=amityvillehorror.htm.

6.   Greg Carson (producer), "Supernatural Homicide" (MGM Home Entertainment, 2005), interview with Dr. Adelman in the special features section of

The Amityville Horror movie. For inaccurate reports that the family had been drugged, see Pranay Gupte, "Slain Family Drugged, Police on L. I. Report." *The New York Times*, November 18, 1974, p. 37.

7. For inaccurate reports that the family had been drugged, see Gupte 1974 (op. cit.); "Suspect in Slaying of Family Reportedly Admits One Killing," *The Times Herald Record* (Middleton, New York), November 16, 1974, p. 2.

8. Carson 2005, op. cit.

9. The Lutzes do not dispute that they beat their children with a wooden spoon shortly after moving into the house. In his book, Jay Anson suggests that this was out of character and evidence that supernatural forces were altering the Lutzes behavior. However, when interviewed years later, Danny Lutz claimed that he was commonly disciplined with a wooden spoon. See Trevor Fehrman, "Growing Up in the Amityville Horror," *Skeptic* (Altadena, CA) 18(3) (2013): 58–59.

10. Jay Anson, *The Amityville Horror* (New York: Pocket Star Books, 2005), p. 290.

11. Anson 2005, op. cit., p. 2.

12. Nick Freand Jones and Craig Collinson (directors), "The Real Amityville Horror," a documentary produced by Nobles Gate Scotland for Channel 4 Television Corporation (UK), released on October 24, 2005.

13. Anson 2005, op. cit., pp. 2–3.

14. Daniel Farrands (director), "Amityville: Horror or Hoax?" a *Histories Mysteries* TV documentary, season 6, episode 10, airing October 31, 2000. In reading Anson 2005 (p. 301), one could get the impression that this event occurred on February 18, due to the vague writing style. It was organized on that date but took place on March 6. See also Jones and Collinson 2005 and Anson 2005 (pp. 3–4).

15. Farrands 2000, op. cit.

16. Farrands 2000, op. cit.

17. Anson 2005, op. cit., p. 302.

18. Anson 2005, op. cit., pp. 302–303; Jones and Collinson 2005, op. cit.

19. Rosemary Ellen Guiley, *The Encyclopedia of Demons and Demonology* (New York: Facts on File, 1979), p. 8; Brian Righi, *Ghosts, Apparitions and Poltergeists* (Woodbury, MN: Llewellyn, 2011).

20. Farrands 2000, op. cit.

21. Farrands 2000, op. cit.

22. Rick Moran and Peter Jordan, "The Amityville Horror Hoax," *Fate*, May 1978: 43–47. See p. 46.

23. Alan Landsburg (producer), "The Amityville Horror," *In Search Of* (TV program), airing October 4, 1979.

24. Anson 2005, op. cit., p. 194.

25. Hoffman 1977, op. cit., p. 242.

26. Alex Drehsler and Jim Scovel, "Fact or Fiction?" *Newsday*, November 17, 1977, p. 4A.

27.   Rick Moran, "Amityville Revisited," *The Fortean Times* 190 (2004): 32–37. See p. 37.

28.   Moran 2004, op. cit., p. 37.

29.   Ric Osuna, *The Night the DeFeos Died: Reinvestigating the Amityville Murders* (Nevada: Noble Kai Media, 2003), p. xix, 351. For the quote, see Ric Osuna, "Lutz vs Weber," accessed November 11, 2013, at http://www.amityvillemurders.com/lutzvweber.html.

30.   "Was 'Amityville' Made Up?" Associated Press article appearing in *The Evening Capital* (Annapolis, Maryland), July 30, 1979, p. 11.

31.   "Was 'Amityville' Made Up?" op. cit.

32.   "Was 'Amityville' Made Up?" op cit.

33.   See Kaplan and Kaplan 1995, pp. 174–86; Joe Nickell, *Entities: Angels, Spirits, Demons, and Other Alien Beings* (Amherst, NY: Prometheus Books, 1995), p. 122; S. T. Joshi, *Icons of Horror and the Supernatural: An Encyclopedia of Our Worst Nightmares*, Volume 1 (Westport, CT: Greenwood Publishing, 2006), p. 274.

34.   Diana Jean Schemo, "'Amityville' Prisoner Says Movie Money Tainted Defense," *The New York Times*, June 25, 1992.

35.   Nickell 1995, op. cit., p. 126.

36.   Rick Moran and Peter Jordan, "The Amityville Horror: The Truth Behind America's Most Infamous Haunted House," *UFO Report* 5(6) (June 1978): 36–39, 74–77. See p. 38. See also Rick Moran and Peter Jordan, "The Amityville Horror Hoax," *Fate*, May 1978: 43–47. See p. 46.

37.   Moran and Jordan 1978, op. cit., p. 45.

38.   Pete Bowles, "Lutz Family 'Horror' Suit Is Rejected," *Newsday*, September 11, 1979.

39.   Guiley 1979, op. cit., p. 8.

40.   Sally Satel and Scott Lilienfeld, *Brainwashed: The Seductive Appeal of Mindless Neuroscience* (New York: Basic Books, 2013), p. 17.

41.   Satel and Lilienfeld 2013, op. cit., p. 17.

42.   "Ames: Separated Spy, Agent Lives," *The Daily Press* (Newport News, Virginia), April 29, 1994, citing the *Washington Post*.

43.   Tim Vasquez, "Another Tall Tale," *Weatherwise* (September–October 2006): 52–56. See p. 54.

44.   Vasquez 2006, op. cit., pp. 54–55.

45.   Anson 2005, op. cit., pp. 245–249.

46.   Vasquez 2006, op. cit., p. 55.

47.   Nickell 1995, op. cit., p. 127.

48.   Vasquez 2006, op. cit., p. 56.

49.   Anson 2005, op. cit., p. 68.

50.   Anson 2005, op. cit., pp. 68–69; Michael Kernan, "The Calamityville Horror," *The Washington Post*, September 16, 1979, pp. D1–D3. See p. D3.

51.   Alex Drehsler and Jim Scovel, "Fact or Fiction?" *Newsday*, November 17, 1977, p. 5A.

52. Dennis Hevesi, "Between the Covers, Some Changes," *Newsday*, September 17, 1978, p. 26.

53. Rick Moran and Peter Jordan, "The Amityville Horror Hoax," *Fate*, May 1978: 43–47. See p. 45.

54. Dennis Hevesi, "Haunted by a Horror Story." *Newsday*, September 17, 1978, p. 12.

55. Alex Drehsler and Jim Scovel, "Fact or Fiction?" *Newsday*, November 17, 1977, p. 4A.

56. Kathleen Lutz, "Exclusive: Wife Tells Chilling Story Behind Our 28 Days of Horror in House Terrorized by Evil Spirits," *The National Enquirer*, December 13, 1977, pp. 1, 28–29.

57. Paul Hoffman, "Our Dream House Was Haunted," *Good Housekeeping* (April 1977): 119, 238, 240, 242. See p. 238; Rick Moran and Peter Jordan, "The Amityville Horror: The Truth Behind America's Most Infamous Haunted House," *UFO Report* 5(6) (June 1978): 36–39, 74–77. See p. 77.

58. Alex Drehsler and Jim Scovel, "Fact or Fiction?" *Newsday*, November 17, 1977, p. 5A.

59. Joe Nickell, *Entities: Angels, Spirits, Demons, and Other Alien Beings* (Amherst, NY: Prometheus Books, 1995), p. 127.

60. Nickell 1995, op. cit., p. 127.

61. Nickell 1995, op. cit., p. 125.

62. Gordon Stein, ed., *Encyclopedia of Hoaxes* (Detroit: Gale Research, 1993), p. 63.

63. Melvin Harris, *Investigating the Unexplained* (Buffalo, NY: Prometheus Books, 2003), p. 202.

64. Hevesi 1978, op. cit., p. 26.

65. Anson 2005, op. cit., pp. 95–96.

66. Anson 2005, op. cit., pp. 187–195.

67. http://murderpedia.org/male.D/d/defeo-ronald.htm, accessed November 3, 2013.

68. Colin Colwell, "Convict Gives Version of Amityville Killings," *Newsday*, June 25, 1992.

69. Diana Jean Schemo, "'Amityville' Prisoner Says Movie Money Tainted Defense," *The New York Times*, June 25, 1992.

70. Curt Suplee, "Dolors to Dollars," *The Washington Post*, December 9, 1977, p. B1, B3. See p. B3 for quotes.

71. Moran 2004, op. cit., p. 34.

72. Moran 2004, op. cit., p. 34.

73. Rick Moran and Peter Jordan, "The Amityville Horror: The Truth Behind America's Most Infamous Haunted House," *UFO Report* 5(6) (June 1978): 36–39, 74–77. See p. 39.

74. Kernan 1979, op. cit., p. D1.

75. Moran and Jordan 1978, op. cit., p. 39.

76. Anson 2005, op. cit., p. 126.

77. Kernan 1979, op. cit., p. D1.

78. Farrands 2000, op. cit.

79. Rosemary Ellen Guiley, "Where Is the Real Story behind the Amityville Haunting?" October 5, 2011, accessed November 10, 2013, at http://www.fatemag .com/inside-fate/bloggers/rosemary-ellen-guiley/where-is-the-real-story-behind-the-amityville-haunting-2/.

80. Moran 2004, op. cit., p. 34.

81. Lawrence Van Gelder, "A Real Life Horror Story," *The New York Times*, October 9, 1977, p. 2, 15. Quote on p. 2.

82. Anson 2005, op. cit., p. 307.

83. William J. Slattery, "Jay Anson: The Man Who Wrote *The Amityville Horror*," *Writer's Digest* (March 1979): 22–26. See p. 26.

84. Hevesi 1978, op. cit., p. 26.

85. Moran and Jordan 1978, op. cit., pp. 45–46.

86. Suplee 1977, op. cit., p. B3.

87. Jones and Collinson 2005, op. cit.

88. Alex Drehsler and Jim Scovel, "Fact or Fiction?" *Newsday*, November 17, 1977, p. 5A.

89. Suplee 1977, op. cit., p. B3.

90. Anson 2005, op. cit., p. 307.

91. See, for example, Jay Anson, *The Amityville Horror* (New York: Pocket Star Books, 2005).

92. Nathan Robert Brown, *The Complete Idiot's Guide to the Paranormal* (Auckland, New Zealand: Penguin Group, 2010), p. 23.

93. Kevin Christopher, "The ABC-ville Horror," *Skeptical Inquirer* 27(1) (2003): 53–54. See p. 54.

94. Christopher 2003, op. cit., p. 54.

95. Guiley 1979, op. cit., p. 8.

96. Jason Lynch, Maureen Harrington, Steve Erwin, and Liza Hamm, "Amityville Ghosts," *People* 63(15) (April 18, 2005).

97. Eric Walters, (director), "My Amityville Horror," a Lost Witness Pictures production airing on Sundance NOW, March 17, 2013.

98. Fehrman 2013, op. cit.

99. Dennis Hevesi, "Haunted by a Horror Story," *Newsday*, September 17, 1978, p. 14.

100. Gary White, "The Real Horror Story," *The Ledger* (Lakeland, Florida), April 25, 2005; Jones and Collinson 2005, op. cit.

101. Ed Lowe, "The Relentless Terror of the Amityville Tourists," *Chicago Tribune*, March 2, 1980, p. H13, 42–43, 47. See p. 43.

102. Lowe 1980, op. cit., p. 42.

103. Lowe 1980, op. cit., p. 47. Italics in original.

104. Lowe 1980, op. cit., p. 47.

105. Barbara Basler Krebs, "Buyer of 'Haunted House' in Amityville Not Dispirited," *The New York Times*, August 1, 1979, p. B4; Joanne Wasserman, "Amityville Horror House Sold for $80,000," *New York Post*, July 31, 1979; "Ask the Globe," *Boston Globe*, October 12, 1980, p. 1.

106. Walter Lippmann, *Public Opinion* (New York: Harcourt, Brace, 1922), cited in F. MacDonnell, *Insidious Foes* (New York: Oxford University Press, 1995), p. 2.

Chapter 6

1. *Unsolved Mysteries,* "Rainboy," first aired on NBC TV, February 10, 1993.

2. Unless otherwise noted, the following quotations are based on interviews from Dimitri Doganis and Bart Layton, "The Rain Man," *Paranormal Witness,* season 1, episode 6, produced by RAW TV, first aired on the Syfy Channel, October 12, 2011.

3. *Unsolved Mysteries* 1993, op. cit.

4. Robert Lenihan, "Mystery Remains Puzzle," *Pocono Record* (Stroudsburg, Pennsylvania), April 5, 1991, pp. B1, B4.

5. Kevin McCaney, "Strange Happenings Being Checked," *Pocono Record,* March 10, 1983, p. 15.

6. Mark Treinen, "All Eyes on the Tube Watching 'Rainboy' Saga," *Pocono Record,* February 11, 1993, p. B1.

7. "S-Burg Man on Povich Show," *Pocono Record,* June 6, 1994, p. 14.

8. Gary Roberts, personal communication with Robert Bartholomew dated December 20, 2011.

9. Lenihan 1991, op. cit.

10. W. J. Kortz, "Stroudsburg Accepts Police Chief's Resignation," *The Morning Call* (Allentown), November 15, 1984.

11. Christina Tatu, "Stroudsburg Mysteries: The Devil and Don Decker," *Pocono Record,* February 5, 2012.

12. *Unsolved Mysteries* 1993, op. cit.

13. Tatu 2012, op. cit.

14. Tatu 2012, op. cit.

15. Sandra Ho (editor), *Moisture Problems in Manufactured Homes: Understanding their Causes and Finding Solutions* (Manufactured Housing Research Alliance, 2000).

16. National Oceanic and Atmospheric Administration (NOAA) (2003), accessed November 10, 2013 at: http://www.ncdc.noaa.gov/oa/climate/research /2003/feb/februaryext2003.html.

17. Kyle Imhoff, personal communications dated December 3 and 20, 2011. Mr. Imhoff works for the Pennsylvania State Climate Office.

18. Pennsylvania State University temperature data for Scranton, Pennsylvania, accessed November 23, 2014 at: http://climate.met.psu.edu/www_prod/ ida/submit.php.

19. Patrick Huelman, interview with Robert Bartholomew dated December 3, 2011.

20. *Unsolved Mysteries,* "Rainboy," first aired on NBC TV, February 10, 1993.

21. Joe Nickell, *The Mystery Chronicles* (Lexington: The University Press of Kentucky, 2004).

22. Tatu 2012, op. cit.

23. *Montgomery Ward Catalogue* 1983, accessed November 24, 2013 at: http://www.flickr.com/photos/wishbook/6137175108/in/set-7215762477666 8919/.

24. Tatu 2012, op. cit.

25. Tatu 2012, op. cit.

26. W. J. Kortz, "9 People Sentenced in Monroe County Court," *The Morning Call* (Allentown), October 28, 1986.

27. Tracy Jordan, "Poconos Restaurant Owner Indicted on Arson Charges," *The Morning Call* (Allentown), October 18, 2012.

28. Tatu 2012, op. cit.

29. Raegan Medgie, "Rainman Charged with Arson," report airing on WNEP (Scranton-Wilkesboro), October 19, 2012, accessed on December 22, 2013, at http://wnep.com/2012/10/19/rainman-charged-with-arson/.

30. Sandra I. Bloom, *Creating Sanctuary: Toward the Evolution of Sane Societies*, revised edition (New York: Routledge, 2013), p. 155.

31. Bruce Jacobs, "Adolescents and Self-Cutting (Self-Harm): Information for Parents" (Cooperative Extension Service, College of Agriculture and Home Economics, New Mexico State University, 2005), p. 1.

32. Bloom 2013, op. cit., p. 155.

33. Lori Plante, *Bleeding to Ease the Pain: Cutting, Self-Injury, and the Adolescent Search for Self* (Westport, CT: Greenwood, 2007), p. 18.

Chapter 7

1. E. Christopher Emmanuel, *Living Divine Harmony* (Bloomington, IN: Balboa Press, 2013), p. 5.

2. Ed Warren, Lorraine Warren, Al Snedeker, and Carmen Snedeker, with Ray Garton, *In a Dark Place: The Story of a True Haunting* (New York: Villard Books, 1992).

3. "The Haunting in Connecticut," Box Office Mojo, accessed 1 May 1, 2014, at http://www.boxofficemojo.com/movies/?id=hauntinginconnecticut.htm.

4. Oliver Jones, "Inside Story: The Real-Life Haunting in Connecticut," *People*, April 4, 2009, accessed July 29, 2014, at http://www.people.com/people/article/0,,20270145,00.html.

5. Jones 2009, op. cit.

6. The two oldest were Carmen's by a previous marriage.

7. Susan Dunne, "Family Tell-All Is Part of 'The Haunting' Set," *The Courant* (Hartford, CT), July 14, 2009.

8. Dimitri Doganis and Bart Layton, "The Real Haunting in Connecticut," *Paranormal Witness*, season 2, episode 7 (2012).

9. Susan Corica and Glenn Smith, "An Unworldly Being," *Herald Extra* (New Britain, Connecticut), August 15, 1988a; Bryant Carpenter, "Southington

Haunting Is Daunting," *Record-Journal* (Meriden, Connecticut), August 13, 1988; Kathy Rivard, "Southington Family Spooked by House," *Bristol Press* (Bristol, Connecticut), August 11, 1988.

10. Corica and Smith 1988a, op. cit.; Carpenter 1988, op. cit.

11. CNN reporter Melissa Long interview with Carmen Snedeker (2009), accessed May 4, 2014, at http://www.youtube.com/watch?v=NTsNC3lxGr0.

12. Carpenter 1988, op. cit.; Corica and Smith 1988a, op. cit.; Susan Corica and Glenn Smith, "Haunted House Claim Clouded by Tenant, Landlord Dispute," *Herald* (New Britain, Connecticut), August 29, 1988b.

13. Joe Nickell, *Entities: Angels, Spirits, Demons, and Other Alien Beings* (Amherst, NY: Prometheus Books, 1995), p. 131.

14. Ed Warren, Lorraine Warren, Al Snedeker, and Carmen Snedeker, with Ray Garton, *In a Dark Place: The Story of a True Haunting* (New York: Villard Books, 1992).

15. "I Was Raped By a Ghost," *Sally Jessy Raphael* show transcript no. 1084 (Multimedia Entertainment, October 30, 1992), airing on American national television.

16. "A Haunting in Connecticut," League of Paranormal Investigators International, interview with Sandy, accessed May 4, 2014, at http://www.youtube.com/watch?v=ioWGiOXbVRQ.

17. The Maury Povich program was taped on March 2, 1992, and aired soon after.

18. This show was taped October 19 but aired on October 30, Halloween Eve.

19. "I Was Raped By a Ghost," op. cit.

20. "I Was Raped By a Ghost," op. cit.

21. Ken Dimauro and Jeanne Starmack, "Demonic Presence Said to Plague Family," *Observer* (Southington, Connecticut), August 18, 1989.

22. Corica and Smith 1988b, op. cit.

23. Dimitri Doganis and Bart Layton, "The Real Haunting in Connecticut," *Paranormal Witness*, season 2, episode 7 (2012).

24. Doganis and Layton 2012, op. cit.

25. Doganis and Layton 2012, op. cit.

26. Doganis and Layton 2012, op. cit.

27. Warren et al. 1992, op. cit., pp. 145–147.

28. Karen Schmidt, "Couple Sees Ghost; Skeptics See Through It," *Hartford Courant*, October 30, 1992.

29. Joe Nickell, "Death of a Demonologist: Ed Warren dead at 79," *Skeptical Inquirer* 30:6 (November/December 2006), p. 8.

30. "Damned Interview: Ray Garton," interview by Ray Bendici in March 2009 in *Damned Connecticut*, accessed May 1, 2014, at http://www.damnedct.com/damned-interview-ray-garton.

31. "Damned Interview: Ray Garton," op. cit.

32. "Damned Interview: Ray Garton," op. cit.

33. "Damned Interview: Ray Garton." op. cit.

34. "Damned Interview: Ray Garton," op. cit.

35.   Kim Newman, "The Haunting in Connecticut," *Sight and Sound* 19(6) (June 2009): 60.

36.   Doganis and Layton 2012, op. cit.

37.   "The Haunting in Connecticut: The True Story with Carmen Reed," interview with Rita Scott from *The Crypt* interview program on Westport Radio in Ireland, accessed July 4, 2013, at http://www.youtube.com/watch?v=kxt3C1g_oyc.

38.   "I was Raped by a Ghost," op. cit.

39.   "I was Raped by a Ghost," op. cit.

40.   "A Haunting in Connecticut," League of Paranormal Investigators International, interview with Sandy, accessed May 4, 2014, at http://www.youtube.com/watch?v=ioWGiOXbVRQ.

41.   "I was Raped by a Ghost," op. cit.; "A Haunting in Connecticut," op. cit.

42.   Doganis and Layton 2012, op. cit.

43.   Doganis and Layton 2012, op. cit.

44.   Doganis and Layton 2012, op. cit.

45.   "The Haunting in Connecticut: The True Story with Carmen Reed," interview with Rita Scott from *The Crypt* interview program on Westport Radio in Ireland, published July 4, 2013, at http://www.youtube.com/watch?v=kxt3 C1g_oyc.

46.   Scott Beaulieu, "Haunting" House Owner: Casper's Not Here. 'A Haunting in Connecticut?' Not Likely, the Homeowner Said," NBC Connecticut, March 16, 2009, accessed 2 May 2, 2014, at http://www.nbcconnecticut.com/news/local/I-Aint-Afraid-of-No-Ghost.html.

47.   "'Haunting in Connecticut' Draws Unwanted Visitors to Real-Life House," Associated Press report in the *New York Daily News*, March 23, 2009.

Chapter 8

1.   Isaac Asimov, *The Roving Mind* (Buffalo, NY: Prometheus, 1997), p. 43.

2.   Annekatrin Puhle and Adrian Parker, "Science in Search of Spirit," in James Houran (editor), *From Shaman to Scientist: Essays on Humanity's Search for Spirits* (Lanham, MD: Scarecrow Press, 2004), pp. 9–10. Quote from p. 10.

3.   Puhle and Parker 2004, op. cit.

4.   Bette Bonder, Laura Martin, and Andy Miracle, *Culture in Clinical Care* (Thorofare, NJ: SLACK Incorporated, 2002), p. 30.

5.   Ruth M. Underhill, *Red Man's Religion: Beliefs and Practices of the Indians North of Mexico* (Chicago: University of Chicago Press, 1965), cited in Shelley Osterreich, *Native North American Shamanism: An Annotated Bibliography* (Westport, CT: Greenwood Press, 1998), p. 48.

6.   See Robert E. Bartholomew, "The Conspicuous Absence of a Single Case of *Latah*-Related Death or Serious Injury," *Transcultural Psychiatry* 36(3) (1999): 369–376; Robert E. Bartholomew, rejoinder to invited replies by Drs. Ronald Simons, Michael G. Kenny, and Robert L. Winzeler on "The Conspicuous Absence of a Single Case of *Latah*-Related Death or Serious Injury," *Transcultural Psychiatry* 36(3) (1999): 393–397; Robert E. Bartholomew, "The

Medicalization of the Exotic: *Latah* as a Colonialism-Bound 'Syndrome,'" *Deviant Behavior* 18 (1997): 47–75; Robert E. Bartholomew, "The Idiom of *Latah*: Reply to Dr. Simons," *The Journal of Nervous and Mental Disease* 183 (1995): 184–185; Robert E. Bartholomew, "Culture-Bound Syndromes as Fakery," *Skeptical Inquirer* 19(6) (1995): 36–41.

7. Blake Smith, Benjamin Radford, and Karen Stollznow (hosts), "The Warren Omission," *Monster Talk* radio show airing on October 16, 2013, accessed May 2, 2014, at http://www.skeptic.com/podcasts/monstertalk/.

8. Smith, Radford, and Stollznow 2013, op. cit.

9. Smith, Radford, and Stollznow 2013, op. cit.

10. "I Was Raped By a Ghost," *Sally Jessy Raphael* TV show transcript no. 1084 (Multimedia Entertainment, airing October 30, 1992) on American national television. Multimedia Entertainment Incorporated, Show 1030-92.

11. "Ed and Lorraine Warren: The Haunting in Connecticut" interview with the Warrens on the *Seekers of the Supernatural* TV program hosted by Tony Sparrow, accessed May 5, 2014, at http://www.youtube.com/watch?v=n8NpfyNhfp4.

12. David Hess, *Science in the New Age: The Paranormal, Its Defenders and Debunkers* (Madison, WI: University of Wisconsin Press, 1993), p. 138.

13. Emily D. Edwards, "A House That Tries to Be Haunted: Ghostly Narratives in Popular Film and Television," in James Houran and Rense Lange (eds.), *Hauntings and Poltergeists: Multidisciplinary Perspectives* (Jefferson, NC: McFarland, 2001), p. 86.

Index

About the Authors

ROBERT E. BARTHOLOMEW is a medical sociologist specializing in paranormal claims. He has published books addressing topics on the margins of science including UFOs (Prometheus), lake monsters (The State University of New York Press), Bigfoot (Hancock House), and strange customs (University Press of Colorado). He has published sixty articles in science journals ranging from the *British Medical Journal* to the *International Journal of Social Psychiatry*. A high school social studies teacher, he has been interviewed in the *New York Times, Smithsonian Magazine, USA Today,* the *Wall Street Journal,* and on the History and Discovery channels. He is featured in a new eight-part National Geographic series on UFOs.

JOE NICKELL is a prominent investigator of the paranormal who holds a PhD in English, focusing on literary analysis and folklore. A former private investigator, he is the author of two dozen books on historical, paranormal, and forensic mysteries, myths, and hoaxes. Joe served as the resident magician at the Houdini Hall of Fame, and he is a respected historical document consultant who has helped to expose famous forgeries, including the purported diary of Jack the Ripper. He has appeared on *Oprah, Larry King Live, CNN with Anderson Cooper,* and *Dateline NBC.*